Barrel of Herri

Cooking Temperatures

Low 150°C

Moderate 180°C

Hot 230°C

Very hot 250°C

3 Teaspoons
=
1 Tablespoon

1 QUART
=
4 CUPS

A HOGSHEAD...........................

63 GALLONS ....

DRAM ᴬᴺᴰ GRAIN

GOOD
FOOD
FOR
YOUR
TABLE

For
Sheila Melrose and May Morgan,
our Mothers

GOOD FOOD

FOR YOUR TABLE

A Grocer's Guide

By
Ian James, Nicholas Selby
and Louisa Chapman-Andrews

SALT · YARD
BOOK Cº

A Pinch

The amount that can
be taken between the
thumb and forefinger

$\frac{1}{8}$ teaspoon

Foreword

When in 1964 I first had a flat in Primrose Hill there were umpteen shops... a dairy and two grocer's besides, a couple of butcher's not to mention greengrocer's, barber's and junk shops galore.

Over the years rising rents and the short-sightedness of estate agents have decimated our real shops and made the ordinary business of living almost impossible without access to a supermarket.

In the last couple of years, though, there've been signs of a change. We still have no dedicated bread shop but we do have a wet fish shop and we do have Melrose and Morgan to the provisions and delicatessen of which one all too easily becomes addicted. Without their fish and chicken pies our lives (or at any rate our menus) would fall apart. Soups are delicious and (though of course I never eat them) so are puddings. So I'm happy... and with no inducement... to commend this book.

It's sometimes a bit pricey. Melrose and Mortgage is one joke (not mine) and Prada for the Larder is another (not mine either). But jokes at least mean that the shop is now an institution. I hope so.

Alan Bennett

Hello

Not long after we opened our first shop in a quiet side street of Primrose Hill in London in the late autumn of 2004, a friend of ours brought in a copy of *Law's Grocer's Manual*. This 800-page tome is, as the title says, a guide for grocers, first published in 1890. It diligently lists hundreds of products that a grocer should stock, where they are from, how they should be sold and – in some cases – recipes, too. It is a fascinating and illuminating record of what it was to be a grocer more than 120 years ago.

Jump 100 years to the UK high street of the 1990s and it's unlikely you would have found many grocers. In fact, you'd be hard-pressed to find any butchers, bakers, fishmongers, greengrocers or cheesemongers either. Supermarkets were here and they were booming.

Then, in the latter part of the decade, a quiet but powerful revolution began. In 1997 the first UK farmer's market was held in Bath, connecting customers directly with farmers and producers of artisan foods. Other towns and cities soon followed and proved that consumers cared enough about the food they ate to go from stall to stall to talk to the producers and so to understand more about it.

In early 2000 we were spending Saturday mornings in Borough Market, London. Here we found farmers and small-scale food producers from all over the UK, selling some of the finest produce we'd ever seen or tasted. Our visits soon became a highlight of the week, as we worked our way around, discovering new sellers and new foods and watching the seasons come and go through the produce on display. This way of shopping for food was completely different to the chore of going to the supermarket and we really enjoyed it.

This experience was one of the inspirations for us in setting up our own food business. Our goal a simple one: to source the very best food the

British Isles had to offer and sell it all under one roof, seven days a week. We were creating a modern grocer.

On our first day we offered artisan baked breads, English orchard fruit and juices from Kent, three English cheeses, organic milk in bottles, loose leaf tea, coffee beans from one of London's then-rare coffee roasters, bags of pulses and grains and whole smoked mackerel, all set out on a long refectory table. At the far end stood two chefs, an oven, grill and hob with a menu for our first day's trading: pumpkin and sage soup, a raised pork pie, red cabbage coleslaw and a treacle tart.

Since then our ethos has changed little, but the range of products we stock has grown, a new shop has been added, an offsite kitchen has been built, recipes tried and tested, some warmly welcomed and others forgotten.

This book aims to share the knowledge and ideas we've gleaned in more than 10 years from the chefs, makers, farmers, importers, distributors, staff and customers we've worked with. Their thoughts, ideas and opinions have helped shape both our business and this book.

This is a guide to ingredients, how to source and how to store. What to buy (and what not to buy) and when. How to make sure your kitchen cupboards are well stocked with useful food so you can always rustle up something good to eat. You'll find historical information about how it is that certain foods have become part of our daily lives and, sometimes, how they've been adopted or adapted from food cultures around the world. There are recipes and ideas that we hope will inspire you to try newthings and challenge some of your own preconceptions. Recipes thatallow you to use just a few storecupboard essentials to create a nourishing meal, or help you preserve what's bountiful today for the shorter days ahead.

There are some reminders and lessons within these pages about how to do things properly. We have all become obsessed with quick results when actually the simple ritual of, for instance, making tea in a teapot with loose leaves, allowing it to brew, then using a tea strainer while pouring – rather than settling for a rushed tea bag in a mug – can give pleasure, let alone a better-tasting cup.

This book also sets out to answer some of the culinary conundrums we can face: what is the difference between couscous and quinoa? Hot-smoked and cold-smoked? And how 'easy' is easy-cook rice? With this knowledge, we hope you will become more confident in the food you buy in shops and make at home.

Armed with this collection of information and ideas, we hope you'll enjoy planning, shopping for and making the food that you eat a bit more. That you'll think a little harder about what you put into your shopping basket, where it comes from, how it has been produced and the price you're paying for it.

We admit that good food costs. It needn't cost the earth, but we should all be willing to pay its true value. By spending just a little bit more, the rewards often come not only in flavour, but your food will probably have been produced or reared in a more ethical way... and it could also last that little bit longer and go that little bit further. That's a choice that you can make and we hope this book will help you make it.

Welcome to our contemporary Grocer's Guide.

BREAD

An Introduction to Bread

Bread seems to have been one of the world's oldest 'prepared' foods, proven to be around an astonishing 30,000 years ago. It remains the staple that pulls all food cultures together; from an English flour-dusted bloomer, to an Indian chapati, to a French baguette, bread is the daily accompaniment to our food around the world.

We grew up on white sliced, delivered by the bread man to the back doorstep, with the odd wholemeal loaf or packet of Ryvita thrown in. How things have changed. These days, everybody is into bread, there has been quite a revolution. We are in the lucky position of having fresh bread at our fingertips... but so, too, are most of you. Artisan bakeries are setting up everywhere. The availability of truly good bread is one thing that has changed for the better in English food culture in recent years.

At home now we always have a sourdough loaf on hand and the freezer is full of ends of sourdough, for toasting emergencies, for bread puddings or for turning into breadcrumbs (see pages 27 and 29). Good bread is not cheap and we want to make sure we use up every last bit. And we love white bread, especially old-fashioned English loaves that you don't see much any more, such as the London bloomer. We recently began exploring rye and wheat-free breads, too. Along with everyone else, we have been thinking about decreasing our wheat and gluten intake and trying breads made from other flours.

When we first opened Melrose and Morgan, only our most discerning customers asked where we sourced our bread, or if we made our own; in the last five years, we have seen a boom in interest in 'proper' bread. Our customers have also learned how to manage their bread: sourdough bought on Saturday will still be good for toast on Wednesday. It stays moist because there's so much water in it.

Of course we make bread, too. These days, at home, we make a lot of little white tin loaves with a pre-ferment (see page 16), left to rise for at least four hours or overnight. We think that baking bread is not difficult and is largely about planning; organising where to fit the different processes into your day is pretty much the hardest bit.

• •

Bread has become an article
of food of the first necessity;
and properly so, for it constitutes
of itself a complete life-sustainer,
the gluten, the starch, and sugar...
and combining the sustaining
powers of the animal and vegetable
kingdoms in one product.

Mrs Beeton, 1861

Your morning loaf is not just a handy vehicle for marmalade, lovely though that might be; bread has been one of the staffs of life throughout history.

Without the domestication of wheat, we may not have made the shift from hunter-gatherers to modern societies. The ancient Egyptians had gods to protect bread and grain; the Roman Empire used the free distribution of bread as a means of currying political favour with its people. Bread has also had huge significance in religious ritual for thousands of years.

Bread is so engrained in our culture that it has permeated language as a metaphor for life's basic necessities – 'breadwinner' and 'putting bread on the table' – and for terms connected to wealth, with 'bread' and 'dough' being common synonyms for money.

Bread has always been at the mercy of social trends. Ever since it has been possible to sift fine white flour from coarse whole grains, civilisations have demonstrated their social standing through the type of bread they eat: fine white loaves for nobility, through to the coarsest brown loaves for the least privileged in society.

When the bread slicing and packing machine was invented in the US in 1928, it and many things following it were declared the 'best thing since sliced bread', and to eat it was to be at the social vanguard. Recently, the Atkins diet of the 1990s made all carbs the enemy, leading to a backlash against our long-trusted loaf.

Thankfully a renewed interest in traditional artisan skills and ancient grain varieties has seen the sourdough and craft bread revolution of the 21st century and a better targeted backlash, not against all breads, but against processed flours, preservatives and high-speed proving techniques that create the less-than-palatable sliced breads that still fill supermarket aisles.

How to Make Bread

•••

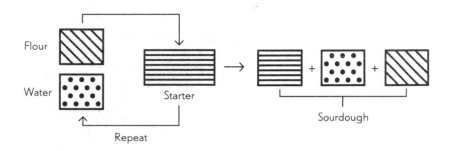

Flour

Water

Starter

Repeat

Sourdough

Unleavened Breads

Often referred to as flatbreads, some of the most famous of these are chapati, tortilla, naan and matzo. Due to the lack of a fermentation process, they are generally quick and easy to make.

Leavened Breads

In these breads, the dough has had a rising agent added. Leavened breads are generally made in more northern cultures, probably because the leavening process requires controlled temperature conditions that are harder to achieve in hot countries. European bakers have a wide variety of styles, from the English farmhouse tin to the Russian black rye loaf.

The leavening process has traditionally been achieved by using either sourdough starters, created by wild yeasts, or baker's yeast, a byproduct of the brewing process. A third way – a pre-ferment – combines elements of both.

Sourdough Leavens

At one time, all yeast-leavened breads were sourdoughs. Produced by a very long fermentation process without the use of cultivated yeast, this bread relies on the naturally occurring yeasts and *lactobacilli* found in flour, beer, on fruit and in the air. Many sourdough starters have been 'alive' for generations and many are said to have a special taste and texture due to their unique characteristics.

In order to bake a sourdough loaf, you need to make a sourdough starter. A flour and water mixture is left to ferment, over as much as a couple of weeks, to cultivate naturally occurring yeasts and lactobacilli. You must 'feed' it regularly with more flour and water and, eventually, you will have a bubbling mass with the right consistency and aroma to make bread.

Baker's Yeast

The development of leavened bread seems to have run in close proximity to the beer-making industry, as the 'barm' (the froth on top of fermenting beer) produces cultures that can be used to make bread.

These days, commercial yeast is used much more widely than sourdough starters, as it has comparatively more consistent and speedier results.

To grow, yeast requires warmth, moisture and food. A small amount of sugar is needed to give it a start, alongside some time to develop in warm water to come 'alive'.

Many modern fast-action yeasts don't require any sugar and can be added straight to the flour in the mixing stage. If you are after a home-made loaf in fairly short order, then these fast-action yeasts do have their place. But we are fans of a more old-fashioned, slow bread-making tradition; good things really shouldn't be rushed, and (for all the reasons above and below) bread ought definitely to be included in that. If you want some home-made bread in a hurry then consider a simple soda bread, which can be baked in around 30 minutes (see page 223). Don't try to rush 'proper' bread making; instead, fit the different processes into your day.

Whichever yeast you choose, during the rising process it produces carbon dioxide, which expands the dough's cellular network and enables it to rise, while also giving bread its characteristic flavour and aroma.

Pre-ferment

Some artisan bakers use baker's yeast to enhance a loaf's character and flavour by mixing a small proportion of a dough's overall ingredients, which are then allowed to ferment over several hours before being mixed into the remaining bread dough. This improves the flavour, falling as it does halfway between yeast-risen and sourdough bread.

Pre-fermentation Gives

Superior flavour: a subtle wheaty aroma
and a pleasing aromatic tang

Increased acidity, which in turn has a strengthening
effect on the gluten structure of the crumb

Increased shelf life: as acidity rises,
so does bread's ability to stay fresh

• •

The Best Thing Since Sliced White?

Most bread on offer in the UK today is still mass-produced by a method
first used in 1961: the Chorleywood Bread Process. This substantially
reduces yeast's fermentation time through a high-energy mechanical
process and the addition of ascorbic acid and fats. It dramatically increases
a baker's yield; taking a loaf from flour and water to sliced and packaged
in just three and a half hours. It also allows a greater proportion of lower-
protein British grain to be used, which had previously been unsuitable.
The process was taken up around the developed world, particularly in the
USA. Many now believe that it's this fast-forwarded fermentation process,
alongside the processing and preservatives, that has made such bread
a nutritional minefield for those with dietary sensitivities. In addition,
we would argue that bread made in this way is not 'real' bread. It looks
and tastes different and shares few of the nutritional qualities. If it's the
convenience of a sliced loaf that you want, go to a craft baker who owns
a slicing machine.

What to Look For When Buying a Loaf

Most of us shop with our eyes when it comes to food.
Walk into any bakery and you'll be met with
a variety of shapes, sizes, colours and smells.
Here's some of the things to look for (or ask about).

Crust

As a general rule,
a crust should be thin.
It can of course be crisp and
crunchy or soft and light
depending on the bread
style. What it shouldn't be
is thick or leathery.
A well-baked bread's crust
should also contain
lots of flavour.

CRUMB

(The soft bit inside.) Again, different
breads and baking techniques result
in different types of crumb. It can be
'tight' or 'open', 'elastic' or 'cakey'.
Sourdough loaves tend to have an
open crumb; yeasted breads have
tighter crumbs. Above all it should be
soft, fresh and carry lots of flavour.

Freshness

Most of us know that fresh is
best and you'll rarely find a
one-day-old loaf on an artisan
baker's shelf. Some breads
do improve on their second
or third day... but that
second or third day should
be on your shelf, not theirs.

Colour

Most well-cooked breads have
gradations of colour over their
crust; it's unlikely that an artisan
loaf will be a perfectly uniform
colour all over. But if it looks
burned or scorched, don't buy it.

Traditional British Loaves

•••

Batch Usually a tall white loaf with soft sides. These loaves are not baked in tins but on large trays next to each other so, as they rise, they butt into each other. As a result, when separated after the bake they do not have crusts on their sides.

Bloomer/London Bloomer A long white loaf with rounded ends, sometimes enriched with milk or butter. The origin of the name is unclear but could be due to the loaf 'blooming' or expanding in the oven, rather than being contained in a tin. Traditionally, the bloomer would have been a 900g (2 lb) loaf with 13 cuts along the top to symbolise the 12 disciples and Jesus. The loaf should have a bottom crust no thicker than a shilling.

Cob A small round loaf with a flat bottom and a domed top with a thick crust. The top can be slashed, either with a cross or with multiple slashes for a chequerboard effect.

Cottage Two loaves in one, this has a small round loaf baked on top of a larger round one. It was a very common and popular loaf in Britain, but is rarely seen today.

Farmhouse, Tin or Split Tin Baked in a tin with a split top and often dusted with flour. The crumb is soft and chewy.

Plait Dough is divided into equal lengths before being plaited together in three or four strands. Breads shaped in this way are sometimes enriched with eggs or butter.

Sandwich Loaf A white, granary or wholemeal loaf baked in a tin with a lid. The resulting square-sided loaf is perfect for making sandwiches.

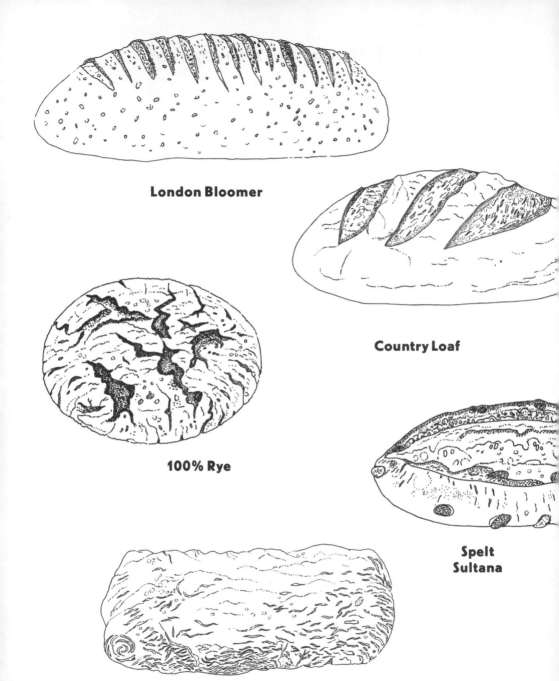

London Bloomer

Country Loaf

100% Rye

Spelt Sultana

Ciabatta

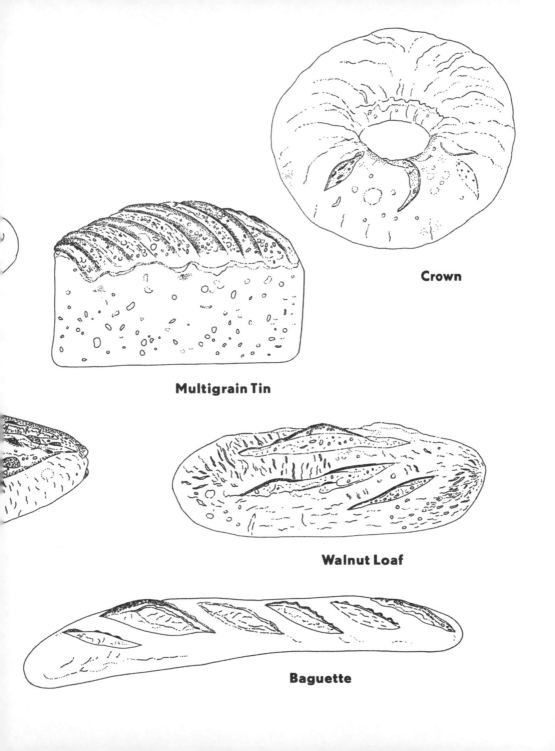

Crown

Multigrain Tin

Walnut Loaf

Baguette

Our Favourite Breads Around the World

•••

Baguette The long thin loaf may in fact be originally from Vienna, but is now totemic of France. It should have a crisp crust, a golden colour and an open crumb. Many artisan bakers are using sourdough methods to make their own versions of baguette.

Brioche Enriched with eggs and butter, creating a richer, softer crumb.

Challah This plaited bread belongs to the Jewish tradition and has a strong religious significance to that faith. It's a yeasted wheat dough made with eggs and sugar.

Chapati An unleavened round flatbread made from wheat, typically found in the Indian subcontinent and cooked in a pan.

Crispbreads More like a biscuit than a bread, these were traditionally made to store over the winter. They can be made from a variety of grains – such as rye, buckwheat, or oats – that carry more flavour than wheat. The Nordic countries are particularly adept at their production.

Grissini These got themselves a bad name as the ubiquitous plastic-wrapped sticks abandoned on the table in Italian-style trattorias. In reality, when eaten fresh, they are crunchy and delightful.

Pumpernickel A German bread with a dark colour, sweet flavour and earthy aroma, this is made from 100 per cent rye flour with a sourdough starter. It's dense and heavy and has lots of flavour.

Tortilla Once these were always made from cornmeal, but now they're usually made from wheat. A flatbread and a staple of Central America for thousands of years, they are similar in style to the Indian chapati.

Gluten

When choosing bread, another factor has become important. People's dietary needs have become more complicated and one of the main digestive antagonists appears to be gluten.

Gluten is found in certain grains, notably wheat. Gluten gives elasticity to a dough, providing its capability to expand when a rising agent is added to make bread light. Gluten-free bread tends to be thick and heavy, yet crumbly and lacking in structure.

Certain grains and flours have less gluten than others. In addition, it's now recognised that the type of gluten found in spelt is of a different make-up to that found in traditional wheat and, for some reason, appears to have a less negative effect on the digestion for some people than regular wheat.

If gluten is a problem for you, a few options remain:

Try spelt, it may cause fewer problems than traditional wheat.

Loaves made from rye typically contain less gluten.

Gluten-free flours have been developed to simulate traditional wheat flours. Potato, rice, tapioca, maize and buckwheat flours sometimes have xanthan gum added to help mimic the binding effect of gluten. Without it, breads made from gluten-free flour can be crumbly.

How to Store and Keep Bread

1

Keep bread away from direct sunlight, at room temperature.

2

Bread that is kept in warm, moist environments is prone to the growth of mould.

3

Don't put bread in the fridge: it will develop mould more slowly, but will also turn stale quickly due to 'retrogradation', where the starch molecules crystallise.

4

Artisanal bread is best stored in a paper bag, as it retains the bread's freshness.

5

The crust on a good sourdough should allow your loaf to stay good for three to four days. Just slice as you need it and turn it cut-side down on the bread board to reduce air exposure.

6

Freeze any excess bread in a freezer bag (just make sure you slice it first; you can toast it from frozen).

7

Breads with added oils or fats – such as olive oil, butter or eggs – will keep for longer.

Flour

...

One of the main ways to vary the bread we eat is to use different flours to make it. These differences can be achieved either through the milling process – which produces different grades of flour from the same grain, from the finest white to the coarsest wholemeal – or through the type of grain that is used.

Traditional stone milling is the best way to ensure the flavour and preserve the nutritional value of flour. Whole grains are ground in a single 'pass' between two mill stones. Nothing is taken away or added and the result is a whole grain flour. However, these days, most flour has been processed through a steel roller mill. These efficiently extract as much white flour as possible from grains. (It probably goes without saying, but white loaves are lighter and more airy than whole grain varieties, but also less nutritious.)

Freshly milled flour isn't white as you might expect, instead it has a yellow tint. However, many of the foods we've become used to eating today wouldn't look great if they used yellow flour. So white flours now often contain additives that make it appear whiter, effectively bleaching it.

Bread Flour Types

Barley Commonly blended with wheat to make bread, this is an Iron Age grain that is rarely used in its pure form to make bread these days.

'Brown' and 'Granary' At its best, 'brown' means bread made with 85 per cent of the whole grain... but all too often it only means that colouring has been added to make white flour brown, so check the label. 'Granary' is a term for commercially made brown flour to which malted wheat grains have been added to increase texture and flavour. Both words often mean very little and we think the products are pretty worthless.

Oats Used to add texture and nutritional value to other flours, oats create a closer crumb in the bread.

Rye Turkish in origin and widely used by the Romans, rye is dark in colour and has a distinctive, pleasantly sour taste. It makes a dense loaf favoured particularly by the Scandinavians and Russians.

Spelt An ancient cousin of modern wheat and widely used by the Romans, this grain works very well in bread making as well as in general baking. It is available in both white and whole grain varieties, which offer more complex, nutty flavours to a loaf. Don't make the common mistake of thinking that spelt is gluten free; it is not.

Strong White Generally a wheat flour. Hard varieties of wheat, with high gluten and protein contents, are milled, then the husks from the whole grain are sifted away. Look for organic and stoneground varieties.

Wholemeal Again generally wheat, made with up to 100 per cent wholemeal flour, giving the full nutritional value of the grain. Loaves made with this should feel quite heavy for their size. A good loaf will develop a rich, sweet smell after a couple of days.

Using Bread in Cooking

For the most part we use bread to sandwich, mop up, or accompany the food we eat. Resourceful cooks also use fresh and less-fresh bread as an ingredient, perhaps most commonly in bread-and-butter pudding. Look a little further, though, and bread in a variety of forms (sliced, crumbed, torn, chopped) ends up in all sorts of dishes...

Orange and Chicory Bread Salad

•••

This is a winter version of our summer panzanella. Use day-old bread, toasted in the oven and allow the warm cubes to soak up the sherry vinegar dressing. Try other winter leaves instead of chicory; watercress would be an excellent substitution. Use a crumbly blue cheese.

Serves 4 as a starter

Ingredients

200 g day-old sourdough bread
2 oranges
2 heads of chicory
1 bunch of tarragon
2 small shallots
25 g walnuts
6 tbsp extra virgin olive oil
2 tbsp sherry vinegar
sea salt and freshly ground
 black pepper
150 g blue cheese

Equipment

sharp knife and chopping board
colander
baking sheet
small bowl
large salad bowl
whisk

Preparation

Preheat the oven to 160°C / 325°F / gas mark 3.

Remove and discard the crusts from the bread, then cut into bite-sized cubes.

Peel and segment the orange.

Separate and wash the chicory leaves.

Wash, pick and chop the tarragon leaves.

Peel and finely chop the shallots.

Roughly chop the walnuts.

Method

Bake the bread cubes and walnuts on a baking sheet in the oven for 10 minutes, then remove and set aside.

Make the dressing by whisking the oil slowly into the vinegar in a small bowl, then add the shallots and season with salt and pepper.

Place the chicory leaves in a large salad bowl, dress with half the dressing and scatter over the warm bread cubes and the orange segments.

Throw over the tarragon leaves and walnuts, then crumble in the blue cheese, drizzle over the remaining dressing and serve.

Savoury Bread Pudding

•••

This is a great way to use up day-old bread. Throw in some grilled crispy smoked bacon for added flavour.

Serves 4

Ingredients

175 g day-old bread (weighed
  with crusts removed)
unsalted butter, for the oven dish
1 large leek
100 g cavolo nero
6 sprigs of oregano
100 g Caerphilly cheese
1 tbsp olive oil
sea salt and freshly ground
  black pepper
2 tbsp white wine
250 ml double cream
250 ml milk
5 eggs

Equipment

sharp knife and chopping board
30 x 20 cm ovenproof dish
box grater
2 large saucepans
medium mixing bowl
deep roasting tin

Preparation

Cut the bread into 2 cm cubes.

Butter a 30 x 20 cm ovenproof dish.

Trim the leek, then wash and chop it.

Remove the stalks from the cavolo nero and wash and shred the leaves.

Pick and wash the oregano leaves.

Grate the cheese.

Method

Cook the leek and herbs in the oil until softened but not coloured, season, add the wine and cook for a few more minutes. Blanch the cavolo nero in boiling water for three minutes, then squeeze out excess water.

Make the custard by whisking together the cream, milk and eggs and season well with salt and pepper.

Toss the leek, cavolo nero and half the cheese with all the bread cubes. Place in the dish, pour over the custard and allow to stand for one hour so the bread absorbs the custard. Sprinkle evenly with the remaining cheese.

Preheat the oven to 180°C / 350°F/gas mark 4. Place the oven dish in a deep roasting tin. Pour enough hot water from the kettle into the tin to come halfway up the sides of the dish, then bake for 50 minutes, until the custard has set and the top is golden brown.

Ginger and
Lime Treacle Tart

•••

For more consistent results, use fresh breadcrumbs. We use ginger to add depth and lime to balance the sweetness. Serve with crème fraîche.

Serves 6

Ingredients

For the sweet pastry

100 g chilled unsalted butter
230 g plain flour, plus more to dust
75 g icing sugar
1 egg, lightly beaten

For the filling

1 lime
25 g crystallised ginger
400 g golden syrup
100 g honey
150 g fresh breadcrumbs
1 egg
1 tsp ground ginger
2 tbsp double cream

Equipment

zester and juicer
sharp knife and chopping board
large mixing bowl or food
    processor
rolling pin
20 cm tart tin with removable base
saucepan

Preparation

Finely grate the zest and juice the lime.

Chop the crystallised ginger.

Method

First make the pastry. Chop the butter for the pastry. Rub the butter into the flour either in a large mixing bowl with your fingertips or in a food processor. Add the icing sugar and egg and bring together into a ball. Roll out to 2 mm thick on a work surface lightly dusted with flour and use to line a 20 cm tart tin with removable base, 2.5 cm deep. Rest in the fridge for 20 minutes. Preheat the oven to 180°C/350°F/gas mark 4. Line the tart shell with baking parchment, weigh it down with raw rice or baking beans and blind bake for 20 minutes until the pastry is cooked through.

Allow to cool.

Heat the syrup and honey gently in a saucepan, then remove from the heat and add the lime zest and the crumbs. Allow to cool for 20 minutes until the crumbs start to absorb the syrup. Beat the egg and both types of ginger with the cream. Add to the bread mixture with the lime juice and give it a good stir. If the mixture seems a bit dry or stiff, add a little more golden syrup. Pour into the tart shell. Place in the oven on the baking sheet and cook for 25 minutes, or until golden brown.

Making and Storing Breadcrumbs

Breadcrumbs can be used in many ways, from coating chicken, chops or fish before frying, to stuffing vegetables, or in various sweet puddings. There should be no need to throw old bread away. Seeded breads and heavy rye breads are not suitable for breadcrumbs; you need a uniform, fine golden crumb.

For fresh breadcrumbs Remove crusts from day-old bread, cut the crumb into cubes and blitz in batches in a food processor to fine crumbs. (Or grate on a box grater.) Store in the fridge in an airtight container for up to one week, or freeze for six months.

For dried breadcrumbs Make the breadcrumbs as above. Preheat the oven to 140°C/275°F/gas mark 1. Spread them on a baking sheet lined with baking parchment and place in the oven for about 30 minutes until golden brown and very dry. They will keep in an airtight container for up to one month.

Using Breadcrumbs as a Coating

Season 50 g of plain flour well and spread on a large plate. Beat 1 egg with 4 tbsp of milk, season and place in a shallow dish. Lay 200 g of fresh breadcrumbs on a large plate. Cover the pieces of food in flour, then shake to remove the excess. Now dip into the egg mixture, then finally coat evenly in the crumbs. Place on a clean plate. Chilling for a short while sometimes helps the coating to stick during cooking. The food is now ready for deep- or shallow-frying.

M

How to Make Proper Toast

•••

Hot, crunchy toast, slathered in butter, is a very lovely thing. Soggy, cold, leathery triangles on a plate are another thing entirely, so it's worth paying a little attention. In matters as fundamental as this we often refer to Delia, on whose advice these key toasting tips are based:

1 Toasters can be hugely convenient, but we find the settings to be precarious and prone to scorching

2 Toast made under the grill will give you more even, trustworthy results and you can get away with some less than perfect bread slicing as well

3 Preheat your grill at the highest setting for 10 minutes before making your toast

4 Slice the bread about 1 cm thick

5 Position your slices on the rack about 5 cm away from the grilling bars; you want the bread to toast quickly so it's crunchy outside but still soft in the middle

6 Let your toast brown to your liking on each side; keep a bit of an eye on it and don't wander too far from the grill while the toasting is in action

7 When the toast is done, transfer to a toast rack to allow the hot steam to escape from the toast vertically without trapping any sog-inducing condensation

8 If you don't have a toast rack, just prop your toast against a jar to allow the steam to escape for about a minute before serving

9 Don't, whatever you do, place your toast immediately flat on a plate as this will collect steam and ruin its lovely crispness

10 Always eat toast as soon as possible after it's made; never make it ahead of time

11 Never wrap toast in a napkin or cover it in any other way as this will also trap steam and make it soggy

12 Use the best-quality bread you can get your hands on and the same applies to the butter. In most cases slightly salted works very well, but the creaminess of unsalted can show off a good fruity jam

13 Sourdough makes very good toast as it is slightly chewy, but an old-fashioned bloomer can make the best toast on earth

14 Slightly stale bread works just as well as fresh for making toast and can actually add to the texture

Toast Toppings

Avocado, Marmite and Chilli Flakes

Peanut Butter, Banana and Runny Honey

Seville Orange Marmalade and Crispy Smoked Streaky Bacon

Sardines, Capers and Pickled Radishes
(see page 449)

Fresh Crab Meat, Cayenne Pepper and Mayonnaise

Beetroot, Curd Cheese and Chilli Oil

Chocolate Spread, Sliced Pear and Crushed Hazelnuts

Scrambled Egg and Lime Pickle

Cinnamon, Sugar and Salted Butter (Grilled on Raisin Toast)

Figs, Crumbly Blue Cheese and Parma Ham

Ploughman's Picnic Loaf

Use a loaf with a good crust. Cut the top off to create
a lid and empty out the crumb (use it for breadcrumbs,
see page 29). Spread the whole inside with Salad cream
(see page 328) and layer in Baby Gem lettuce leaves,
sliced cucumber and tomatoes, sliced boiled egg, grated
Cheddar and smoked ham, sprinkling baby pickled
onions or dolloping good chutney between each layer,
until full. Pop the top on, then slice and serve.

Brown Betty

Preheat the oven to 180°C/350°F/gas mark 4. Roast a
dish of peeled and cored pears in the oven, dotted with
unsalted butter, a sprinkling of ground cinnamon and
another of muscovado sugar. Remove when softened
and glossy and stir in a handful of chopped pecans. Blitz
a handful of rolled oats and a handful of day-old bread
together. Dress with a few spoons of melted unsalted
butter, honey, a little sugar and a pinch of salt. Cover the
pears with this topping. Bake for about 25 minutes, or
until golden. Serve with ice cream.

CHEESE

An Introduction to Cheese

There aren't many people that don't like cheese of one sort or another; whether they're enjoying it on top of a pizza, tucking into a big dish of cauliflower cheese or carefully selecting a hand-made washed rind sheep's milk cheese from a specific dairy. But now, with ever-increasing numbers of cheeses being created, it can be hard to navigate the choices available. Hopefully, we can help with that in this chapter.

Of course the cheese on the top of the pizza could be the finest artisan pecorino, or part of a 100-tonne batch produced by a machine. But there's one constant between those two extremes: milk.

Cheese is made from all types of milk: cow's, goat's, sheep's, buffalo's, camel's, mare's... even yak's and reindeer's. Add to that the effect of different climates and soil types and you have a near-limitless variety. But, whatever the type of milk and wherever you are in the world, similar methods are applied to turn the milk into cheese.

Cheese-making in the British Isles

We have a long history of cheese-making in this country that probably started with the Norman invasion. Along with William the Conqueror came Cistercian monks who brought expertise from France, the country that seems to have created the foundations of our cheese-making today. In those early days, sheep were the usual source for cheese-making. It was only after the 16th century that farming methods changed and cows were kept for their milk instead. In time, regional cheeses started to be produced such as Cheshire, Lancashire, Cheddar and Wensleydale. The recipes created back then are pretty similar to the cheeses of the same names today. With the arrival of the industrial revolution, the country's milk started to be taken by train into the towns and cities. Cheese-making took advantage of the technical advances and mass production began.

Two world wars later and the impact of rationing meant that artisan cheese-makers were a dying breed. Further damage was done in the 1960s and 1970s with the rise of supermarkets, who needed a consistent product available all year round. This brought along another level of mass production and a further loss of artisan practices.

Today we are in a very different position. In 2013, 903 cheeses from the UK were entered in the British Cheese Awards. Alongside a revival in other artisan food practices has come a demand for artisan, locally made cheeses. Some have found favour abroad too, such is their quality.

Cheese-making Today

As you'll witness from the list later on in this chapter (see pages 42–43), we're pretty good at making all sorts of cheeses, from classic regional cheeses, to those influenced by other countries' cheeses, to new and exciting ideas developed by a new generation of cheese-makers who want to make their mark. It is easy enough to meet cheese-makers these days at many farmer's markets, those individuals who take the time and care to produce amazing cheeses, effectively by hand. They've studied their craft, tried and tested new methods, in some cases cared for the animals too... and produced a wonderful array of hand-made cheeses, some of which can take up to two years of tender care before being sold and enjoyed. These are the craftspeople – along with the bakers, the smokers, the coffee roasters – who are changing the way we think about food in this country today.

Buying Cheese

The explosion of interest in cheese has, of course, led to a modest rise in specialist cheese shops. At the same time, supermarkets have begun to stock much improved ranges and – sometimes – local cheeses, too. If you're lucky enough to have a cheesemonger close to you, use them and support them. They will make your buying decisions easier as well as introducing you to new cheeses and giving useful advice.

You may be buying cheese for a simple lunch, for a celebratory supper, or just to make a sandwich. You may need it to make a cheese sauce for a cauliflower, or perhaps a chunk of Parmesan to grate on your pasta. Whatever your need, it's worth paying a little more attention and selecting a cheese that's been made by hand, even for the cheese sauce, as the quality and flavour will surpass any mass-produced product that goes by the same name.

So use the services of your local cheese specialist and use their knowledge to help you make the right choices.

One of the great things about going to a cheese shop or counter is that you normally get a chance to try the products before you buy. Always ask for a taste of the cheese before committing to the purchase: you need to make sure they are in good shape and that you like them. Be wary of any cheesemonger who refuses this.

Also, it's worth buying little and often, rather than getting big chunks of cheese. The seller will hopefully have better storage conditions than you have at home and be more expert in the care of those cheeses, so let him or her look after them. Try to buy in season too... do you really need fresh mozzarella in the middle of winter?

How an Artisan Cheese is Made

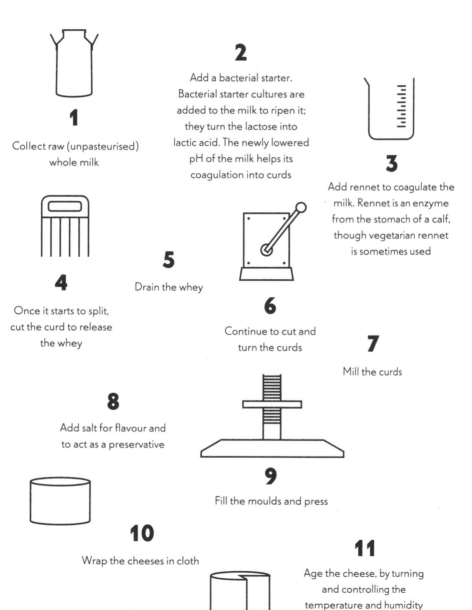

1
Collect raw (unpasteurised) whole milk

2
Add a bacterial starter. Bacterial starter cultures are added to the milk to ripen it; they turn the lactose into lactic acid. The newly lowered pH of the milk helps its coagulation into curds

3
Add rennet to coagulate the milk. Rennet is an enzyme from the stomach of a calf, though vegetarian rennet is sometimes used

4
Once it starts to split, cut the curd to release the whey

5
Drain the whey

6
Continue to cut and turn the curds

7
Mill the curds

8
Add salt for flavour and to act as a preservative

9
Fill the moulds and press

10
Wrap the cheeses in cloth

11
Age the cheese, by turning and controlling the temperature and humidity

Types of Cheese

•••

Fresh Cheese

Fresh cheese can be recognised by its lack of rind or mould and soft, spreadable nature. As the name suggests they're for eating now, not keeping. Some are made from milk, others from whey. Serve them chilled.

Cream cheese has a high fat content due to the combining of cream with the milk. It's often used in cheesecakes and forms a very popular icing on top of carrot cake.

Cottage cheese is the curds, drained of most of their whey but not pressed to form a mass. Eat with heritage tomatoes and lots of black pepper, or summer berries and runny honey.

Curd cheese is the first step in all cheese-making (see page 37) and can be eaten at this stage, once the whey has been drained. Use in baking, both savoury and sweet (such as in the famous Maids of Honour tarts) or to add interest to salads.

Fromage frais is a curd cheese that is creamy and soft; many serve it with dessert. It has typically sour notes but is very creamy in the mouth. It usually has less fat than curd cheese or cream cheese.

Ricotta is typical of Italy and traditionally made from the whey of sheep's milk that has already been used to make cheese. The whey is heated to near-boiling, then passed through a cloth. What's collected in the cloth is left to cool and set. It's used in cannelloni, stuffed into courgette flowers and can be made into cheesecakes as well as served simply with summer fruits.

Mozzarella is traditionally made in Italy from buffalo's milk, but there are now many versions made from cow's milk. Once formed into a solid, it is stretched and kneaded to a spongy consistency. With mozzarella, the fresher the better. Don't waste a good-quality cheese on pizza; serve it with tomatoes, large pungent basil leaves and the best olive oil to hand. For an extra special treat try burrata, a speciality of Puglia, which is a soft thick skin of buffalo mozzarella surrounding a liquid buffalo cream that flows out on cutting.

Chèvre refers to a group of fresh goat's cheeses. They range in shape, appearance and flavour: mild and creamy when young, they become drier and more acidic as they age. Serve as part of a cheese board, use to make an interesting cheesecake, add to an omelette or serve as a dollop on top of a soup. Take your pick

Soft Cheese

Soft cheeses require time to reach their maturity and full flavour. In appearance most would recognise them as a Brie or Camembert-type cheese, as they are usually round and covered by soft white rind. You can describe the rind as having 'bloomed'. The bloom or mould comes from the addition of particular bacteria during the cheese-making process. The moulds are perfectly safe to eat and two particular bacteria used are *Penicillium candidum* and *Pencillium camemberti*. Once the cheese has been formed and the bacteria added, the cheeses are placed in specific climatic conditions, which allow them to ripen. They are carefully cared for during this process until they are ready to be sold and eaten. Once at home, these cheeses have a limited shelf life.

Hard (and Semi-Hard) Cheese

These cheeses are also defined by their texture, which comes from a lack of moisture. This is probably the broadest group of cheeses. The cheeses can be further classified by:

Semi-hard and hard (uncooked) these are made by cutting the curds to remove the whey and then pressing in moulds to squeeze out more liquid. Cheshire is a semi-hard, while Cheddar is a hard.

Semi-hard and hard (cooked) the milk is first heated to encourage the whey to drain away and make drier curds. They are then put under extreme pressure and left to ripen for a very long time. Gruyère is a semi-hard, while Parmesan is a hard.

Blue Cheese

These are defined by veins of blue mould running through them. These days bacteria are injected directly into the formed cheese and allowed to grow. The bacteria find their way into any cracks or holes that have been left during the cheese-making process. Two bacteria are generally used: *Pencillium roqueforti* and *Pencillium glaucum*. Blue cheeses can be soft or hard and made with cow's, sheep's or goat's milk. The blue veins create a distinctive, strong smell and they're often referred to as 'big cheeses', as their salty, sharp flavour errs on the side of powerful.

Washed Rind Cheese

The cheeses can be soft or hard and are detectable from both their smell and appearance. While maturing, the cheeses are 'washed' in a salty brine which encourages the growth on the rind of the *Brevibacterium linens* mould. This creates a characteristic red-orange rind and produces some of the smelliest cheeses. If you can deal with the aroma, it's worth it, as you're treated to some of the most complex-flavoured and interesting cheese.

Flavoured Cheese

We're not big fans of these. If you want fruit or nuts with your cheese, serve them on the side. Also, the idea of smoked cheeses doesn't appeal; the smoking will cover up any distinguishing flavours. Don't bother.

Cheese Seasons

•••

In our desire to have everything available all year round, no matter what the temperature or season, we've come to depend on having our food available 'on tap'. However, when you start to consider it, cheese is the product of milk and milk is the product of animals that eat grass... and grass doesn't grow all year round. Couple this with the fact that the animals also produce milk for their young and, when their young are old enough, their mother's milk starts to run out until the next newborn comes along. So, our expectations of having any cheeses all year round are a little unreasonable.

Different cheeses are available at different times of the year and any cheese changes its flavour profile throughout the year.

A good cheese shop should be making some decisions for you by stocking only what is in season. However, here are a few pointers:

Sheep and goats produce milk for between eight to 10 months each year, usually stopping in winter. So fresh, soft, young goat's and sheep's milk cheeses are more likely to be available in spring, summer and autumn. In spring, animals should eat sweet new grasses and flowers, producing milk that is floral, herby and grassy. In the summer the pastures are more lush with beta-carotene, giving the milk a richer colour and flavour. At the end of the autumn and into winter, hay and grains become their staple diet, giving a stronger and more earthy flavour.

How and when a cheese is aged also affects the end flavour. For example, Stilton is thought best made with summer milk and aged for between three to five months, hence its strong links to Christmas. And sometimes we should listen to our appetites more carefully; there's a reason we crave light fresh cheeses in summer and hard flavoursome cheeses in winter.

Cheeses from the British Isles

Berkshire

Waterloo	Soft	**COW**	Rich, buttery, salty	**U**	**V**	Firm-to-oozing
Wigmore	Soft	**SHEEP**	Mild, sweet, yeasty	**U**	**V**	Smooth, creamy

Co. Cork

Ardrahan	Washed rind	**COW**	Earthy, pungent, smoky	**P**	**V**	Firm, soft and sticky
Coolea	Hard	**COW**	Nutty, sweet, long-lasting	**P**	**NV**	Gouda-like, smooth

Co. Tipperary

Cashel Blue	Semi-soft	**COW**	Rich, tangy	**P**	**V**	Creamy

Cumbria

St James	Washed rind	**SHEEP**	Rich, meaty	**U**	**NV**	Dense, moist

Devon

Beenleigh Blue	Semi-soft	**SHEEP**	Tangy, sweet, strong	**P**	**V**	Soft, creamy
Harbourne Blue	Soft	**GOAT**	Clean, fresh, strong	**P**	**NV**	Dense, crumbly
Ticklemore	Hard	**GOAT**	Delicate, herby, cool	**P**	**NV**	Light, moist, crumbly

Gloucestershire

Stinking Bishop	Washed rind	**COW**	Strong yet subtle	**P**	**V**	Creamy, oozing

Hampshire

Tunworth	Soft	**COW**	Sweet, nutty	**P**	**NV**	Creamy, chalky

Herefordshire

Ragstone	Soft	**GOAT**	Lactic, lemony	**U**	**NV**	Smooth, creamy

Lancashire

Kirkham's Lancashire	Hard	**COW**	Lemony, tangy	**U**	**NV**	Moist, crumbly

Nottinghamshire

Colston Bassett Stilton	Semi-soft	**COW**	Strong, full, tangy	**P**	**NV**	Soft-to-crumbly
Stichelton	Semi-soft	**COW**	Complex, fruity, salty	**U**	**NV**	Creamy

Somerset

Cardo	Washed rind	**GOAT**	Pungent, meaty	**U**	**V**	Fudgey
Gorwydd Caerphilly	Semi-hard	**COW**	Lemony, mushroomy	**U**	**NV**	Creamy, crumbly

Montgomery Cheddar	Hard	**COW**	Nutty, rich, sweet	**U**	**NV**	Dry, grainy
Tymsboro'	Soft	**GOAT**	Lemony, herbaceous	**U**	**NV**	Smooth, chalky

West Midlands

Berkswell	Hard	**SHEEP**	Nutty, sweet, spiky	**U**	**NV**	Grainy

Yorkshire

Hawes Wensleydale	Semi-hard	**COW**	Mild, lactic	**P**	**NV**	Smooth, dry, moist

Cheeses from the Continent

Jura

Comte	Hard	**COW**	Sweet, nutty	**U**	**NV**	Dense, moist

Loire

Crottin de Chavignol	Soft	**GOAT**	Rich, nutty	**U**	**NV**	Dense, crumbly

Midi Pyrenees

Roquefort	Semi-hard	**SHEEP**	Sweet, tangy	**U**	**NV**	Crumbly, moist

Normandy

Brie de Meaux	Soft	**COW**	Strong, savoury	**U**	**NV**	Creamy, oozing
Camembert	Soft	**COW**	Strong, earthy	**U**	**NV**	Buttery, supple

Lombardy

Gorgonzola Dolce	Semi-hard	**COW**	Sweet, salty	**U**	**NV**	Silky

Various

Parmigano Reggiano	Hard	**COW**	Sweet, nutty, salty	**U**	**NV**	Solid, crumbly
Pecorino	Hard	**SHEEP**	Rich, salty	**P**	**NV**	Dense, crumbly

La Mancha

Manchego	Hard	**SHEEP**	Nutty, savoury, sweet	**P**	**NV**	Compact, dry

Canton de Vaud

Gruyère	Hard	**COW**	Sweet, nutty	**U**	**NV**	Dense, smooth

U Unpasteurised	**P** Pasteurised	**NV** Non-Vegetarian	**V** Vegetarian

Cheeses from the British Isles

On pages 42–43, you will find some of our favourite cheeses, that we've got to know and that go down well with our customers. They offer the full range of cow's, goat's and sheep's, hard, soft, washed rind and blue. The flavours and textures will differ from cheese to cheese as well as with the season. Our notes on those pages offer an indication of what to expect, but different producers have varying production methods, so please check the label or ask the seller for advice. This particularly refers to issues of pasteurisation and whether animal or vegetarian rennet has been used. (It is advised that pregnant women shouldn't eat cheese made from unpasteurised milk.)

Cheeses from the Continent

Our foreign travels, as well as ease of transportation, have increased the range of cheeses available to us and we now expect to be able to buy and enjoy cheeses from farther afield. Our own (limited) knowledge only extends as far as some of the cheeses available on the Continent.

In terms of production methods and styles of cheeses, they are similar if not the same as those produced in the UK. However, there are a few stars that stand out and deserve to be enjoyed. And to be fair a Parmesan-style cheese tastes like it should because it's made in a certain geographical area... trying to make it here just wouldn't work.

The list on pages 42–43 is a very basic and pared-back range but we think these are some that we should all be eating from time to time.

Storing Cheese

When you buy a piece of cheese from a specialist shop it will usually come carefully wrapped in waxed paper. When you get it home it should stay in that paper until you need it and you should hang on to the paper to re-wrap any that is left. Cheese does not like being wrapped in plastic. Some large retailers wrap it in plastic first then put an outer waxed paper coating around it, so discard the plastic and wrap it in the outer paper.

Very few of us have a cellar or larder these days and we have to rely on the fridge to do the job they used to do. When keeping cheeses in the fridge:

1

Keep them wrapped in their waxed paper

2

Place a damp cloth in a lidded plastic container, sit your cheeses on the cloth and place the lid on top

3

Keep blue cheeses in a different box as their aroma can permeate the others

4

Keep the sealed box in the lower part of the fridge until required, checking every few days on their condition to ensure no new moulds are developing

5

If you can't be bothered with the box, keep the wrapped cheeses in the salad drawer of the fridge with the vegetables, where the humidity will help

CHEESE

BOARD

Putting Together a Cheese Board

•••

Creating a cheese board throws up all sorts of possibilities. Whatever the occasion, go with a limited selection of best-quality cheeses, rather than try to recreate a cheese counter. For some, a single piece of cheese is all a meal needs to complete it. If you're entertaining a group of six to eight, then three cheeses are plenty. If there's a crowd, five is enough. As a rule, allow 80g for each person at the end of a meal, or if it is a big element of the meal, allow 100–150g depending on the cheese.

When putting together a cheese board, ask the cheesemonger's advice. They'll know what's good that week and will suggest cheeses you may not have tried before, or new combinations. Or just buy cheeses you know you like; as long as they're not all very pungent and fight with each other. The obvious and safest bet is to go for:

Hard Cow	**Soft Sheep or Goat**	**Blue**
Montgomery Cheddar	Wigmore or Ragstone	Stichelton

There's something for everyone here and none would be too challenging for any guest. There are other ideas to try:

Geographical	**Milk Specific**	**Variety Specific**
choose a group of cheeses from a particular location, such as the West Country, Wales or Ireland	choose three goat's cheeses or three sheep's cheeses and enjoy their differences	try three washed rind cheeses or three blues

There is no 'correct' combination to make the perfect board. If you buy artisan-made cheeses in good condition your cheese board will be good.

How to Serve

Cheese (except fresh cheese, see page 38) should be removed from the fridge at least two hours before you require it to allow it to reach room temperature. Place the cheeses on the board you wish to serve them on, remove their paper wraps and cover with a damp, clean tea towel or cloth.

Having the right tools makes serving cheese easier. A knife with holes is good for soft cheeses (to stop them sticking to the blade), or one that is very thin and narrow. Use a robust knife for hard cheeses. If you're in the habit of buying chunks of Parmesan, a stubby, sharp knife will prove useful.

Serve with a biscuit, fresh fruit or a chutney, remembering that the cheese is the star, so the accompaniments mustn't out-do it.

Fruit to Serve with Cheese
•••

It's not essential to serve fruit with cheese, but if you want to here are a few suggestions. You don't need to go over the top. Keep it very simple; one type of fruit is more than enough:

Apple sharp, crisp, nothing too sweet. Suited to hard cheeses

Pear works well with all blue cheeses, particularly Stilton and Stichelton

Dates try a fresh Medjool date with a soft goat's cheese

Muscat Grapes wait for these floral-scented flavour bombs at the end of the summer and pair them with any soft and mild cheese

Figs fresh Turkish figs in the summer were made to go with the lighter soft cheeses, both cow's and goat's

Summer Berries strawberries, blackberries and raspberries all suit fresh cheeses, particularly ricotta

Chutney, Pickle, Jelly

•••

Equally, it's not compulsory to provide chutney, though there are times
when a cheese cries out for a dollop of the stuff. Fruity, sweet, acidic
chutney goes well with lots of hard cheeses. Anything too hot or spicy
tends not to work as the flavours start to compete... but sometimes the
softer and milder cheeses can take the contrast of a sharp and spiky jelly
or pickle.

Pickled Fruits
with blue

A Sharp Jelly with a Chilli Kick
with soft or fresh cheeses,
particularly goat

Onion Marmalade
a great all-rounder

Sweet and Acidic Fruit Chutney
marries with strong
and mild hard cheeses

Wine and Cheese Matching

•••

Don't assume that it's always got to be red wine or port. It's accepted
knowledge now that white wines – including some sparkling wines – make
as good partners as reds, if not better.

White
soft cheeses and
stronger flavours

Red
hard cheeses and
milder flavours,
but nothing creamy

Dessert
all manner of
cheeses

Port
perfect with
the blues

Biscuits for Cheese

•••

We're rather overwhelmed by the choice of cheese biscuits these days. There are now all shapes, sizes and flavours trying to grab our attention with different flours, seeds, nuts and fruits. When it comes to choosing a biscuit to go with cheese, the flavour of cheese shouldn't compete with that of the biscuit. Simplicity should prevail. Some of the classics include:

Bath Oliver An 18th-century physician, Dr William Oliver, from Bath, invented this recipe as an alternative for Bath buns which he thought were making his patients fat. They are made from flour, butter, yeast and milk, are a pale cream colour and have a very small rise. He bequeathed the recipe to his coachman, a Mr Atkins, with £100 and 10 sacks of finest flour. Mr Atkins set up in business making them and made his fortune.

Cream Cracker Another biscuit that has a long history; this one was invented by Joseph Haughton at his home in Dublin and manufactured by William Jacob, an Irish baker, around 1855. They don't contain cream; the name relates to the method of production where the ingredients are 'creamed' together.

Oatcake Certainly the oldest of our classics, these may have been around since Roman times, Everyone has their own favourite version: thick, thin, buttery, dry, coarse or fine, rounds, squares or triangles. Traditionally, they consist of fine oatmeal mixed with flour, but we think they need a bit of butter (see page 107). Apparently the Queen enjoys one at breakfast.

Charcoal Biscuits Another very English biscuit; Charles Ryder in Evelyn Waugh's *Brideshead Revisited* ate these black thins while cramming for his exams at Oxford. They were originally produced by a London baker, John Longman Bragg, in the late 19th century and contained a small amount of charcoal added to aid digestion. They have a chalky texture.

Cooking with Cheese

•••

Choosing the right cheese to cook with is a skill. Not all cheeses react well to cooking, though some seem to have been made for it. We all know to use Parmesan on pasta, but do we know which is best for cheese on toast or grating on top of our lasagne? Some theory to guide us:

Risotto

Chèvre, fresh cheeses,
Parmesan, pecorino, ricotta

Pasta

try blues, Parmesan, pecorino, soft goat's, Tallegio

Melting Cheese

for a toasted cheese and ham sandwich,
lasagne or potato gratin, it must be high in fat,
but not too hard or dry. Gruyère works well;
it's also the traditional cheese used in fondue

Cheese Sauce

try Cheddar, Comté, Emmental,
Gruyère, Parmesan, Stilton

Quiche

Cheddar, Comté, Gruyère, Wensleydale

Salads

blues, chèvre, curd cheese, feta

Seeded Rye Cracker

•••

Often the biscuit is just the means of getting the cheese from your plate to your mouth in one go. They can be plain, even cardboard-like, other times there's just a bit too much going on in the flavour department which is lost on the cheese. So here are three simple biscuit recipes that are neither cardboard in consistency nor will fight with the cheese.

These are as good with a chunk of Caerphilly as they are with houmous. Take your pick.

Makes 6 large crackers

Ingredients

25 g cold unsalted butter
125 g plain flour,
   plus more to dust
100 g rye flour
½ tsp sea salt
½ tsp baking powder
125 ml whole milk
50 g mixed seeds (poppy,
   linseed, sesame)

Equipment

sharp knife and chopping board
mixing bowl
rolling pin
baking tray
baking parchment
wire rack

Preparation

Preheat the oven to 180°C/350°F/gas mark 4.

Chop the butter and keep it chilled.

Method

In a mixing bowl, rub the cold butter into the flours, salt and baking powder. Gradually add the milk to make a soft dough that is slightly wet. Knead it a little until the stickiness has gone.

Tear off small amounts of the dough and roll out on a lightly floured surface as thinly as you can using a rolling pin.

Sprinkle with the seeds and roll once more to embed them into the dough.

Place on a baking tray lined with baking parchment and bake for about 15 minutes, until crisp when broken in two. Transfer to a wire rack to cool completely. Don't worry too much about the shape, you can break the sheets into shards and serve.

Keep in an airtight container and eat within one week.

Digestive Biscuits

•••

For those of you who have never tried a piece of Cheddar or blue cheese on a digestive, this is for you. The slight sweetness of the biscuit brings out the best in the cheeses. And you can always use them up with your tea. We've used a spelt flour here; it has a good nutty taste.

Makes 15

Ingredients

100 g cold unsalted butter
100 g medium oatmeal
100 g spelt flour, plus more to dust
1 tsp baking powder
60 g light soft brown sugar
¼ tsp sea salt
20 ml milk

Equipment

sharp knife and chopping board
mixing bowl (optional)
food processor (optional)
cling film
rolling pin
round or square biscuit cutter
baking tray
baking parchment
wire rack

Preparation

Chop the butter and keep it chilled.

Method

Mix all the dry ingredients together in a mixing bowl, or in the bowl of a food processor.

Rub in the butter, or pulse-blend it in. Add the milk to bring the mix together, but don't over-work the dough.

Press into a flat disc, wrap in cling film and chill in the fridge for 30 minutes.

Preheat the oven to 180°C / 350°F / gas mark 4.

Roll out the dough on a lightly floured surface to no more than 5 mm deep, thinner if you can. Cut your biscuits out with a round or square cutter and prick each with a fork a few times. (You can freeze them at this point.) Place them on a baking tray lined with baking parchment.

Bake for 15 minutes, until coloured on the edges, then transfer to a wire rack to cool completely.

You can of course cover these with melted chocolate if you're in that sort of mood (not to eat with cheese).

Keep in an airtight container and eat within one week.

Fig and Walnut Oatcakes

•••

A simple biscuit. The butter makes it nice and crumbly. Again, any cheese you fancy works on top of one of these.

Makes 20

Ingredients

60 g chilled unsalted butter
50 g dried figs
50 g walnuts
125 g fine oatmeal, or medium oatmeal
60 g plain flour, plus more to dust
1 tsp baking powder
¼ tsp sea salt
1 egg white

Equipment

box grater
sharp knife and chopping board
food processor
mixing bowl
cling film
rolling pin
round or square biscuit cutter
baking tray
baking parchment
wire rack

Preparation

Grate the butter coarsely.

Remove and discard the stalks from the figs and chop them. Chop the walnuts as well.

If you have medium oatmeal, blitz it in a food processor for three minutes.

Method

Mix all the dry ingredients (except the figs and walnuts) together in a food processor.

Add the butter and pulse-blend until the mixture looks like crumbs. Now add the figs and walnuts, then the egg white and pulse-blend once more, just until the dough comes together.

Press into a flat disc, wrap in cling film and chill in the fridge for 30 minutes.

Preheat the oven to 180°C/350°F/gas mark 4.

Roll out the dough on a lightly floured surface to 3 mm thick. Cut into rounds or squares (you can freeze them at this point). Place them on a baking tray lined with baking parchment.

Bake for 15 minutes: the biscuits should be firm to the touch. Transfer carefully to a wire rack to cool completely.

Keep in an airtight container and eat within two weeks.

Onion Marmalade

•••

This is a lovely pickle for all sorts of cheeses. We serve it with Wensleydale buttermilk scones (see page 114) filled with rocket and curd cheese. Our method is different to most others because we don't cook the onions in butter or oil beforehand. The secret to success is to know when to remove it from the heat. Keep tasting it as it cooks and use your judgement.

Makes 5 jars

Ingredients

1 kg white onions
6 cloves
10 black peppercorns
10 allspice berries
50 g sea salt
900 g granulated sugar
450 ml cider vinegar
1 tbsp fennel seeds

Equipment

sharp knife and chopping board
5 x 200 ml jam jars with lids
muslin
string
mixing bowl
saucepan

Preparation

Peel and slice the onions 2 mm thick.

Sterilise five 200 ml jars (see page 408).

Tie the spices (except the fennel seeds) in a piece of muslin with string.

Sprinkle the salt over the onions in a mixing bowl and leave for two hours. Rinse and drain thoroughly.

Method

Simmer the sugar and vinegar in a saucepan, adding the spice bag.

Add the onions and cook gently for about one hour until reduced and thickened and the remaining liquid is a deep golden colour. Discard the spice bag. Now add the fennel seeds and cook for a final five minutes. Remove from the heat.

Quickly pot and seal while it is still hot.

Welsh Rarebit

There is much written about what cheese to use in this dish; however, we recommend that you use anything that's left in the fridge as long as it tastes good. Try a strong cheese such as Cheddar married with something like a young soft cheese or even a cream cheese. Melt 25 g of unsalted butter in a small saucepan with 1 tbsp of plain flour, slowly whisk in 100 ml of stout and 1 tsp of English mustard. Cook for one minute, until smooth. Melt in 150 g of grated cheese, a dash of Worcestershire sauce and a grind of black pepper. Remove from the heat and beat in an egg yolk. Leave to one side while toasting two slices of bread under the grill on one side, then flipping to give the other side a half-toasting with just a little colour. Spread the cheese mixture right to the edges of the half-toasted sides and grill for three minutes until it becomes a bubbling mass. Allow to cool for a few minutes before cutting in half and eating. Makes 2 slices.

Use Up Your Rinds

Don't throw away Parmesan rinds when you have finished grating. They are excellent flavour enhancers and give depth to casseroles, or soups such as Minestrone soup (see page 362), or slide into a cheese sauce to bolster the flavour. The rind will hold together while it cooks and allow the cheese to melt away. Remove any remaining rind with a slotted spoon before serving.

M

Goat's Cheese Straws with Anchovies and Fennel Seeds

Take a block of shop-bought puff pastry and roll it out into a 2 mm-thick rectangle. Lay on to a sheet of baking parchment and chill for 30 minutes to make it easier to handle. Spread liberally with a soft tangy goat's cheese, scatter with drained and chopped anchovies and add a sprinkling of chilli flakes and crushed fennel seeds. Fold over in half and press down, using a rolling pin. Brush lightly with beaten egg and chill for 30 minutes. Preheat the oven to 180°C/350°F/gas mark 4. Cut into 1 cm-thin strips; sprinkle with poppy and sesame seeds. Place on a baking tray lined with baking parchment and bake in the hot oven for 20 minutes until golden brown, turning a few times to ensure they dry out and are crisp and flaky. Serve as a pre-supper snack with drinks.

Marinated Feta

Sterilise a 500 ml jar and lid (see page 408). Cut 200 g of feta into 2 cm cubes. Layer it in the jar with ½ tsp of dried oregano, 1 sliced garlic clove, a few pink peppercorns and a bay leaf. Cover with a good extra virgin olive oil and repeat the layering until the jar is full, tapping out any air bubbles. Push a dried chilli down the side. Chill for one week before serving (make a note of the sell-by date of the cheese on the jar and don't worry if the oil 'sets'; it will liquefy at room temperature). Serve with salads, grilled pork, or charred aubergines and tomatoes.

M

CHOCOLATE

An Introduction to Chocolate

Where once it was wine, then cheese, swiftly followed by coffee, the new dinner party hot topic is chocolate: dark, milk, percentage of cocoa, or the latest chocolate tasting you attended.

We're not talking Mars Bars here. We're talking high-quality, small-batch bars, sometimes from a single estate, made by a growing collection of artisan producers.

Long before these developments, most of us were content with a slice of our auntie's chocolate layer cake at Sunday afternoon tea. One of our grandmothers had a sweetshop, so bars of Fry's Chocolate Cream and weighing out boiled sweets from glass jars were part of childhood. We still eat chocolate almost every day and feel slightly cheated if there isn't any in the house. That's when we go to the kitchen cupboard to sneak the cooking chocolate. But we are still learning about proper, good-quality chocolate... and enjoying the lessons. We are such fans that we have even started to produce our own bars and the process has given us a deeper understanding of the fascinating complexities of chocolate.

There's something about chocolate. Try finding someone who doesn't like it. Or count the friends who say that they're 'addicted' to it. Then of course there are the purported health benefits of eating it on a daily basis.

We don't think you need to buy super-high-end chocolate. We just like it made with care and without added fats. As you snap a piece of chocolate and it melts on your tongue, you can tell how well it has been made.

These days, artisan chocolatiers are springing up in larger cities, often proponents of the bean-to-bar process where chocolate of a single origin can be traced back to source. Some are producing bespoke chocolate of hitherto unknown intensity – almost a flavour overload – of which you can truly only eat a small square. People are increasingly willing to spend more on a bar of good-quality chocolate to treat themselves, rather than chomping through a whole sugary and fatty commercial bar.

Scientists have discovered that chocolate contains substances that can have an effect on our brains: tryptophan, used by the brain to make serotonin; phenylethylalamine, which promotes feelings of attraction, excitement and nervousness; and theobromine, a weak stimulant that can produce a (legal) high. But whether you're using it to bake or cook with, or merely to enjoy in any number of confectionery guises, we're not eating chocolate for a daily dose of vitamins or minerals, proteins or carbs, or anything else it can do for our bodies. We're eating it for pleasure...

Stimulants and fashion aside, we are here to help you work out what to buy and how to make the best use of it. But first, a little bit of history...

• •

Cacao

The cacao tree grows in equatorial regions around the globe, particularly in South and Central America including the Caribbean, in West Africa, Indonesia and Malaysia.

A cacao tree usually produces a crop of pods twice a year, with each tree producing 20–30 pods. A single cocoa pod produces 20–60 cocoa beans. A whole tree's worth of pods produces enough beans to make 450g of chocolate, which is six or seven standard-sized bars.

Aztec king Montezuma offers the Spanish Conquistador Cortés a cup of bitter chocolate to drink. Cortés introduces cacao and the drink to the Spanish court of King Philip. The Spanish add sugar and vanilla to the drink.

First mention in the UK of cacao in the book *The Indian Nectar* by Dr Henry Stubbs. He had witnessed it first hand in Jamaica, where it was considered a medicine and was used by apothecaries.

Pope Pius V is introduced to a chocolate drink, but doesn't like it!

1500 **1600** **1700**

Pre-1500s

Mayans and Aztecs use cacao beans to trade with and to make a chocolate drink for warriors and kings.

London coffee houses starting to serve a chocolate drink. Fans include Samuel Pepys.

The Italians find it agreeable and coffee houses in Venice and Florence start to sell a chocolate drink. France follows.

Irish physician and explorer Sir Hans Sloane comes up with the addition of milk instead of water to the drink, effectively creating a forerunner of modern-day drinking chocolate.

JS Fry and Sons produce the first chocolate bar in a shape and form we're more familiar with today, although it wouldn't have tasted as nice, as it would have essentially been a rather rough mixture of cocoa and sugar.

Chocolate confectionery outsells sugar confectionery for the first time.

Swiss chocolatier Daniel Peter uses Nestlé's dried milk powder to create the first milk chocolate bar.

Sales of chocolate worldwide reach $113 bn.

1800

1900

2000

Cacao cultivation spreads from Central and Southern America to West Africa and Indonesia as demand grows.

Chocolate was included in the rations of troops fighting the First World War.

Varieties of Cacao Beans

...

Forastero The most widely cultivated, accounting for about 90 per cent of cocoa production. Originating in the Amazon, the beans are now widely grown in South America and West Africa. The high-yielding tree makes a lower-grade cacao and is used for commercial chocolate making and baking. But as with any produce, terroir plays its part and Forastero from São Tomé and Ivory Coast has more complex, prized flavours.

Criollo Probably first cultivated by the Mayans. Today it's one of the more prized beans, produced largely around the Indian Ocean. It has spicy, floral, delicate notes and is used to make fine chocolate.

Trinitario A hybrid of Criollo and Forastero, named after they naturally cross-pollinated in Trinidad in the 17th century. They are not widely grown but are a more complex bean with fruit, floral, wood and tobacco flavours.

Porcellana So called for its colour, this white bean is a strain of Criollo, native to Venezuela. It's highly prized and grown in very small quantities. It has an intense flavour, with notes of roasted almonds and sweet olive oil. The world's entire crop is currently purchased by one producer: Amedei.

Production

Cocoa pods are left to ferment, then the seeds or 'beans' are extracted, cleaned and roasted. The roasting allows the beans to develop flavour in a similar way to coffee beans, in addition to reducing moisture.

Once roasted, the husks of the beans are removed, leaving the kernels or nibs. These are ground to a paste between rollers, which also releases the fat or cocoa butter. The paste is known as chocolate mass.

Once the mass has cooled and hardened it is essentially unsweetened chocolate. To make dark chocolate, sugar and cocoa butter are added and the mixture is passed through steel rollers to a fine powder. Finally it goes through the 'conching' process: the powder is placed in a shell-like heated trough and a heated roller passed back and forth. This takes from several hours to up to a week, during which flavours develop, moisture content is reduced and flavourings, often vanilla, are added. It can now be made into couverture (see page 68) or undergo a final process of tempering.

In the tempering process, the chocolate is heated and cooled to exact temperatures to produce a smooth and glossy product.

Confectionery

Today, chocolate is generally sold in three forms: dark, milk and white. Many consider that the most sophisticated-tasting is dark chocolate, as it is usually less sweet than milk or white chocolate and can be bitter and have more complex flavour notes. To be officially called dark chocolate it must contain no less than 35 per cent cocoa solids and not contain milk. But it is 70 per cent that is the magic number for many consumers, with any less not considered 'real' chocolate. You can go as high as 100 per cent, but those bars are very much an acquired taste.

In the UK, to be called milk chocolate, it must have no less than 20 per cent cocoa solids. It can be described as being sweet and creamy.

White chocolate contains no cocoa solids and some would say it is just not chocolate. What it does contain is cocoa butter, milk and sugar.

Chocolate Trends

•••

Bean-to-bar

Apart from being great marketing speak, this phrase points to a commitment to do things properly; to go back to the source and ensure every process along the way is carried out to make the best chocolate bar possible, with no short cuts. Some producers have bought cacao plantations and will charter wind-powered boats to deliver their ethically produced crop to their manufacturing plants. (This is generally small-scale and not undertaken by global manufacturers.) The result is high-quality, complex-flavoured and covetable chocolate.

Single Origin Chocolate

In the same way that wine growers and coffee producers have recognised the value and quality of wine or coffee from a single estate or plantation, now you can find chocolate from specific regions – or even farms – from a particular type of cacao bean. As a result, this chocolate has unique flavour notes and aromas.

Fairtrade

This movement aims to ensure producers are fairly rewarded. Often as part of a co-operative, farmers are guaranteed prices for their crops, as well as being given support in other areas of their lives, whether in improving growing conditions and farming efficiencies, or providing education for children. Some chocolate brands base their entire range on this ethical production and make it their raison d'être, whereas others may offer fairly traded chocolate among their other products. All Fairtrade chocolate will advertise itself as such on the packaging, allowing us, the consumers, to make our own choices.

Place a small piece of good-quality chocolate on the centre of your tongue and close your mouth. Chocolate is a rare food that melts at body temperature, so within seconds it will start to melt on your tongue.

As it melts, push your tongue up to the roof of your mouth and you'll detect different notes and flavours that may remind you of other foods.

perhaps Nuts, Coffee, Spices, Fruits or

Tobacco

When tasting chocolate, it's been concluded that there are more than 600 different aromas and flavour compounds.

Don't confuse a high percentage of cocoa as being a sign of a better-quality chocolate. It simply denotes the percentage of cocoa solids used. In the same way, you wouldn't expect a wine to be better merely because it has a high percentage of alcohol.

Cooking with Chocolate

...

Look in the baking section of supermarkets for cooking chocolate, as confectionery chocolate has different properties and can produce unexpected results when cooking. Also, substituting a milk chocolate for a 70 per cent chocolate could have disastrous effects on your baking, so always follow the recipe suggestions.

Cocoa Powder

This has had most of the cocoa butter removed and is virtually fat-free. Use for drinking chocolate, cakes, biscuits, pastry, or confectionery.

Couverture

This comes in blocks, bars or small pellets ('nibs' or 'chips'). It contains a lot of cocoa butter (31 per cent minimum) which makes it perfect for cooking, as it melts beautifully to a smooth, glossy liquid that's easy to work, for use in ganaches, desserts and cakes. Couverture needs to be 'tempered' if you want a glossy finish and a good 'snap' (see page 71). (Some can be purchased already tempered, to save you the trouble.) Different types of couverture have varying cocoa mass and cocoa butter percentages and use beans from various regions and continents. All these variables produce couvertures of different flavours, some bitter, some fruity, others floral and spicy. Choose yours to suit what you're making.

Cocoa Nibs

These are roughly crushed, roasted cocoa beans without their husks. They're hard, bitter and have little sweetness. They can be used for anything from sprinkling over salads to adding to biscuits and brownies.

Chocolate in Savoury Dishes

For some cuisines, adding chocolate to a savoury dish is normal, such as in the famous and complex chilli-spiked Mexican mole sauce. The chocolate is bitter rather than sweet and only added in small quantity to a vast array of spices and smoked chillies, so is not the predominant flavour. It also helps to smooth out the sharp flavours of the spices, at the same time adding depth. The Italians also use chocolate and you'll sometimes find a recipe that uses cocoa powder in a sauce or ragoût with game.

Coconut and Rum Chocolate Cake

•••

Rather exotic and perfectly easy to make. The success lies in gentle folding of the mixture. It is flourless so will keep for one week in an airtight container... if it lasts that long. Replace the rum with milk if you want.

Serves 8

Ingredients

For the cake

160 g unsalted butter, plus
  more for the tin
200 g dark chocolate
160 g golden caster sugar
40 g desiccated coconut
160 g ground almonds
25 ml dark rum
4 eggs, separated

For the icing

25 g unsalted butter
60 ml coconut milk
225 g icing sugar
10 g toasted coconut flakes

Equipment

20 cm loose-bottomed cake tin
box grater
mixing bowl
saucepan
electric mixer
wire rack

Preparation

Butter and line a 20 cm loose-bottomed cake tin.

Grate the chocolate and place it in a mixing bowl.

Preheat the oven to 180°C/350°F/gas mark 4.

Method

For the cake, melt the butter in a saucepan, then pour it over the chocolate in the bowl to melt. Stir in half the sugar, all the coconut, ground almonds and rum and the egg yolks.

Whip the egg whites with the remaining sugar in an electric mixer on full speed until firm peaks are formed. Stir one-third of them into the chocolate mixture. Gently fold in the remaining egg white, using a metal spoon or spatula and keeping as much of the volume as you can.

Bake for 30 minutes in the middle of the oven, then leave to cool on a wire rack.

To make the icing, melt the butter in a saucepan and set aside to cool slightly. Beat the coconut milk and icing sugar together until combined, then beat in the melted butter. Spread evenly over the cake and decorate with toasted coconut flakes.

Very Dark
Chocolate Biscuits

•••

We use spelt flour in this recipe to add more flavour. If you don't have any to hand, either use all plain flour or experiment with wholemeal. You can freeze the raw mixture when you have rolled the balls; just defrost, then bake as below.

Makes 30

Ingredients

200 g dark chocolate
100 g plain flour
80 g plain spelt flour
35 g cocoa powder
1 tsp baking powder
½ tsp salt
200 g unsalted butter
160 g light muscovado sugar
1 egg
1 tsp vanilla extract

Equipment

sharp knife and chopping board
sieve
electric mixer
cling film
baking trays
baking parchment
wire rack

Preparation

Chop the chocolate finely with a sharp knife.

Method

Sift together the flours, cocoa, baking powder and salt. Melt the chocolate over a bain-marie (see right).

Beat the butter and sugar together in an electric mixer until lightened but not fluffy. Add the egg and vanilla and beat again. Mix in the chocolate, then fold in the dry ingredients. Wrap in cling film and rest in the fridge for 30 minutes.

Preheat the oven to 180°C / 350°F/ gas mark 4. Roll the biscuit dough into 30 g balls; you should get 30 of them. Space them out over a couple of baking trays lined with baking parchment. Bake in the oven for 12 minutes. Leave to cool slightly on the baking trays, then carefully transfer to wire racks with a palette knife to cool completely.

Tempering Chocolate

This gives a glossy finish. Using a digital thermometer, heat 250 g of chocolate in a heatproof bowl over a pan of simmering water to 45°C. Then cool to 26°C, by gently stirring off the heat on a cool surface. Return to the heat, taking the chocolate up to 30°C, then remove immediately. It's now ready to use.

Melting Chocolate
Over a Bain-marie: the Rules

Always use a heatproof bowl to melt chocolate; metal or Pyrex are good choices. The bowl should fit over the pan, but should not touch the water. The water should be just simmering very gently, not boiling. Chop the chocolate into small chunks, add to the bowl and use a spatula to keep it moving, to ensure an even melt. Remove the chocolate as soon as it has melted or it will overheat. Avoid getting water into the chocolate as this may tarnish the finish.

Quick Chocolate Truffles

Blitz 150 g of dark chocolate in a food processor until granular. Heat 100 ml of double cream, 2 tbsp of Somerset cider brandy, or any dark rum or brandy to hand and 1 tbsp of muscovado sugar until almost boiling, then slowly pour over the chocolate, blending until you have a paste. Cover and chill for 45 minutes. Once chilled, roll into small bite-sized balls of about 15 g each and dust with cocoa powder. Makes about 15.

M

Chocolate Spread

Blitz 50 g of blanched, toasted hazelnuts in a food processor. Add 20 g of icing sugar and 100 g of melted dark chocolate and blitz again. Add 40 ml of hazelnut or light groundnut oil with ¼ tsp vanilla extract. Blitz until smooth. Pot into a sterilised 200 ml jar (see page 408) and store in a cool place (not in the fridge).

Chocolate Gingers
and Fruit and Nut Rounds

Buy the best-quality crystallised ginger and half-dip it into Tempered chocolate (see page 71). Allow to set on a piece of baking parchment.

Using the tempered chocolate, make 5 cm discs of melted chocolate on baking parchment. As the chocolate is setting, push toasted pistachios, yellow raisins and cranberries into the pools of chocolate. Allow to set and serve with coffee after supper. Try using almonds and sour cherries, or any other good-quality dried fruits and nuts that are hiding in the back of the kitchen storecupboard.

Spiced Hot Chocolate

Add a few crushed green cardamom pods, some fennel seeds, pink peppercorns or mellow chilli flakes to simmering milk and allow to infuse for five minutes before passing through a sieve. Then pour it over your chocolate as usual. Add a pinch of sea salt to bring out the flavour.

M

Quick Chocolate Sauce

Heat 150 g of dark chocolate, 100 ml of double cream, 30 g of demerara sugar and 30 g of unsalted butter in a pan over a low heat. Once melted, beat in 50 ml of hot water and a pinch of sea salt and continue to beat until emulsified. Serve in a warmed jug. Makes 300 ml, or six servings.

Storecupboard Stars

70% CHOCOLATE

both for eating and as couverture, the latter in button form for easy melting

COCOA

POWDER

Storing a Cake in the Freezer

1

First ensure your cake has fully cooled. Do not ice it.

2

Place a large piece of cling film on a work surface and wrap over the top of the cake, tightly.

3

Take another piece of cling film and lay it on the table. Turn the cake over and wrap cling film over the top again, ensuring all air has been expelled and the cling film is secure.

4

Remember to label the cake with its baking date.

5

A cake can usually be stored in the freezer for up to three months.

Chocolate Cream Icing with Raspberries

Melt 125 g of dark chocolate over a bain-marie (see page 71). Whip 250 g of double cream to soft peaks with ½ tsp of vanilla extract. Fold together with half a punnet of raspberries. Spread through the middle and over the top of the cake. Scatter the remaining raspberries over and dust with icing sugar.

Pour-over Chocolate Icing

Melt 90 g of unsalted butter in a saucepan over a low heat. Stir in 3 tbsp of milk, 20 g of cocoa powder and ½ tsp of vanilla extract. Whisk this into 190 g of sifted icing sugar. Add 40 g of finely chopped nuts. Pour over a cake and allow to set.

Sour Cream Icing

Melt 150 g of dark chocolate in a bain-marie (see page 71). Once melted, turn off the heat. Beat in 150 ml of sour cream. Sift over 100 g of icing sugar and 1 tsp of vanilla extract and continue to stir. Leave to cool until icing reaches a spreadable consistency.

Chocolate Fudge Icing

Set a saucepan over a low heat and dissolve 125 g of caster sugar into 125 g of double cream. Do not boil. Pour over 100 g of grated dark chocolate in a bowl and stir to melt, then beat in 75 g of unsalted butter until glossy. Cover with cling film and allow to cool and thicken, then apply to a cake with a palette knife.

An Introduction to Coffee

It's how billions of us start our day and often finish a good meal; 'having a coffee' is a euphemism for taking a break and the drink is a well-known social lubricant. Coffee – arguably one of the world's greatest flavours and aromas – is at once evocative and exotic. The scent of a cup is filled with the thrilling anticipation of that first sip and at the same time comforting, welcoming and homely.

Few ingredients arouse so much passion and debate, or in fact have such a colourful past. Revered throughout history, becoming the subject of JS Bach's 'Coffee Cantata', a potent symbol of political protest and even blessed by a pope, coffee has also been disapproved of, banned and demonised over the centuries. In truth your morning cup is as much cultural and historical icon as it is hot, rejuvenating drink.

Discovered in north-east Africa, some records suggest as early as the 9th century, coffee first made its way to the Yemen before it was introduced to Constantinople in 1453. By 1475 the world's first coffee shop, Kiva Han, opened, followed shortly by a Turkish law which stated that a woman could divorce her husband if he failed to provide her with a daily quota of the black stuff.

Brought to the Continent in the late 1600s, coffee quickly took hold across Europe. At one point, 3,000 coffee shops existed in London alone. Influential places, they were seats of debate and political force frequented by artists, intellectuals, bankers and businessmen. Lloyd's of London and the London Stock Exchange both started life as coffee houses.

While the rest of Europe clung on to their coffee culture, the next coffee surge in the English capital wasn't until the 1950s and 1960s, after the first espresso machine landed in Soho in 1952 and a new crop of coffee houses attracted a hipster, bohemian crowd of artists, writers and actors.

These days, London is awash once more with coffee shops and not only big chains; a renewed interest in specialist coffee beans and artisanal micro-roasteries means that coffee is at last well and truly ingrained in the British culture.

Growing up, it was instant Nescafé that first characterised coffee as we knew it; drunk at 11am coffee mornings. By our mid teens in the early 1980s, hanging out in an Italian-style café called Café Roma in our home town – one that offered a 'frothy' coffee, no less – felt very grown up. Their attempt at a cappuccino was far from the real thing, but we loved it.

At home the Melita Coffee Maker was followed by the cafetière, but it wasn't until we arrived in London in the late 1980s that we started to taste coffee resembling anything like that which we've become accustomed to today. A visit to Milan at around the same time was where the first real espresso was tasted, standing up in a bar and downed in one. No surprise then that an Italian stovetop coffee maker found its way back home in our luggage at the end of that trip.

Today, we're a sucker for a flat white when out and about, while at home it's generally a simple filter or a stovetop cup which seems to deliver the required results without too much geekery.

Choose the Right Grind

•••

There are four main types of grind, each yielding a particular coffee strength, as well as requiring a particular type of coffee maker:

Coarse

Primarily used for the cafetière, where longer steeping is required

Medium

For filter and automatic drip pot brewers

Fine

Produces a strong coffee for use with espresso or stovetop machines. Can be used in a regular coffee maker, but leaves sediments

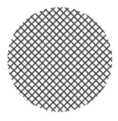

Extra Fine

Used to make Middle Eastern or Turkish coffee in a small pot called an ibrik. Often mixed with cardamom

Some coffee shops and independent retailers now offer to grind your beans to suit your coffee-making equipment – whether cafetière, stovetop or espresso machine – thus giving you the freshest grind to your exact needs. Search them out and take advantage!

Know Your Beans

•••

Whole Beans To get the best from your coffee, you need to buy whole beans for grinding at home. Grinding coffee releases its essential oils, setting free its aromas and flavours, which quickly begin to deteriorate. The more rapidly you can use freshly ground coffee, the more lively and flavourful the resulting cup will be.

Spotting Quality Good-quality beans are consistently uniform in colour, smooth with no cracks and all the beans should be whole with no broken pieces. Depending on the roast, they could be matt or shiny. Look for a medium to dark colour, as a very dark roast can be disguising an inferior-quality bean.

Single-estate Beans An increased interest in sustainability and the provenance of coffee has seen beans selected for their unique qualities from individual farms. This growth in single-estate beans has in turn given rise to an interest in specially selected seasonal coffees only available at certain times of the year. Increasingly on offer through artisan coffee roasters who sell online and ship to your door, but you should also look out for recommended coffees of the month in your local specialist coffee shop. If they don't have them, suggest they start.

Ethical Sourcing (Fairtrade) Coffee is a commodity and one of the world's most heavily traded. A byproduct of this is that its trade has not always been fair to the (often) developing communities that work to produce it. Direct trade with brokers, who work specifically with coffee growers, builds mutually respectful relationships that intend to benefit individual producers or co-operatives in coffee-producing countries, which can't be a bad thing.

Terroir

...

The concept of terroir – or the specific geographic conditions that affect a crop's flavour and characteristics, traditionally applied to wine – can be applied to coffee as well. While flavours can be identified that distinguish, say, Kenyan from Colombian coffee, roasting, grinding and coffee-making technique can also affect the flavour, so it's by no means the only factor. But there are certain things you can start to identify from particular coffee-growing regions, so you can find the coffee best suited to your tastes:

South America

Colombia Medium-bodied coffees with mellow acidity and a definite nutty, caramel-like sweetness, Colombia is frequently rated among the top three coffee-producing countries in the world.

Bolivia Left out of the top-end coffee market until relatively recently, Bolivia actually has the perfect terrain for coffee trees to flourish, producing a fruity cup.

Brazil The largest producer of Arabica beans, therefore with a range of qualities on offer. Those worth drinking are typically nutty, chocolatey and bittersweet with a mild acidity. Look for 'Pulp Natural', coffee that has been through a process that leaves some of the 'cherry' (the pulpy fruit around the coffee beans) on the beans to develop a more full-bodied, milk chocolate sweetness with some spiciness.

Galapagos Islands Some of the world's best organic coffees come from these Islands, where coffee trees thrive in the unspoiled, clean air.

Venezuela The best-quality coffees are grown on the Colombian border and have bright, clean, crisp flavours and low acidity.

Central America

Costa Rica Reproached for being middle-of-the-road due to the country's vast coffee proliferation and cash- rather than quality-conscious production methods. The less-good coffees are rather mild and soft in flavour... in other words: boring.

El Salvador Once thought of as balanced and sweet... but not very inspiring, El Salvador has come up in the world with some really interesting single-estate coffees.

Guatemala Some say these are the best coffees in Central America. Good Guatemalan coffees have clean fruit flavours, with bright floral hints.

Honduras The quality of coffees from Honduras ranges vastly. The good ones have anything from sugar cane sweetness and mildly fruity acidity, to deeper caramel tones and lower acidity, perfect for espresso.

Nicaragua A wide range of flavours, some mildly citrussy and others with a pronounced acidity.

Africa

Burundi Very similar to coffees grown in neighbouring Rwanda, beans produced here are fruity – particularly reminiscent of red fruits – and sweetly citrussy.

Ethiopia Huge differences in biodiversity and two very different processing techniques give Ethiopian coffees more variety than most. 'Natural' processing allows the cherry to be dried around the coffee bean before it is removed, giving the coffee rich, sweet and fruity wine-like flavours. 'Washed' processing removes the cherry completely, soon after picking, bringing out more delicate floral notes which have a lightness that can be thought of as very similar to tea.

Kenya Coffee plants are grown in the full strength of the sun without shade, so the beans have big, bold flavours with a tartness sometimes like blackcurrants, a savouriness that resembles tomatoes and often tropical fruit flavours. Regarded by many coffee aficionados as the best.

Rwanda Light and tea-like, Rwandan coffees can be top class.

Tanzania Typically rich-flavoured and medium bodied, the coffee most people associate with Tanzania is the peaberry; however, there are many more standard beans worth looking out for.

Other Parts of the World

Indonesia On the whole full-bodied and low on acidity. Sumatran coffees tend to bring about a strong 'love / hate' response, with anything from a rich, toasted unsweetened cocoa flavour to a smoky, earthy or – some say – mushroomy complexity. Javan coffees are typically rich and full-bodied with a herbal undertone, while Sulawesi varieties are typically sweet with warm, spicy notes.

Papua New Guinea Often these coffees have complex-yet-mellow chocolatey flavours and deserve to be recognised separately from Indonesian coffees.

The Pursuit of Perfection

We have long planned every journey – particularly the morning run to office or meeting – with a view to the best coffee route. The risk of missing out on our morning dose or – worse – experiencing an inferior cup is simply too much to bear.

There's no doubt, the joy of a properly made cup of coffee is one of life's true pleasures, but while we are avid coffee lovers, we are not caffeine fiends. One very good cup a day is, and should be, enough. It stands to reason, then, to insist that cup must be the best you can possibly get, whether it's home-made or sipped while out and about.

Seeking out and frequenting local artisan establishments is a must, of course. Also, home brewing – and the perfecting of the art – is something of an obsession for us. Coffee filtering, percolating, plunging and grinding devices have been purchased in their dozens over the years. Honed down to relative perfection, we can now share the lessons we have learned to help shortcut the hard work and reveal some of the expensive mistakes that inevitably get made in the pursuit of (coffee) nirvana. Be warned, a degree of precision is required, but once you are in the habit of enjoying consistently delicious brews, you won't mind a bit.

Drinking Occasions: Know Your Roasts

More versatile than one might imagine, coffee is of course mostly enjoyed hot with rich, darker roasts providing the strong, thick, sultry hit of espresso many of us like to start the day with.

More surprising perhaps are the lighter roasts coming on the market that, when filtered, offer a cleaner, more refreshing 'tea'-like experience, with a lightness that makes them very palatable for afternoon drinking. Lighter roasting allows more of the integrity of the bean to shine through, giving more complex flavours and less bitterness. As a result, only the best-quality beans are used. Mellow fruitiness and a pleasant acidity is conjured from the beans, making for a more sophisticated alternative to its more brazen dark-roast cousin.

The concept of chilling coffee is by no means new, the 'Frapp-enised' high street being testament to our year-round obsession with the coffee bean. However, consider a much more grown-up and refined light roast cold extraction next time you fancy a chilled coffee: steep coarse-ground beans in cold or room temperature water for at least 12 hours, then strain (see page 91).

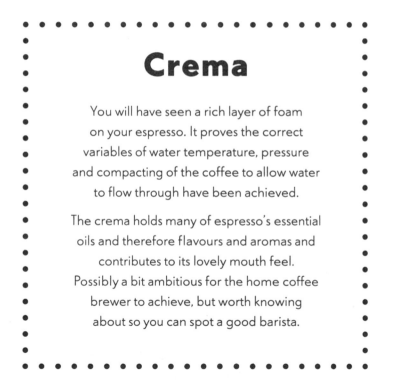

Crema

You will have seen a rich layer of foam on your espresso. It proves the correct variables of water temperature, pressure and compacting of the coffee to allow water to flow through have been achieved.

The crema holds many of espresso's essential oils and therefore flavours and aromas and contributes to its lovely mouth feel. Possibly a bit ambitious for the home coffee brewer to achieve, but worth knowing about so you can spot a good barista.

Coffee-making Methods at Home

•••

FILTER

These days reinventing itself as the 'pour over'. Lighter roasts work best here. If you are using filter paper then first wet the paper so that it doesn't absorb so many of the coffee's essential oils. Put in your coffee, then pour over a small amount of water to let the coffee lightly expand or 'bloom'. After 20 seconds, very slowly pour on the rest of the water in a circular motion.

CAFETIERE

These work best with medium roasts. Warm the pot with boiling water and then dry it. Put in the coffee and, as with filter, pour over a small amount of water to allow the coffee to 'bloom'. Wait for 20 seconds, then pour in the rest of the water and stir. Allow to stand for three to four minutes before plunging.

STOVETOP

Very slightly coarser-ground dark espresso roasts work best here. Once the pot comes to the boil, reduce the heat to very low and let the coffee come through slowly. If it continues to boil furiously it will burn the coffee and make it taste bitter and scorched.

SIPHON

If you've seen something looking more like a science experiment than a coffee-making device in your local artisan coffee house, then you've probably discovered the siphon. Popularised by California coffee geeks in recent years, it was a technique first used before the Second World War. Water vapour is forced through the grinds into another chamber where the coffee is brewed, resulting in a very pure, clean cup.

ESPRESSO

Dark roast espresso coffee is needed here. Get to know your machine; the pressure is important and might need adjusting to let the coffee come through at the proper rate. Also, the amount of coffee and the coarseness of the grind may need to be adjusted slightly.

AEROPRESS

Home brewing has been given a boost by the introduction of the Aeropress, which uses air pressure to extract more flavour from the coffee. Some say it can offer a very close result to a professionally made espresso, for little cost.

ESPRESSO

MACCHIATO

LATTE

FLAT WHITE

AMERICANO

WATER

ESPRESSO

PICCOLO

SILKY FROTH

MILK

ESPRESSO

CHOCOLATE

CAPPUCCINO

SILKY FROTH

CREAMY MILK

ESPRESSO

MOCHA

SILKY FROTH

MILK

CHOCOLATE

ESPRESSO

A Consistent Cup

•••

Weighing ground coffee to the gram is the way the professionals get their consistent results, but if you find that a bit of an ordeal, we've found that American measuring cups make a very handy substitute. As a general rule we use the ratios here and grind our beans fresh every time. Of course everyone likes their coffee differently, so use this as a starting point and increase or decrease the amount of water to get the strength you like:

To Make

Use

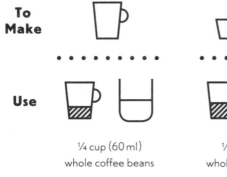

¼ cup (60 ml)	⅓ cup (80 ml)	½ cup (120 ml)
whole coffee beans	whole coffee beans	whole coffee beans
350 ml water	500 ml water	700 ml water

And so on... This equates to 60 g of ground coffee per 1 litre of water. 20 g is around 1 heaped tbsp.

Freshly Ground

To get the best flavour and freshness, always grind whole beans as you need them. Use fresh-ground coffee as soon as possible after it has been ground; even 10 minutes' exposure to the air can reduce a great cup to a merely good one.

Freshly Drawn Water A lot of emphasis is put on the quality of the coffee beans, and rightly so. However, it's worth remembering that a cup of coffee is 99 per cent water, so it's important you use fresh and – ideally – filtered water.

To Boil or Not to Boil Boiling water can destroy the delicate flavours. Water at 95 – 97°C is ideal to allow proper extraction without diminishing the flavour-giving essential oils. Once boiled, cool the water for around 30 seconds before using.

Squeaky Clean Make sure your equipment is thoroughly clean. Leftover residues, oils and coffee grounds can impart unpleasant flavours. If you have a coffee maker, you should clean it with a vinegar and water mix at least once a week.

Steaming Milk Unless you are the proud owner of a professionally tuned coffee maker and have been taught by a barista, then – frankly – attempting to create silky milk in your flat white at home is a bit of a waste of time. If you must have milk, quickly scorch some in a pan and add it unapologetically to a small amount of strong coffee to make a simple café con leche.

Iced Home-brewed Coffee

Put ⅓ cup of ground coffee in a cafetière. Pour over 1½ cups of cold water (preferably filtered). Stir and chill overnight, with the plunger in the up position. The next morning, take a glass, fill with ice cubes and pour in cold milk until about two-thirds full. Push the plunger down and pour over the cold brewed coffee, adding sugar if required. Makes 2 glasses.

Cooking with Coffee

•••

Besides drinking it, coffee offers the home cook a variety of interesting routes for kitchen experiment:

Ices and Granitas Marrying well in rich ice creams (cream is an obvious match), coffee also works very well with vanilla-, fudge-, raisin- and rum-infused concoctions. It's also excellent in refreshing granitas, often with liqueur added to make an icy post-supper digestif.

Baking and Desserts Great both as the star of the show in classics such as coffee and walnut cake and for bringing out subtle richness and depth as a background ingredient in chocolate cakes. Chocolate is arguably coffee's best friend, but experiment with malty, caramel flavours, too. It also pairs very well with warm, aromatic spices such as cardamom and cinnamon. Nuts love coffee, as do dried fruits and – surprisingly – orange juice and zest, with which it adds a complex undertone to chocolate puddings and desserts.

Silent Savoury Star Used sparingly, that ability to bring out depth without overpowering means that coffee can also be a clever cook's addition to rich meat stews and casseroles, particularly with dark ale stocks, venison and beef.

Marrying Flavours Considering the complex variety of flavours and aromas found in coffee itself, from nutty to chocolatey, floral and fruity, malty and toasted, sweet and caramelly, to grassy, herbal, spicy and woody notes, you can start to think more creatively about the kinds of flavours that might work with coffee as a cooking ingredient. Restaurants have recently popularised the use of coffee in surprising combinations with anything from bacon and mustard to popcorn and liquorice.

COFFEE BEANS

A container of your favourite variety or blend of coffee beans and a dedicated coffee grinder to give you fresh coffee whenever you want it.

COFFEE GRANULES

1 jar of good-quality freeze-dried coffee granules (for baking purposes only!)

If in doubt, buy your ground coffee in small quantities, just enough for you to use over the next one or two weeks

Essential oils start to break down as soon as a bean is roasted, so store whole beans in an airtight container in a cool, dark, dry place

Storing your coffee in a cupboard near the oven may well be too warm.

DON'T REFRIGERATE OR FREEZE

Mocha Madeleines

•••

These are delicious for breakfast as well as during the day. (Make the batter the night before and chill, ready to use in the morning.) If you don't have a madeleine tray, use a shallow muffin tray. Success lies in a gentle folding technique, to capture the air that has been introduced.

Makes 12

Ingredients

125 g plain flour, plus more
   for the tray
2 tsp cocoa powder
2 tsp baking powder
125 g unsalted butter, plus
   more for the tray
2 tbsp instant coffee
2 tbsp milk
1 tbsp demerara sugar
3 eggs
100 g golden caster sugar

Equipment

sieve
mixing bowl
12-hole madeleine tray
  (or see recipe introduction)
saucepan
electric mixer
spatula or large metal spoon
piping bag (optional)

Preparation

Sift together the flour, cocoa and baking powder into a mixing bowl.

Butter and flour a 12-hole madeleine tray (or see recipe introduction).

Method

Dissolve the coffee in the milk. Melt the butter and demerara in a saucepan set over a medium heat, making sure the sugar dissolves. When it bubbles and browns slightly, remove and stir in the dissolved coffee. Set aside.

Beat the eggs and caster sugar in an electric mixer until the mixture is thick and doubled in volume and has reached the 'ribbon' stage (this means it will hold a figure of eight when you squiggle the mixture back into the bowl); it may take several minutes. Fold in the sifted ingredients and the coffee mixture using a spatula or large metal spoon.

Cover and leave to settle for three hours, or chill and leave overnight if you plan to bake for a breakfast.

When ready to bake, preheat the oven to 180°C/350°F/gas mark 4. Pipe or spoon the batter into the prepared tray and bake for 15 minutes, or until firm to the touch. These are best served warm, but will keep for a few days in an airtight container.

Coffee and Sour Cherry Trifle

•••

Serving a trifle at a supper party is guaranteed to bring a gasp of delight from at least one guest. Choose a glass serving bowl for maximum effect and serve in little bowls, allowing room for second helpings.

Serves 8

Ingredients

100 g sour morello cherries
50 ml dark rum
30 g dark chocolate
40 g whole almonds (skin on)
175 g trifle sponge (or leftover
  Mocha madeleines, see left)
5 leaves of gelatine
125 g demerara sugar
600 ml strong coffee (or 6 tbsp
  of instant coffee dissolved in
  600ml of hot water)
300 ml real vanilla custard
  (see page 113), cooled, made
  with 1 extra tsp of cornflour
  to thicken
200 ml double cream

Equipment

mixing bowls
vegetable peeler
sharp knife and chopping board
baking tray
glass serving bowl
small saucepan

Preparation

Soak the cherries in the rum in a small bowl, for a few hours or overnight.

Shave the chocolate, or chop it into shards.

Preheat the oven to 140°C/275°F/gas mark 1. Spread the almonds on a baking tray and roast for 20 minutes. Cool, then chop.

Method

Cut the sponge into small cubes and scatter into a glass serving bowl. Soak the gelatine in a small bowl in cold water to cover for about five minutes.

Heat a small saucepan and dissolve the sugar in the coffee. Remove from the heat, squeeze the excess water from the gelatine and whisk the softened leaves into the hot coffee to dissolve. Scatter the sponge with the rum-soaked cherries and pour over the coffee. Allow to set in the fridge.

Cover with the cold custard. Softly whip the cream (see page 105). Paddle the cream over the custard and scatter with the chocolate and almonds.

Coffee and Hazelnut Fudge

•••

Everybody loves fudge. That's a fact, even in these days of sugar-free diets. The secret is just to have a little at a time. This recipe is ideal to wrap and offer as a gift. Beating in chocolate at the end gives a luxurious finish. We use freeze-dried instant coffee to give a good coffee flavour. Make sure you hit 120°C (248°F) before you remove the pan from the heat, or your fudge won't have the correct consistency.

Makes 500 g

Ingredients

120 g dark chocolate
250 g golden granulated sugar
75 g golden syrup
80 ml double cream
30 g unsalted butter
1 tbsp instant coffee dissolved
   in 1 tsp of hot water
125 g hazelnuts

Equipment

20 cm square baking tin
baking parchment
sharp knife and chopping board
heavy-based saucepan
jam or sugar thermometer

Preparation

Line the sides and base of a square baking tin measuring 20 x 20 x 3 cm with baking parchment.
Finely chop the chocolate.

Method

Put the sugar, golden syrup and cream in a heavy-based saucepan set over a low heat, stirring from time to time to dissolve the sugar. When the sugar has dissolved, increase the heat to a gentle rolling boil and cook until 120°C (248°F) has been reached on a jam or sugar thermometer. Don't stir at this stage.

Remove from the heat, beat in the chocolate, butter and coffee, then finally the hazelnuts.

Quickly and carefully pour into the prepared tray before it sets.

Once cooled, cut into 3 cm squares and keep in an airtight container for up to three months.

DAIRY

An Introduction to Dairy

Our green and pleasant land is dotted with dairy farms. The ideal climate of wet and warm weather gives rise to plenty of grass and, grass being a cow's favourite food, enables them to produce the milk we've come to rely on every day. And milk is just the beginning as once you have milk you also have butter, yogurt and cream as well as cheese.

These dairy products form the backbone of most Western cooks' armoury of ingredients. It's rare that a visit to your local shop or the supermarket doesn't involve a purchase of at least one of these staples. Once back at home they can be enjoyed in their simplest and most unadulterated forms, or become part of the most complex dishes.

Also, dairy products have earned a place in our hearts as the ingredients of our treasured British comfort foods. The nursery foods of childhood were often based around the dairy, from cauliflower cheese to blancmange or rice pudding and strawberry jam. Today, with our food horizons expanded, the dairy plays a much wider role in the foods that we can make and enjoy.

Does a Cup of Hot Milk Help You Sleep?

Milk is rich in the amino acid tryptophan, which is said to aid sleep by promoting the production of melatonin and serotonin, hormones that help to regulate the sleep pattern and promote feelings of well-being

Milk

•••

It's hard to imagine a time when we didn't rely on a bottle or carton of milk in the fridge. Today, milk is a kitchen staple; whether you're adding it to your cup of tea or coffee, pouring it over your cereal, blending it into milkshakes or smoothies or using it to bake or cook with, let alone pouring an ice-cold glass to enjoy on its own.

Before the mid-19th century, milk didn't often find its way into the cities. But, along with the industrial revolution, came the railway network, that suddenly allowed milk to be transported hundreds of miles overnight. By 1900, the Great Western Railway Company was transporting more than 25 million gallons of milk annually.

Cow's milk is now produced on an industrial scale in most parts of the Western world, with specific breeds of cow selected for maximum yields (Holstein Friesians being the most popular in the UK and the USA) and, with large-scale 'factory' farms on the horizon – and some already here – milk production feels anything but 'artisan'.

However, there are a number of dairy farmers who still believe in the old principles and produce milk from herds of various cattle breeds, chosen for the quality rather than the quantity they can produce. Many of these are practising organic farming methods, or at least putting the welfare of the animal first. If you look carefully, you should be able to find retailers who are following these principles, too.

All of the milk on general sale has been pasteurised and many larger-scale producers have taken to homogenising the milk, too. Homogenisation is the process in which the fat in the milk is evenly distributed throughout the liquid by a mechanical process, rather than being allowed naturally to rise to the top. It's said that the process can help the shelf life of the product, rather than adding any other particular benefits. Some say consumers prefer it that way; however, there is also debate as to whether this process makes it harder or easier to digest.

Gold-top Milk

The UK's Channel Islands have traditionally bred Jersey and Guernsey cows that give a particularly rich and creamy-tasting milk. It does have a higher fat content than whole milk but is great as an occasional treat. It's available both on the islands and in the mainland UK and you'll see the layer of cream that sits at the top of the bottle or carton. It's sometimes called 'breakfast milk'.

Sterilised and UHT ('Long-life') Milk

Both of these have been heat treated to a point where all harmful bacteria have been killed. Neither needs to be refrigerated until they are opened for use. The extreme heat process alters (for the worse) both the taste of the milk and its nutritional benefits.

Evaporated and Condensed Milk

Both of these have undergone heat treatment that extends their useful life and, in the same way as UHT, results in changes to their flavour. In the days before fridges were common, they were a staple. Condensed milk also has sugar added before being canned. There's probably less need for these styles of milk today, although some baking recipes call for them.

Whole or Full-fat

As its name suggests, nothing is added nor removed. In the UK it should have a minimum fat content of 3.5 per cent.

Skimmed

With the majority of the fat removed, this has an average fat content of just 0.1 per cent. Skimmed milk has a watery appearance and less of a creamy taste.

RAW MILK

This is milk that has not undergone a process of pasteurisation. Until pasteurisation was widely introduced in the late 19th century, all milk was raw milk. However, at that time milk was deemed responsible for the transmission of a number of infectious diseases, including tuberculosis, as well as certain food pathogens. Pasteurisation prohibits the growth of these harmful bacteria and so prevented these diseases from being spread through milk. In recent years there has been a movement that has extolled the benefits of non-pasteurised milk so now, through careful monitoring and licensing, raw milk can again be purchased by the public, usually direct from the farmer.

Buying Raw Milk

You'll find it at farmer's markets, or direct from a farm. Its proponents say it tastes better and has lost no nutrients. (But it is advised it should not be drunk by pregnant women, children or those with compromised immune systems.)

Semi-skimmed

With a fat content of 1.7 per cent, this is now the most popular milk bought in the UK.

Alternatives to Cow's Milk Products

•••

Goat's Milk

Some people assume that goat's milk is unpleasantly strong in flavour and aroma. The reality is that goat's milk is mild tasting and shouldn't smell any stronger than your average carton of cow's milk. The historical issue of strong-smelling goat's milk is in fact due to the way that goats were kept: male goats are by nature rather strong-smelling and, if kept together with the females, particularly at milking time, their musky smell can permeate the milk. With modern methods of farming, this rarely happens now. Many people readily buy goat's milk cheeses, yet for some reason they're put off by the idea of goat's milk yogurt and butter. Besides any health arguments (some believe those who suffer intolerant reactions to cow's milk find goat's milk products less problematic), it's worth giving goat's milk a try. Milk, yogurt, butter and cream are now all available from many food retailers.

Sheep's Milk

In Northern Europe it was only after the Black Death that the cow started to replace sheep as the more popular provider of milk. And it's only in recent decades that some UK farmers are once again rearing sheep for their milk. Ewes bred for milking are typically fed on organic grass, grain and silage, living outdoors during the day but with a snug barn to sleep in at night. The milk has a pure white colour and has the added benefit of being more stable at high temperatures than that of cow's, making it ideal for cooking. The flavour does vary from breed to breed and according to the diet they've received; some can be described as being quite floral in flavour, whilst others are nutty.

Plant Milks

All sorts of plants and most nuts can be used to make a dairy-free alternative. Most will be familiar with soy, rice and almond milks.

Soy Milk Made by boiling soaked, ground soy beans. It's an important part of Asian cuisine, as well as a drink in its own right. Soy milk can be made into yogurt, cream, cheese or tofu.

Rice Milk Made using brown rice, this is probably the most watery of the dairy alternatives, but does have a naturally sweeter taste than others. When buying commercial brands, read the label carefully to check for added sweeteners.

Nut and Seed Milks Gentle and mild in flavour, these are not quite as flavoursome as animal milks, but their fat and protein content can make them a good alternative in cooking or baking for those who really need to avoid dairy. When baking with them, a bit of 'try and see' may need to be undertaken, but it's certainly worth a shot. Beware of seemingly healthy nut milks that have added sweeteners and flavourings. Those worth a try include almond milk and coconut milk (see page 296 for more on nut milks).

Cream

•••

As described earlier, unhomogenised whole milk settles with time to create two distinct parts: the cream at the top and less fatty part at the bottom. Traditionally cream was collected by letting the milk stand and form into the two parts, but today the cream is separated from the milk by centrifugal force into different grades of cream, from the thickest (double) to the lightest (single). As with milk, all cream is pasteurised, unless bought from a raw milk producer.

Double

With 48 per cent butterfat, this is the cream used most in cooking, either to thicken sauces, or whipped to serve with and decorate puddings and desserts. It also freezes well, though it will not whip as firmly after freezing.

Single

The lightest cream on the market with 18 per cent butterfat, this can be used in cooking and as a pouring cream, as an accompaniment to dessert.

Clotted

With 55 per cent butterfat, this is the cream traditionally served with a scone. Famous in Cornwall and Devon in the south west of England, the cream is collected from herds that feed on the lush pastures that naturally have high levels of carotene and this is what gives the cream its yellow hue. It has a much higher density than double cream and has historically been made by leaving the whole milk in shallow pans for the milk and cream to separate. Once separated, the cream is very gently heated to 82°C, then left to cool overnight. The next day the thick and unctuous cream can be skimmed off and packed.

Whipping

This 35 per cent butterfat product does what it says: it whips. It's just a bit lighter than double cream. It's probably a bit cheaper, too, but requires more effort in the whipping!

Crème Fraîche

The preferred way for the French to serve their cream, hence the name. It's a thick cream with a bacterial culture added, which produces a slight acidity. There are times when it's preferable to cream and we think it's perfect with a chocolate or other rich dessert. It's also used on the savoury side of the kitchen, in sauces and dressings when that bit of sourness helps.

Sour Cream

Produced in the same way as crème fraîche – by adding a bacterial culture – but with a lighter cream. Its sourness means that it's generally used in savoury cooking: on baked potatoes with chives; or in beef stroganoff. Across the pond, it's essential with Mexican food. Make a cheat's version by adding a squeeze of lemon juice to a tub of single or double cream.

Softly Whipped Cream

Nothing beats softly whipped cream. Use a large clean bowl and a balloon whisk. Sweeten double cream with icing sugar, if you want, and whisk slowly until it thickens to a billowing consistency. If you over-beat the cream, it will seize. If this happens, add more cream to loosen it and continue to beat (carefully this time). It will hold for a few hours in the fridge before serving.

M

Buttermilk

This is a byproduct of the butter-making process (see page 107). When making butter, there's a point in the process when the liquid and solids suddenly separate, the liquid part being the buttermilk.

Buttermilk is really only used in baking, typically scones, soda breads and pancakes. The acidity of the liquid, when combined with the bicarbonate of soda in those recipes, creates carbon dioxide and thus expands the mixture to create the 'rise' that's needed.

Today, commercially produced buttermilk is made by adding a live culture to low-fat milk to sour it slightly. Some argue that these commercially made buttermilks bear little comparison to the ripe and tangy buttermilks they remember from their childhood.

Buttermilk is widely available now, due to the resurgence in home baking, but if you need a quick alternative that produces the required rising effect in your baking, try this:

Making Buttermilk

Add 1 tbsp of lemon juice to 100 ml of whole milk and leave to stand for 15 minutes at room temperature. The mixture should thicken slightly and you should see small curdled particles sitting on the top. This won't give the same tangy flavours, but provides the required rise.

Butter

•••

Butter has been prepared down the centuries as a way of extending the life of milk. Originally, several days' worth of cream would have been skimmed from various batches of milk. The age of the cream would have meant that it would have started to sour as the lactose or milk sugars contained within were converted to lactic acid, thus giving a fuller, riper flavour. The cream was churned, which resulted in the fat globules sticking together while the liquid element, known as buttermilk, was forced out. The resulting solid mass we know as butter was then patted into shape.

Today, commercial butter production incorporates bacterial cultures into fresh cream to speed up the ripening process. The cream is then churned and follows the same process that's been followed for centuries, but in great stainless-steel vats, some taking as much as 7,000 litres at a time. Usually, it lacks the lactic acid tang of the old-fashioned varieties.

Today, you can buy three main types of butter: salted, slightly salted and unsalted. The salt has a preservative effect and so extends the shelf life. Which you use is a matter of taste, although our choice is always unsalted as you can use it in baking without introducing a salty flavour to baked goods. If you do want a little more seasoning once you've spread your crusty loaf with butter, you could always add a sprinkle of salt yourself.

Ghee

This ingredient, often used in Indian recipes, is produced in a similar way to clarified butter, but the butter is allowed to caramelise before the milk solids are removed, to give it a nuttier flavour. Ghee can be purchased in supermarkets as well as in ethnic stores.

Clarified Butter

This is another important ingredient when it comes to cooking. It is easy to make, it just takes a little care. It is often called for to seal potted meats, fish or terrines. It can also be used in baking, to make an omelette, for serving with crab or lobster, to add to rice dishes or just poured over any steamed vegetables such as artichokes or asparagus. The aim of clarifying is to remove the milk solids and water to leave a clear golden fat that can be heated to a higher temperature than regular butter. (Unclarified butter burns at a lower temperature, so is hard to fry with.)

Place the required amount of unsalted butter in a heavy-based saucepan over a low heat; remember you will lose 25 per cent of the butter in this process. Cook until you see foam on the surface, then keep cooking until the foam stops forming. Skim the foam with a slotted spoon, then pass the butter through a double layer of cheese cloth to remove any remaining solid particles. Pour into a jar and cool, seal and store in the fridge.

Creaming Butter

Creaming butter when baking is an important technique to master, as this is where air is introduced to your batter mix. Always use butter at room temperature. Beat the butter on a medium speed, introducing the air gently. (Use the whisk attachment if making a very light sponge.) The butter should be pale and fluffy and, if you have added sugar, it should have dissolved into the beaten butter. Now it's time to add the eggs.

M

Making Butter

...

Try to source a good-quality cream from a local producer. It's simple enough to make and, as the byproduct is buttermilk, you can also make a batch of Buttermilk scones (see page 114) or Soda bread (see page 223) when you have finished churning. It makes about 300 g of butter.

1

Place 600 ml of double cream in a brilliantly clean electric mixer and beat with the whisk attachment at medium speed.

2

Keep watching, as the buttermilk will soon fall away from the solids and you will see it splashing about in the bottom of the bowl.

3

Turn the mixer off, strain off the buttermilk and reserve it for baking.

4

Remove the solids from the bowl, place them into a clean sieve and run them under the cold tap to remove all impurities that could sour the butter.

5

Shake out the water, return the solids to the mixer (with ½ tsp of fine sea salt if you want salted butter). Beat again.

6

Drain away any further liquid as you did before, if any appears. Your solid mass is now butter.

7

Transfer to a clean ramekin or other dish and cover with cling film. This will keep for about two weeks in the fridge if you have used salt, less if not, or three months in the freezer.

Yogurt

•••

Look into any supermarket chiller cabinet and you're expected to choose between hundreds of different varieties and flavours of yogurt. Where to begin? Set? Thick? Low-fat? Strained? Live? Bio? Sheep? Goat? Cow?

Yogurt is milk that has had bacterial cultures added to it. The bacteria have the effect of souring and thickening the milk as the lactose is converted to lactic acid: in this case, milk ferments into yogurt. The sourness is often balanced with sweet-tasting fruits or other sugars.

One of the questions we get asked regularly is whether the yogurt we sell is 'live'. Nearly all yogurt is live, the live element being the bacteria, which are introduced into the milk to make the yogurt. (A few manufacturers produce long-life yogurts that are pasteurised after this introduction, which effectively kills off the bacteria and hence are no longer live.) Just to complicate things, when people ask if yogurt is live, what most of them really mean is whether they contain certain types of bacteria which are considered to aid the flora in the human stomach. These yogurts can often be identified by the word 'bio' or 'probiotic' on the packaging. You can choose between the following:

Natural A smooth yogurt made from traditional cultures which produce a tangy taste. Usually available in whole and low-fat varieties.

Natural Bio Yogurt (probiotic) Again these are available in whole and low-fat varieties. They generally have a milder and creamier taste due to the addition of the probiotic cultures. One of the strains – *Lactobacillus acidophilus* – is recognised as important to replenish the digestive system.

Natural Set Set yogurt is made with traditional cultures and sometimes known as French yogurt. It is fermented in the pot in which it is sold.

Greek and Greek-style Yogurt Made from cow's or sheep's milk. It has had quite a high proportion of its whey (the liquid part) strained off, which creates a thick, mild, very creamy result. It has a higher fat content than other yogurts (around 10.2 per cent), but that's still a lot lower than cream.

Cooking with Yogurt

As well as providing you with your morning 'fix', yogurt is used in the kitchen in any number of ways: in marinades to help tenderise; in salad dressings as an alternative to mayonnaise; in baking as an alternative fat to butter; or in sauces and dips. It's often considered a great 'cooler' with hot and spicy foods: a dollop of natural yogurt on your curry often does the trick. Be careful when adding yogurt to sauces to be heated, as it can curdle. (It's worth taking the yogurt out of the fridge and bringing to room temperature before adding to a pan.)

Making Yogurt

•••

1

Boil 600 ml of whole milk. Leave to cool, monitoring its temperature with a thermometer. When it has reached 42°C, stir in 2 tsp of live natural yogurt.

that are required to transform the milk into yogurt need a constant warmth in order to grow. A clean Thermos flask is a good option to keep the milk at the correct temperature.

2

Place into a very clean bowl and cover with cling film. Leave to develop in a warm spot at about 24°C – 29°C for about 14 hours (wrap in a towel if the temperature is inconsistent). The bacteria

3

Once the yogurt has thickened and formed to your liking, place in a clean jar and store in the fridge.

Cooking with Milk

It's preferable to use whole or semi-skimmed milk when cooking, as skimmed milk, with its 0.1 per cent fat content, adds little flavour to a cooked dish. Be careful when heating milk and follow recipe instructions. Milk boils very easily and this can result in an unpleasant flavour and a skin forming on top. Always heat milk gently to avoid scorching, keeping an eye on it throughout. Try to use a wide-based pan, rather than a narrow deep pan, as the greater surface area of the base will help prevent the milk from boiling over the sides.

Pasteurisation

The French chemist and microbiologist Louis Pasteur (1822–1895) is responsible for the improved shelf life of many foods. Pasteurisation involves heating a liquid to a high temperature (72°C/162°F) for a matter of seconds, before cooling quickly. Unlike sterilisation, which is intended to kill all micro-organisms and adversely affects the taste and quality of the product, pasteurisation reduces the number of potentially harmful bacteria, as long as it is kept within certain conditions and – importantly – it doesn't have such an adverse effect on the flavour. As milk is such a great medium for microbial growth, pasteurisation allows its shelf life to be extended.

Storage

Fresh milk should always be kept in a fridge. It can also be frozen, then defrosted in a fridge for 24 hours.

Real Vanilla Custard

•••

Making your own custard may seem daunting, but it really is very easy.
We have added cornflour to this recipe to help stabilise the custard
as you cook it and to help the mixture thicken.

Makes 600 ml

Ingredients

5 egg yolks
1 vanilla pod
250 ml double cream
250 ml whole milk
75 g golden caster sugar
2 tsp cornflour

Equipment

mixing bowls
sharp knife and chopping board
saucepan
whisk

Preparation

Separate the eggs (retain the whites in the fridge
for another recipe, see page 414 for inspiration).

Split the vanilla pod down the middle and scrape
out the seeds with a small knife.

Method

Gently heat the cream and the milk with the vanilla
seeds and pod in a saucepan, whisking to distribute
the seeds. Remove the vanilla pod. Whisk together
the egg yolks, sugar and cornflour, then pour on the
hot milk, whisking constantly.

Return to the pan and cook very slowly, whisking
continuously until the mixture thickens.

Serve from a warmed jug, or it can of course be
eaten cold (as all the best custards are).

Wensleydale Buttermilk Scones

•••

We fill these scones with whipped cream cheese, rocket and Onion marmalade (see page 56), but they are also excellent served with a hot soup. The important rule with scones is to keep the handling of the dough to a minimum, as this will result in a light texture.

Makes 8–10

Ingredients

300 g self-raising flour, plus more to dust
½ tsp bicarbonate of soda
½ tsp cream of tartar
pinch of English mustard powder
½ tsp sea salt
50 g unsalted butter
100 g Wensleydale cheese
50 g Parmesan cheese
1 egg
250 ml buttermilk, plus more if needed

Equipment

sieve
mixing bowls
sharp knife and chopping board
box grater
baking sheet and baking parchment
rolling pin
5 cm pastry cutter
wire rack

Preparation

Sift the flour, bicarbonate of soda, cream of tartar, mustard powder and salt into a bowl.

Chop the butter and keep it chilled.

Grate the cheeses.

Crack and beat the egg, adding a splash of water and a pinch of salt.

Preheat the oven to 190°C / 375°F / gas mark 5.

Line a baking sheet with baking parchment.

Method

Rub the butter into the flour mixture with your fingers until the mixture resembles crumbs. Stir in the grated cheeses. Make a well in the centre of the mixture and pour in the buttermilk.

Bring the mixture together quickly, adding a little more buttermilk if required.

Roll out on a floured surface to about 3 cm deep.

Cut into circles with a 5 cm pastry cutter and glaze with the beaten egg.

Bake in the hot oven for 15 minutes, then remove and cool on a wire rack before serving.

RECIPE
114

EGGS

What it Says on the Egg Box

···

Organic

Always free-range, these must be fed on an organically produced diet and ranged on organic land with no more than six hens per square metre in a maximum flock size of 3,000 birds.

They must have nest boxes and adequate perches of 18 cm per hen and be able to roam outside for at least eight hours a day and must also have outdoor shade.

Free-range

Must have continuous daytime access to runs which are mainly covered with vegetation and with a maximum stocking density of 2,000 birds per hectare.

The maximum flock size is 16,000 birds divided into colonies of no more than 4,000 each.

They must have nest boxes and adequate perches of 15 cm per hen and be able to roam outside for at least eight hours a day and must also have outdoor shade.

Barn

Birds move freely around the barn; maximum stocking density is nine hens per square metre.

There must be one nest box per five hens – or communal nests – and adequate perches of 15 cm per hen. Electric lighting must be provided to give an optimum day length.

The maximum flock size is 32,000 birds divided into colonies of no more than 4,000 each.

Caged

Battery cages were banned; but colony cages were introduced.

Each hen must have 0.75 square metres with nesting boxes, perches to sleep on and an area in which to scratch.

Most colony cages are designed to hold between 40 and 80 birds.

Maximum density is 80 birds per caged colony, that is 60 square metres per caged colony.

How Fresh Are Your Eggs?

1

Gently place an egg
in a bowl of cold water:
it will float to
varying degrees

2

If it lies on the bottom
the egg is very fresh

3

If it stands up and bobs
on the bottom,
it's a little older
but still good to use

4

If the egg floats
on the surface, it should
be thrown away

Brown or White Shells?

Chickens with white ear lobes lay white eggs, whereas chickens with
red ear lobes lay brown eggs. That's it! There is no other difference,
only the appearance.

Storing Eggs

Store at a constant temperature lower than 20°C (68°F). In most domestic
kitchens, the fridge is the best place to keep them, but take them out of
the fridge for 30 minutes before cooking for the best results.

Store away from strong-smelling food, as egg shells are porous, and never
use cracked or broken eggs.

BAKED

CODDLED

CURRIED

DEVILLED

FRIED

HARD-BOILED

PICKLED

POACHED

RAW

SCRAMBLED

SOFT-BOILED

SOUFFLÉD

TRUFFLED

SMALL

53 g and less

4½ minutes

Softish white
and runny yolk

6 minutes

Well-set white
and runny yolk

8 minutes

Hard-boiled
and good to slice

12 minutes

Hard-boiled
and good to grate
or mash

How to boil an egg

Once the water is boiling, add the medium eggs, at room temperature. The water should then simmer, rather than be allowed to boil vigorously. If a shell cracks while cooking, add 1 tbsp of vinegar to help prevent too much egg escaping.

MEDIUM

53–63 g

LARGE

63–73 g

VERY LARGE

73 g and more

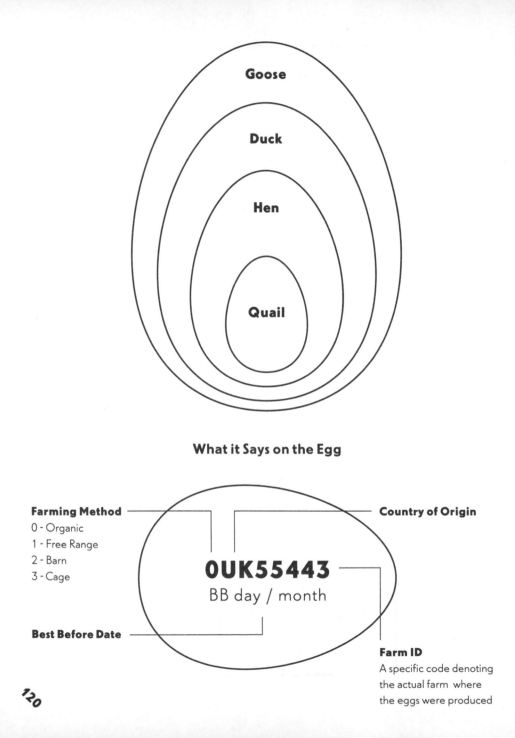

Goose

Duck

Hen

Quail

What it Says on the Egg

Farming Method
0 - Organic
1 - Free Range
2 - Barn
3 - Cage

Country of Origin

0UK55443
BB day / month

Best Before Date

Farm ID
A specific code denoting
the actual farm where
the eggs were produced

Baked Vanilla Cheesecake

•••

We sell this in individual rounds and also make large versions around Christmas with cranberries and orange. We have adjusted this recipe over the years to get the balance just right between sweetness and texture. So this is it: the best baked cheesecake in London.

Serves 6

Ingredients

1 vanilla pod
100 g unsalted butter, melted, plus more for the tin
175 g Digestive biscuits (see page 54)
170 g caster sugar
2 tsp cornflour
500 g cream cheese
4 eggs
100 ml double cream
175 g crème fraîche

Equipment

sharp knife and chopping board
20 cm springform cake tin
baking parchment
food processor or blender
food mixer
mixing bowl
whisk

Preparation

Split the vanilla pod and scrape out the seeds.

Line a 20 cm springform cake tin with baking parchment and butter the sides.

Blitz the biscuits to crumbs in a food processor or blender.

Preheat the oven to 140°C/275°F/gas mark 1.

Method

In a food mixer fitted with the paddle attachment, beat together the sugar, cornflour, cream cheese and vanilla seeds. Add the eggs and whisk for a minute. If you don't have a paddle, mix by hand until combined and all lumps are removed. It's important not to introduce too much air into the mixture.

Whisk both creams together, then add to the mix.

Add the melted butter to the biscuit crumbs, stir well, then press into the prepared tin. Pour in the cream cheese mixture.

Bake in the oven for one hour, until slightly risen. The edges will be golden, but it should still have a wobble in the middle.

Allow to cool, then remove from the tin, cover and refrigerate for up to five days. Serve with fresh summer berries.

Mayonnaise

Take a clean bowl and sit it on a damp cloth to avoid movement. Whisk two egg yolks at room temperature with a pinch of salt.

Measure 250 ml of light oil, either sunflower, olive or groundnut. Very slowly, whisking constantly, pour in a thin stream of the oil.

Success here is down to how well the oil is incorporated. Should the mixture split, add 2 tbsp of hot water and continue to whisk. Once the oil is incorporated, whisk in 1 tsp of Dijon mustard and 1 tbsp of white wine vinegar. Taste for seasoning.

Try Any of These Added to Home-made Mayonnaise

Finely grated zest of 1 unwaxed lemon, 1 tsp of chopped capers, 1 tsp of chopped cornichons and chopped dill, to serve with fish.

Crush three large garlic cloves and add with lots of freshly ground black pepper and a handful of chopped watercress to serve with steak.

Roast and finely chop 50 g of walnuts, stir through and serve with grilled asparagus.

Stir through the same amount of yogurt to make a great tangy dressing for salads or coleslaw.

Add 2 tbsp of chopped tarragon and serve with roast fish or chicken.

M

7

FISH

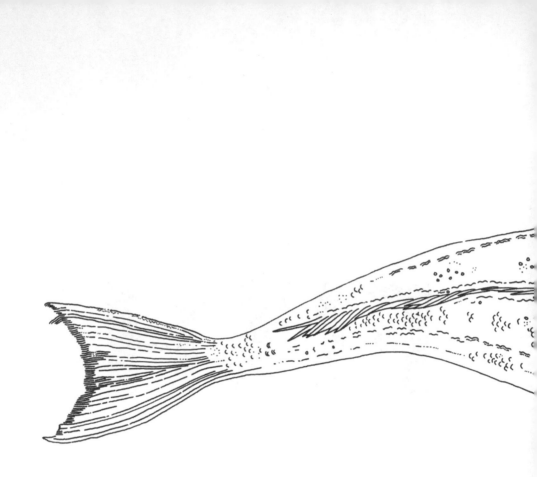

Grey Gurnard

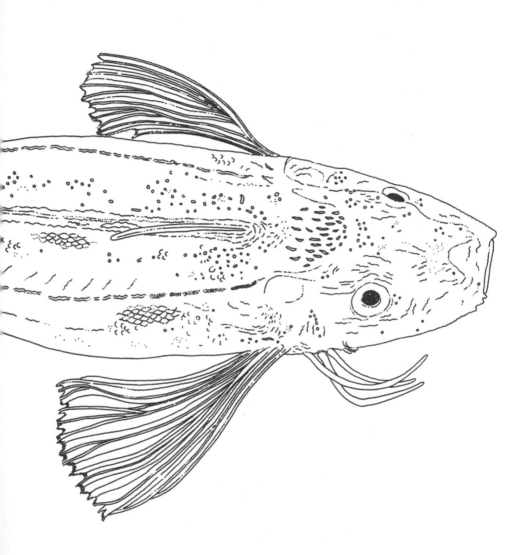

An Introduction to Fish

We're fortunate that we are an island nation, surrounded by seas that have over the centuries provided us with a bountiful and valuable source of food. Our ancestors have cured fish for a couple of thousand years at least; widely available fresh fish is a more recent affair. It proved so popular that we're now suffering the consequences of decades of overfishing. Good work is being done to repair that damage and there may come a time when our seas are full once more.

In culinary terms we're known as the nation who invented fish and chips and, as delicious as a freshly landed beer-battered fillet of pollock (please, not cod any more) is, our talents extend a little further. Anyone for stargazy pie, smoked eel, Morecambe Bay potted shrimp, Scottish smoked salmon, Colchester oysters, Arbroath smokies, cullen skink or Cromer crab?

Fish and shellfish in all their forms provide a wealth of nutritional benefits as well as giving variety and scope in the kitchen. This chapter is here to help you become a more confident shopper and user of fresh fish and, at the same time, to celebrate our rich heritage in all manner of cured and preserved fish. And, of course, to offer some thoughts and suggestions as to how we can use them in our kitchens.

Buying Fish

This can be a bit of a minefield. There's a wide range of fish and shellfish that are readily available, but which one suits your needs? Then there are questions about sustainability. And is it the correct season to be buying a particular fish (see chart, page 130–131)? There's also the question of whether to go for convenience and buy a pre-packed product or something from the frozen section, or whether you can summon up the courage to go and ask for something from the fresh fish counter. These days many of us are quite happy to go and choose a pre-packed piece of fish from a chiller cabinet, in a packet which tells you the price, where it's from and hopefully what to do with it when you get home. The problem is that it just never looks that nice.

On the other hand, the fish on the counter generally looks really inviting, but is not priced or portioned and doesn't come with any instructions. What to do? Well, the high streets have a secret weapon: fishmongers.

A visit to a fishmonger will leave you feeling less intimidated than when you walked in and, hopefully, with some fish in your basket. A fishmonger can tell you a lot more about that fish than the information written on the pre-packed version... and also it's likely you'll be getting really fresh fish.

So next time you fancy a piece of fish, go to a fishmonger or a fish counter, summon up the courage and ask questions to help you make the right decisions. (Don't forget you're under no obligation to buy.) If a particular fish catches your eye, those questions should go something like this:

What is it?
Where is it from?
When was it caught?
How do I cook it?
Does it need filleting, if so can you fillet it?
How much do I need?
What does it cost?

Make a friend of your fishmonger and use them to help you. If you can't get to a fishmonger, or you shop online, there are excellent resources available from the Marine Conservation Society and the Marine Stewardship Council. Both have helpful websites that can advise on what you should and shouldn't be eating from a sustainability point of view, have accreditation schemes to help you make the right choices, and provide information about where to buy and what to look for. The Marine Conservation Society even have a mobile App to help you make the right choices while you're on the move.

Buying Seasonal Fish

We're all pretty well rehearsed these days in the story of what fruits and vegetables to buy at different times of year. But did you know there's a good time and a not-so-good time to be buying fish? It primarily comes down to avoiding fish during their breeding or spawning times. On pages 130–131 is a chart which will help. (Please note this chart is for wild fish, not farmed, so you won't find salmon on the list as it is available all year round due to it being farmed. It also doesn't apply to frozen or canned fish.)

If you're building a relationship with your fishmonger, they will be able to advise you on these matters, too.

Aïoli
Beurre Blanc
Brown Butter
Caper
Harissa
Hollandaise
Lemon Mayonnaise
Marie Rose
Mornay
Parsley
Pesto
Tartare
Tomato (Not Ketchup!)
White Wine

		JAN	FEB	MAR	APR	MAY
F	**Black Bream**	●	●	●		
I	Cod	○				○
S	**Coley**				●	●
H	Dab	○	○	○		
	Dover Sole	●	●	●		
	Flounder	○				○
	Grey Gurnard	●	●	●		
	Haddock	○	○			○
	Hake	●				●
	Lemon Sole	○	○	○	○	
	Mackerel	●	●			
	Plaice				○	○
	Pollock					●
	Red Mullet	○	○	○	○	○
	Sardine	●	●			
	Sea Bass	○	○			
S	**Cockle**	●	●			
H	Crab, Brown				○	○
E	**Crab, Spider**	●	●	●		
L	King Scallop	○	○	○		
L	**Lobster**	●	●	●	●	●
F	Mussel	○	○	○		
I	**Prawn, Cold Water**	●	●	●	●	●
S	Prawn, Dublin Bay	○	○	○	○	○
H	**Queen Scallop**	●	●			
	Razor Clam	○	○	○	○	
	Whelk	●	●	●	●	●

JUN	JUL	AUG	SEP	OCT	NOV	DEC
●	●	●	●	●	●	●
○	○	○	○	○	○	○
●	●	●	●	●	●	●
	○	○	○	○	○	○
	●	●	●	●	●	●
○	○	○	○	○	○	○
		●	●	●	●	●
○	○	○	○	○	○	○
●	●	●	●	●	●	●
			○	○	○	○
		●	●	●	●	●
○	○	○	○	○	○	○
●	●	●	●	●	●	●
		○	○	○	○	○
			●	●	●	●
	○	○	○	○	○	○
			●	●	●	●
○	○	○	○	○	○	○
	●	●	●	●	●	●
				○	○	○
				●	●	●
			○	○	○	○
●	●	●			●	●
○	○	○				○
●	●	●				●
				○	○	○
●	●	●	●			

What to Look For When Buying

...

Fresh Fish

The eyes should be bright and clear, not faded or sunken

The skin should be shiny and moist, not dull or dry

The gills should be blood red, not brown

The cavity, if the fish is gutted, should be clean

The body should be firm, not flabby

The fish should have a sea-fresh smell; it shouldn't smell 'fishy'

Fillets should be neat, compact and firm

White fish should have a whitish translucency and no discoloration

Shellfish

Lobsters, crabs and prawns should feel heavy

Shells should be tightly closed or, if open, should close quickly when firmly tapped. They shouldn't be cracked or broken (discard any that are)

Smoked Fish

The flesh should feel firm, look glossy and not be sticky

How Much to Buy

Fresh Fillets

180 – 200 g per person

A delicate fish such as plaice would be at the lower end of the scale, while the upper is for meatier salmon

Whole Fish

350 – 450 g per person

A 700 – 900 g fish would feed two

Shellfish

about 500 g (in their shells) per person

Smoked Fish

250 g of smoked salmon serves four people as a starter

Storage

Fresh fish should ideally be eaten on the day of purchase. It can be kept for up to two days in a refrigerator, but it does deteriorate fairly quickly. Fresh fish can be frozen on the day you buy it, though it's never quite as nice as when eaten fresh.

Smoked or cured fish can usually be kept for slightly longer, but do go along with any instructions or use-by dates on the packaging.

When keeping fish in the fridge, ensure that it is covered and on a plate. You need to prevent any drips on to cooked or prepared foods stored beneath to prevent cross-contamination. For this reason, fish should be kept at the bottom of the fridge if possible, with cooked and prepared foods on a higher shelf.

Smoked fish should be well wrapped to help stop its aroma permeating any porous foods in the fridge, such as eggs.

Sustainable Fishing

Much has been reported on the state of our oceans. They have been overfished and are put at risk through pollution and climate change. We're paying the price, with certain species in danger. If we want to keep eating fish, there are some simple new rules. The Marine Conservation Society and the Marine Stewardship Council websites can help guide us through these troubled waters to avoid further damage.

We need to change our eating habits to buy and eat a far more diverse range of fish and we need to accept that increasing amounts of the fish we eat will be farmed. We also need to ensure that we do not support certain practices that have a detrimental effect on fish stocks.

Farmed vs Wild

There have been lots of mixed messages about this subject in recent years and the debate continues.

At present there are certain species which have sufficient stock so, if they are fished responsibly, we can keep on eating them. And there are fish that are now farmed, due to the overfishing that happened in previous years. Aquaculture farming, as it is called, is now a complex and large industry. It's not only salmon being farmed, but also cod, sea bass, trout, tuna, prawns, oysters and turbot, among others. Our advice is to look for fish and shellfish that have been certified by the Marine Stewardship Council (you'll see their blue logo on packets of fresh fish) or for the RSPCA Freedom Foods logo.

Fishing Methods

Much of the fishing carried out worldwide is performed on an industrial scale. There are certain methods which are considered preferable.

Most of the damage to fish stocks over the recent decades has been due to particular types of nets and to dredging. Both have not only caught the fish intended for your plate but lots of other marine life, too. It's generally recognised today that 'line-caught' fish is one of the more sustainable methods and you'll often see fish labelled so.

Smoked, Canned, Salted and Pickled

This is where your storecupboard can come into its own. By whatever method fish has been preserved, you suddenly have a whole range of fish and flavours to turn to when you are looking to rustle up a sandwich or supper. We've been using many of these preserved fish for thousands of years and they're still as valuable today.

Fresh Water Fish and Shellfish

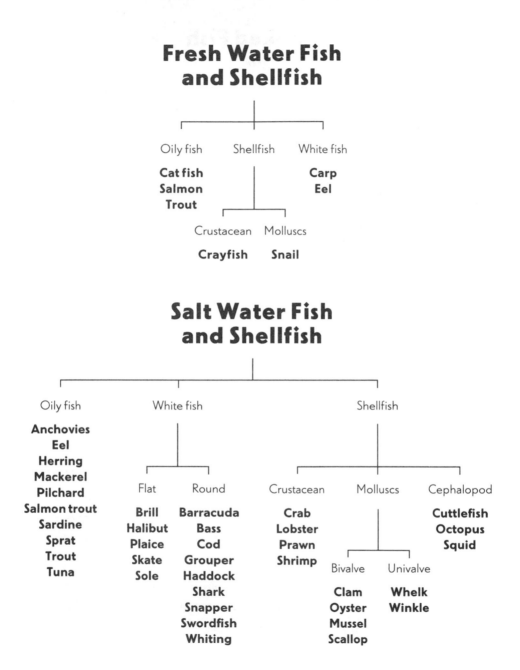

Fresh Water Fish and Shellfish

Oily fish
- **Cat fish**
- **Salmon**
- **Trout**

Shellfish

White fish
- **Carp**
- **Eel**

Crustacean
- **Crayfish**

Molluscs
- **Snail**

Salt Water Fish and Shellfish

Oily fish
- **Anchovies**
- **Eel**
- **Herring**
- **Mackerel**
- **Pilchard**
- **Salmon trout**
- **Sardine**
- **Sprat**
- **Trout**
- **Tuna**

White fish

Flat
- **Brill**
- **Halibut**
- **Plaice**
- **Skate**
- **Sole**

Round
- **Barracuda**
- **Bass**
- **Cod**
- **Grouper**
- **Haddock**
- **Shark**
- **Snapper**
- **Swordfish**
- **Whiting**

Shellfish

Crustacean
- **Crab**
- **Lobster**
- **Prawn**
- **Shrimp**

Molluscs

Bivalve
- **Clam**
- **Oyster**
- **Mussel**
- **Scallop**

Univalve
- **Whelk**
- **Winkle**

Cephalopod
- **Cuttlefish**
- **Octopus**
- **Squid**

Smoked Fish

...

Smoking is an ancient food preservation method, likely invented as fish hung drying over fires in the huts of our ancestors. Antimicrobial and antioxidant, wood smoke forms a barrier on the outside of food, slowing the process by which the oils within it turn rancid. However, smoke alone doesn't fully preserve food; curing or drying is needed as well so it can be kept at ambient temperatures.

These days food is smoked for flavour and texture, rather than purely for preservation. We now enjoy it for the unique characteristics it brings out in salmon, kippers and Arbroath smokies, sprats and mackerel.

Different woods impart their own flavours, so many fish smokers use fruit and other aromatic woods to create more dimensions. Some also use peat, or wood from whisky barrels, to impart another layer or a sense of luxury.

Cold Smoking

This is quite an art, requiring a level of skill and equipment that, we feel, means it is best left to the professionals. Kippers, bloaters and smoked salmon are cold-smoked using the same methods that have been used for hundreds, perhaps thousands, of years.

The smoking takes place at a low temperature, typically between 20–30°C (though it can be as low as 4°C) in a controlled environment; either inside a machine, or by enclosing under earth, or in smoke houses. This allows the smoky flavour to permeate the fish, but does not cook it or draw out excess water or fat, so it remains very moist.

Before smoking, salt-cured fish need to be air-dried to create a tacky outer layer called a pellicle. This protects the fish from the smoke but also allows the smoky flavour to adhere to the surface.

Hot Smoking

This involves exposing the fish to heat as well as smoke in a controlled environment and typically at around 50–80°C. Any higher than this and the fish will shrink, buckle and become very dry.

As with cold smoking, air-drying prior to smoking is preferable so that the smoke can fully adhere to the flesh. However, it is perfectly possible to hot-smoke fresh fish in a matter of minutes with no air-drying at all and it can be a really interesting way to add flavour and character to a piece of oily fish such as salmon or trout.

• •

Smoked Fish Goes Well With

Beetroot	**Lemon**
Brown Bread	**Orange**
Crème Fraîche	**Sherry Vinegar**
Eggs	**Watercress**
Fennel	**Waxy Potatoes**
Horseradish	**Yogurt**

Smoked Salmon

Some say the best comes from Scotland, others Scandinavia. We think some very good smoked salmon comes out of both. How you slice and serve it, however, is what sets it apart.

The traditional Scottish method sees the salmon sliced horizontally along the length of the fish into paper-thin slices; the Nordic fashion is for thicker slices cut vertically, so each slice has both the aroma from the strongly smoked outer flesh and the softer, less pungent flesh nearer the bone.

Both are delicious. We like the paper-thin slices for topping buttered brown bread and for canapés and the thicker, vertical slices for eating 'solo', as you would sashimi.

In either case, look out for a smoke house that displays their artisan skills. Salmon is heavily farmed, making it relatively cheap, but smoked salmon is and should remain a luxury. Choose top-quality organic and artisanal smoked fish and put your money where your mouth wants to be. You do get what you pay for and we think that means enjoying it on high days and holidays, when splashing out can be justified.

Kippers

Very good value and incredibly nutritious due to their omega fatty acids, their smell can be pungent, but they are worth it. A knob of butter and some black pepper on a fried kipper is most delicious. With a cup of English Breakfast tea on the side, of course. Kippers are produced across the UK, but probably the most famous is the Craster kipper. This renowned product is still oak smoked by a fourth-generation family business in their original smoke houses at Craster in Northumberland.

Arbroath Smokies

A hot-smoked haddock prepared using traditional methods dating back to the late 1800s, within a five-mile radius of Arbroath. It holds an EC Protected Geographical Status that defines an area which centres around the fishing village of Auchmithie. The smoking takes place inside a whisky barrel, filled with beech and oak. Layers of wet jute sacks cover the top. The resultant deep, strong smoky smell and taste is what makes these distinct. Keep things simple when serving: remove the bone, smear with butter and grill with bacon.

Smoked Eel

The richest, oiliest smoked fish with a firm, meaty texture and intense smoky flavour. Considered a delicacy in many Northern European countries, it is also – as are many eel dishes – popular in Japan. It benefits from being paired with something acidic to cut through the richness such as a sauce with crème fraîche and horseradish, or a salad with waxy potatoes and watercress.

Smoked Sprats

A speciality of Suffolk for centuries. Sprats are a small oily silver fish related to herring and lend themselves to being a great finger food, whether you choose to eat them with the head (the traditional way) or not.

Smoked Trout

A lovely light alternative to smoked salmon. It is often better value, too, and has a more delicate flavour. As with much smoked fish, it pairs very well in a salad of bitter leaves and roasted beetroot, with a sharp dressing made from yogurt or crème fraîche, lemon and horseradish. If you can't eat it all for supper, it's brilliant jammed between slices of brown bread for lunch the next day.

Smoked Mackerel

A rich oily fish and a wonderful source of omega fatty acids. It is hot smoked, adding a deep flavour and is a wonderfully versatile ingredient. A brilliant fridge standby, its oiliness means the texture becomes almost creamy when used to make a quick pâté with yogurt, crème fraîche, lemon, chives and dill. Look out for whole smoked mackerel on the bone if you can get it. The vac-packed fillets are fine for emergencies, but the whole fish are a world apart flavour- and texture-wise.

Salted Fish

•••

Salting, like pickling, is one of the oldest preservation methods. Fish is salt-cured and left to dry until the moisture is fully extracted.

In order to prepare salt fish for cooking, it needs to be rehydrated and most of the salt removed through overnight soaking and subsequent boiling. The aim is never to remove all of the salt; enough salt should remain so you can taste it, or you can end up with a bland piece of fish.

Salt Cod

Salt cod has long been produced in the North Atlantic countries such as Iceland, Norway and the Faroe Islands but, with overfishing, these days the term refers to any meaty white fish such as pollock, ling or haddock. It would traditionally have been dried outdoors on the rocks or wooden frames, but these days it is by indoor heater.

In Spain, salt cod is widely used and called bacalao. The French use it in brandade – one of the most satisfying dips for summer crudités you can make – and in Italy it is baccalà and is eaten on Christmas Eve. It is also a staple in the Caribbean, forming the Jamaican national dish of ackee and saltfish.

Anchovies

The Marmite of the fish world, maligned and adored in turn, these small silver fish are the ultimate secret ingredient. It is amazing what an anchovy can do to a leg of lamb, or indeed a piece of pork: anchovy haters won't detect fishiness, just an intense savouriness. They also work wonderfully with eggs, hard cheeses, tomatoes, garlic, herbs and bring a sophisticated sweetness to sautéed cabbage. The list goes on.

Anchovies are an essential ingredient in Worcestershire sauce and nam pla (Thai fish sauce). They can come preserved both in oil and salt and as a handy paste in a tube. The salted jarred anchovies are considered the best; they are gutted and dried before being packed in salt to draw out the excess moisture, ensuring a firmer, meatier texture as well as a more concentrated flavour. Don't forget that they are sold whole this way, so must be filleted and washed to get rid of excess salt. But whether it's for a Caesar salad dressing (see page 148), or to season a piece of roasting lamb, the effort is well worth it.

· ·

Anchovies Go Well With

Capers	**Lemon**
Chilli	**Parmesan**
Courgettes	**Parsley**
Cream	**Pasta**
Garlic	**Pork**
Lamb	**Tomatoes**

Pickled Fish

•••

As with canning and smoking, the art of pickling fish began as a way of preserving it. The first reports date back to the medieval era, when fish was prepared, then transported in wooden barrels. From East to West, Japan to Peru, Jews to Catholics, pickled fish makes its way across all cultures.

The ceviche of South America is a delicacy of cured raw fish in citrus juice and it is thought that the Spanish escabeche was an evolution of that, with the fish first fried before marinating in a vinegar mixture. But probably the biggest influence in Northern Europe came from the Scandinavians and Baltic countries, whose fishing industry generated the need to find ways of keeping fish fresh. Generally it is the fattier fish that work best for pickling.

Herrings

The Danes are some of the biggest fans of herring or 'sild'. Eaten on rye bread with a little butter and washed down with schnapps and a light lager chaser on the side, they make an incredibly good party snack. In fact you need nothing more for an extremely good night. Pickle your own herring, make sure you buy a light Danish rye loaf and keep your schnapps and your lager ice cold.

Pickled Fish Goes Well With

Beer	**Dill**	**Red Onion**
Butter	**Hard-Boiled Eggs**	**Rye Bread**
Cucumber	**Mustard**	**Sour Cream**

Canned Fish

•••

The process of canning is said to date back to the late 18th century in France, when Napoleon Bonaparte tried to find a way of preserving food for his armies by offering a prize for the best invention. The winner was Frenchman Nicolas Appert, who found a way to preserve food in glass jars. It was an Englishman, Peter Durand, who applied those principles to tin cans and the first canning factory opened in England in 1813. Canned fish are sealed in airtight tins or jars which are sterilised at high temperatures to destroy microorganisms and enzymes before cooling; the process also vacuum-seals the container.

Many fish are not robust enough to withstand the heat. Others have high protein levels which keep them intact. Bones are left in where possible, which also helps. They turn soft and are a good source of calcium.

Salmon

Very different to the fresh or smoked variety, but is a great staple. Eaten with the bones, it is high in calcium and nutritious. You can buy pink or red salmon, also known as sockeye. These are merely different varieties; the red is generally thought to have a firmer texture. It is fantastic for making fishcakes; try it mixed with a little smoked salmon, some dill and a few capers.

Sardines

Sold packed in oil, water or sauce. The fish have their heads and gills removed before cooking, drying and canning. They are tightly packed in flat cans... which has given rise to the familiar metaphor for a crowded situation. Pilchards are just big sardines.

For us, nothing beats a late-night snack of sardines on wholemeal toast: the perfect nutritious storecupboard fall back.

Tuna

By far the most popular canned fish sold today and, thankfully, brands are now using responsible fishing. Sold in brine or oil, the best is white or albacore. Don't be concerned you are hitting a culinary brick wall with this ingredient: there is some very good tuna in cans – though more often in glass jars – that make wonderful fishcakes.

Fish Roes

•••

Fish roes are the eggs from a mature female fish. They are incredibly rich in micronutrients and omega-3 fatty acids. The most commonly known roe is that of the sturgeon – caviar – but across the world, different fish roes are central to a lot of dishes.

Beluga Caviar

Made from the roe of the beluga sturgeon, this is the most luxurious of foods. There are caviar imitators but the real deal is usually handled with a non-metallic spoon and eaten as is, or served simply on toast. What more would you want for one of the most expensive foods sold? Other caviars are used in a variety of ways as garnishes and additions to many dishes.

Bottarga

Tuna or mullet roe that has been pressed, sun-dried and salt-cured, this is a speciality ingredient in Southern Italy, Sicily and Sardinia. It is usually shaved or grated over food as a seasoning and is very potent. It is good sliced thinly and laid over a simple plate of halved hard-boiled eggs, a few dressed bitter leaves and torn lamb's lettuce.

Cod's Roe

This is blanched and often smoked to produce a firm product. The whole roe should be poached and cooled before eating cold, or sliced, coated and fried until crisp. Smoked cod's roe is the basis for Greek taramasalata (see page 147, though that was traditionally made with smoked mullet roe); it is a simple, tasty dip with garlic, lemon, olive oil and breadcrumbs. Another of our late-night saviours is brown buttered toast topped with cod's roe that has been sautéed gently in butter. Very good indeed.

Juniper and Gin-cured Salmon

•••

This is very simple, but you have to plan for it a day ahead. Thinly slice it diagonally towards the skin, so you can enjoy the flavours and textures of the different layers that the spiced salt has permeated. You don't need to cure a whole side; you can start with half a side and halve the cure.

Serves 8–10

Ingredients

1 skin-on side of salmon
  (about 1 kg)
50 ml gin
2 tbsp juniper berries
1 orange
1 unwaxed lemon
small bunch of dill
300 g rock salt
150 g golden granulated sugar

Equipment

tweezers
mortar and pestle
zester
sharp knife
chopping board
cling film
2 baking trays

Preparation

Run your hands along the salmon to feel for the pin bones; remove them with a pair of tweezers. Pour and rub the gin into the flesh.

Crush the juniper berries in a mortar and pestle.

Finely zest the orange and lemon.

Wash, pick and chop the dill fronds and stalks.

Method

Mix the salt, sugar, juniper, zests and dill.

Lay the salmon skin side down on a long sheet of cling film. Apply the salt mixture to cover the entire pink flesh and pat it down firmly. Grab one end of the cling film and tightly wrap the fillet, using more cling film if necessary. Place between two baking trays and weigh down to make sure there is good contact. Place in the fridge for 24 hours.

Unwrap and brush away the salt mixture thoroughly with a dry kitchen cloth.

Leave at room temperature for a couple of hours before serving, to allow the natural oils to be released. Slice and serve with Horseradish sauce (see page 279) and rye bread.

This keeps in the fridge, well covered, for two weeks.

RECIPE
145

Potted Shrimps

•••

We pot our brown shrimps in a hollandaise sauce; we think it gives a better eating quality than setting straight into clarified butter. This is rather controversial, but we think it's worth breaking from tradition now and then. Best served with thinly sliced wholemeal bread and a wedge of lemon.

Serves 6

Ingredients

1 shallot
3 sprigs of tarragon
3 sprigs of parsley
1 nutmeg
125 g unsalted butter
60 ml white wine
25 ml white wine vinegar
1 blade of mace
4 black peppercorns
1 egg yolk
sea salt and freshly ground
   black pepper
squeeze of lemon juice and
   ½ tsp unwaxed lemon zest
300 g peeled brown shrimps
40 g Clarified butter
   (see page 108)

Equipment

sharp knife and chopping board
nutmeg grater
saucepan
heatproof bowl and whisk
4 small ramekins

Preparation

Thinly slice the shallot.

Wash the herbs and pick the leaves.

Grate a pinch of nutmeg.

Chop the butter and chill it.

Method

Boil the wine, vinegar, tarragon, shallot, mace and peppercorns and reduce by half. Set a heatproof bowl over a saucepan of very gently simmering water. The bowl should not touch the water. Put the egg yolk and the vinegar reduction in the bowl and whisk until it thickens and will hold ribbons of the mixture on its surface for a few seconds. Move the bowl on and off the heat to avoid splitting the sauce.

Whisk in the butter one cube at a time. Season and add a squeeze of lemon juice. Allow to cool but not set.

Mix the shrimps with the parsley, lemon zest and grated nutmeg. Fold in the hollandaise and check the seasoning one more time. Pot into ramekins and allow to set in the fridge for 30 minutes.

Pour over the melted clarified butter and set. Keep chilled until ready to serve. This will keep for five days, as long as the seal of clarified butter remains unbroken.

Taramasalata

•••

Often overshadowed by houmous, we think it's time taramasalata made a comeback. Not the dyed bright pink version you see on the supermarket shelves, but this simple, utterly delicious recipe. Most good fishmongers will stock smoked cod's roe. It will keep in the fridge for a week in an airtight container. Sprinkle with toasted onion seeds to serve.

Serves 6

Ingredients

1 lobe (250 g) smoked cod's roe
juice of ½ lemon
250 ml olive oil

Equipment

sharp knife
chopping board
food processor
juicer

Preparation

None. Just invite some friends over and tell them to bring some chilled wine.

Method

Leaving the skin on, chop the roe into chunks and place in a food processor and juice in the lemon. Blitz until smooth. Trickle in the oil, still whizzing, as if making a mayonnaise.

When the mixture starts to seize, loosen it by adding 50 ml of hot water, a little at a time, then continue with the oil until it has all been used and the mixture is light and mousse-like. Chill before serving.

Canned Fishcakes

Drain a 225 g jar of tuna in oil. Mix with a 120 g can of sardines in oil, drained, finely grated unwaxed lemon zest, chopped dill and 400 g mashed potato. Season well. Fold in a beaten egg. Shape into 6 cakes, dust with polenta and chill to firm up. Fry in 1 tbsp of hot oil on both sides to colour. Bake in an oven preheated to 180°C/350°F/gas mark 4 for 10 minutes. Makes 6.

Cider-steamed Mussels with Fennel

Sweat 1 finely sliced onion and 1 garlic clove, 1 chopped fennel bulb and thyme leaves in 2 tbsp of oil. Season. Throw in 1 kg of mussels and 250 ml of cider. Cover. Cook for 10 minutes, shaking from time to time. Remove the mussels with a slotted spoon and keep warm while you reduce the juices, adding chopped parsley and lemon juice. Pour over the mussels. Serves 4 with chips.

Smoked Mackerel Pâté

Beat 250 g flaked smoked mackerel with 50 g of yogurt, 50 g of crème fraîche, the juice of ½ lemon and 1 tsp each of chopped chives and dill. Season and add more lemon if needed. Serves 4.

Caesar Salad

Mix 4 tsp of anchovy paste, 2 crushed garlic cloves and ½ tsp of English mustard powder. Whisk in 2 tbsp of Worcestershire sauce, 1 tsp of white wine vinegar and 1 egg yolk. Drizzle in 125 ml of olive oil. Season. Use to dress a Romaine lettuce. Add warm croutons, anchovy fillets and shaved Parmesan. Serves 2.

M

FRUIT

AND

VEGETABLES

An Introduction to Fruit and Vegetables

Fresh fruit and vegetables are our signifiers of the seasons. Each month brings a new fruit or vegetable to our shopping baskets; the trick is to make the most of them and really appreciate them when they are here. In some months, such as September, we're overwhelmed by the choice and variety, while in the late winter we long for the first signs of spring and a new season's crop. Sometimes our appetites signal the changes too: the first apple of the season; parsnips after the first frost; or healthy brassica greens at the end of the winter.

In our shops, rather than offer a whole panoply of fruit and veg, we've tended to 'hero' the season's new arrivals or star players: asparagus in April, damsons in August, or pumpkins in October. Likewise, in this chapter, we offer a reminder of the highlights and what you should be looking for each month in the greengrocers or supermarket.

With some careful planning and a few tricks up your sleeve, you really shouldn't be tempted by green beans from Kenya or strawberries from Brazil, offered year-round in certain stores. Without even touching on the ethical arguments, the fact is they rarely have any flavour. A strawberry picked unripe and air-freighted to this country cannot compare to a fruit grown and sun-ripened either in your own garden, or by a local farmer.

Of course, we can't grow everything we need in our own backyard. Sometimes we have to look a little further for fruit and vegetables that provide the nourishment and variety we need. We want citrus fruits from Southern Europe to help the year along; the import of these has been going on for centuries and Sicilian lemons, clementines, blood, navel and Seville oranges are firmly rooted in British culinary tradition because of that; while at the height of summer we can't ignore luscious peaches, nectarines or apricots from the same regions.

To truly make the most of fruit and vegetables when in season, we often find ways either to extend their life or transform them into something new.

Fruits can be turned into compotes, stewed or stored in syrup, captured in cordials, made into jam or marmalades, even pickled. A freezer offers options, too. In warmer climes, other food cultures have been drying fruits for centuries and we've traditionally imported and made the most of these in winter months; our Christmas puddings and mince pies would be nothing without the dried vine fruits of the Levant, while the candying of orange, lemon and other 'exotic' fruits lends further opportunities in the short days of winter.

Vegetables can be pickled, frozen, or some can even be left in the ground until needed. Others can be canned in water or brine and some preserved in oil.

Whatever the season, fruit and vegetables offer infinite opportunities, from the simple to the most complex.

Seasonal Fruit and Vegetable Calendar

If you're lucky enough to grow up with a vegetable patch in your own back garden, you soon get to understand what's in season when. However, the desire for choice all-year-round has confused many a shopper. To help, in this chapter we highlight a fruit and vegetable for each month of the year, which we think you should be taking advantage of to enjoy it at its best. You'll also find a general guide to the other fruit and vegetables to be eating each month of the year. Overleaf is a more general chart of the seasons for the most common vegetables and fruits.

VEGETABLES	JAN	FEB	MAR	APR	MAY
Artichokes					
Asparagus					●
Beetroots	○				
Broad Beans					
Brussels Sprouts	○				
Cabbages	●	●	●		
Carrots					
Celeriacs	●	●			
Chillies					
Courgettes					
Cucumbers					○
French Beans					
Jersey Royals				○	○
Jerusalem Artichokes	●	●			
Kale	○				
Leeks	●	●	●		
Parsnips	○	○			
Peppers				●	●
Purple-sprouting Broccoli			○	○	
Radishes				●	●
Runner Beans					
Salad Leaves				●	●
Spinach			○	○	○
Spring Onions			●	●	●
Squashes					
Swedes	●	●	●		
Sweetcorn					
Tomatoes					●
Wet Garlic					
Wild Mushrooms					

JUN	JUL	AUG	SEP	OCT	NOV	DEC
○	○	○	○	○		
●						
○	○	○	○	○	○	○
●	●	●				
					○	○
				●	●	●
○	○	○	○	○	○	○
					●	●
		○	○			
●	●	●	●	●		
○	○	○	○	○		
●	●	●	●			
					●	●
					○	○
					●	●
			○	○	○	○
●	●	●	●	●	●	●
●	●	●	●	●		
	○	○	○	○		
●	●	●	●	●		
○	○	○				
			○	○	○	○
				●	●	●
		○	○	○		
●	●	●	●	●		
○	○	○				
			●	●		

FRUITS	JAN	FEB	MAR	APR	MAY
Apples	○	○	○	○	
Blackberries					
Blood Oranges	○	○	○		
Blueberries					
Cherries					
Clementines					
Cranberries					
Currants					
Figs					
Forced Rhubarb	●	●	●		
Gooseberries					○
Grapes					
Lemons	○		○		
Med Stone Fruits					
Navel Oranges					
Outdoor Rhubarb				●	●
Pears	○	○	○	○	
Plums					
Pomegranates	○	○	○		
Quinces					
Raspberries					
Seville Orangs	●	●			
Sicilian Lemons				○	
Strawberries					●

In the Kitchen

Some fruit and vegetables are available all year round and are part of a well-stocked kitchen. Try to always have:

Carrots	**Lemons**
Celery	**Onions**
Garlic	**Potatoes**
Leeks	(...and a packet of frozen peas doesn't hurt either)

What to Look For
When Buying Fruit and Vegetables

If you have a greengrocer, support them. Much supermarket fruit and veg comes pre-packed for their convenience (not yours), was picked before it was ripe and stored until the supermarket was ready for it. If you're buying in season, you will find produce that tastes as it should. The price will be good, too. Look for firm, plump fruits and remember: ripe fruit smells ripe. If it looks wrinkled, is soft or bruised, don't bother. Veg should look fresh and feel firm. Leaves should be vibrant, not dull.

How to Store: Chilled vs Not Chilled

Our advice is to buy enough for a week and replenish as needed. Modern homes are not designed to store fresh foods beyond the refrigerator. Generally, soft fruits are better chilled, but remove from the fridge an hour before eating for maximum flavour and aroma. Others are better kept in a cool (not cold), dark place. Or in a plentiful bowl of fruit on the countertop. A warning about bananas: they give off ethylene which makes fruit close by ripen more quickly, so store them away from other fruit.

January

•••

January King Cabbage

Handsome, tight heads of crunchy purple-tinged leaves that are sweet in flavour. The purple colouring comes from anthocyanins that are produced when the air temperature fluctuates. This cabbage is perfect when cut into quarters or sixths and roasted or braised.

• •

Brassicas provide greens for our plates in autumn, winter and early spring and the family includes:

Brussels Sprouts　　**Cauliflower**

Broccoli　　**Kale**

(and sprouting broccoli)　　(curly and cavolo nero)

Cabbage　　**Kohlrabi**

(red, white, savoy, spring
and winter greens and hispi)

When buying, look for fresh, vibrant-coloured leaves and tight, firm heads. All can be cooked by a variety of methods, from steaming, to baking, to braising. Many can also be enjoyed raw as an ingredient in a salad. Some of our favourites include:

Cauliflower With a creamy cheese sauce

Cavolo Nero Always trim off tough stalks, add to soups or stews or pasta

Red Cabbage When freshly picked use in a winter slaw, or braise long and slow with spices

Savoy Cabbage An alternative to white cabbage for a summer slaw, or braise or roast with lots of butter

Seville Orange

More than any other, this fruit heralds the start of a new year in the kitchen. In late January the first boxes arrive from Spain and marmalade production begins. What sets these oranges apart from the rest is their bitterness; you wouldn't want to take a bite out of one of these! They make a very good marmalade, partly due to their high pectin levels which help it to set. Marmalade can of course be made with other types of oranges, but there's something about a bitter-sweet Seville orange marmalade. Seville oranges can also be used in savoury dishes such as the French classic duck à l'orange.

The season is short – so start looking around the middle of January – and it's often over by the end of February. Don't be afraid to freeze whole Sevilles, if you have room in the freezer. It's a great way of spreading your marmalade production throughout the year, rather than producing all the jars you need in one go.

Seville Orange Marmalade

Whole Fruit Method

•••

I think it is safe to say we have become obsessed with marmalade over the years. Not just the making, but the eating of it at every opportunity. As with all jam making, it is ultimately the quality of your fruit that will define the flavour you capture in the jar. This is a whole fruit method that uses every part of the fruit apart from the pips and has a lovely full flavour.

Makes six 330 ml jars

Ingredients

1 kg best-quality Seville oranges
2 kg golden granulated sugar
150 ml lemon juice, plus more
  if needed

Equipment

6 x 330 ml jars with lids
plate
your largest saucepan with a lid
sharp knife and chopping board
sieve
jam thermometer
jug or funnel

Preparation

Sterilise the jars (see page 408). Set aside until ready to pot the marmalade.

Wash the fruit thoroughly.

Place a plate in the freezer.

Method

Place the whole oranges in your largest pan with two litres of water. Bring to the boil very gently, partially cover, then cook for two hours, until completely soft when pierced with a knife. Allow to cool. You should have about 1 litre of liquid left. Cut the oranges in half, scoop out the flesh and push it through a sieve. Add to the poaching liquid. Set over a medium heat, add the sugar and lemon juice and heat to dissolve. Slice the skins neatly.

Add the skins. Increase the heat to a setting point of 104.5°C (220.1°F). Stir once or twice, but not too much as stirring cools the pot. Spoon a bit on to the chilled plate and see if it wrinkles when you push a finger through. If not, return to the heat with 50 ml more lemon juice for 10 minutes. Repeat until you have the set. Cool for 10 minutes to allow the peel to distribute, then pot into hot jars using a jug or funnel. Seal. Label and eat within 18 months.

February

...

Purple-sprouting Broccoli

This brassica is a close cousin of the tighter headed, more common calabrese or green broccoli. Don't worry too much about the lower leaves that come with it, it's the tender purple heads that hold the sweet flavour. If left to develop, these purple heads would in fact turn into heavy heads of yellow flowers. You'll also see some white-sprouting broccoli from time to time that's more delicate in flavour.

Both are the easiest of vegetables to overcook and are best steamed to prevent spoiling. A round-ended knife, rather than a sharp-pointed knife, is the best tool to check if any vegetable is sufficiently cooked.

Mire Poix

(pronounced mirh-pwah)

Sometimes described as the Holy Trinity of French cooking, this is onions, carrots and celery in the ratio of 2:1:1, sautéed in butter, used as a base for soups, stews and sauces and for braising meat and fish. Sweat 200 g of onion with 100 g of carrot and 100 g of celery, all finely chopped, in unsalted butter over a gentle heat. Season with salt and cook until translucent, but without colour. The vegetables will release their natural sugars.

M

Root Vegetables

These are the vegetables to celebrate in the winter months, when there's less growing above ground. Some happily remain in the ground all winter and some benefit from the frost that helps turn their starches into sugars.

Beetroots	Jerusalem Artichokes	Salsify
Carrots	Parsnips	Swedes
Celeriacs	Potatoes	Turnips

Puréed, mashed, roasted, baked, in soups or stews... the choice is yours.

Rhubarb

Love it or loathe it, there's no mistaking a rhubarb in its slender, pink forced form (often called 'champagne' rhubarb). It is a tender, sweet stem that brings colour to late winter. It is grown in the Rhubarb Triangle around Wakefield in great, darkened sheds in which rhubarb grows tall, then harvested by candlelight. In the kitchen, rhubarb is most often cooked for pudding, but can go with a savoury dish such as mackerel. The trick is not to stew it to mush. Roast gently with orange juice, spices (try ginger, vanilla or cardamom) and sugar. Add to yogurt at breakfast, serve with cakes or – our favourite – mix with Muscovado meringues (see page 414) and whipped cream to make an Eton Mess-style pudding. Outdoor rhubarb is picked in summer, though lacks the same delicacy and colour.

Rhubarb and Cardamom Vodka

Finely chop 450 g of rhubarb and place in a sterilised 1.5-litre jar (see page 408). Dissolve 100 g of granulated sugar in 750 ml of vodka, pour it over the rhubarb, add six crushed cardamom pods and leave in a dark cupboard for a month. Stir from time to time. Pass through muslin into a sterilised bottle. Serve with ice, soda and a strawberry.

March

•••

Leeks

Leeks stand strong and sturdy in the ground, braced against the frost and snow. They lend their mild, sweet flavour to casseroles, soups and other comforting dishes. If an onion seems too strong, a leek will generally do.

When preparing leeks, it's important to ensure the soil is removed. Gritty leeks are unacceptable in the pot or on the plate. Thorough cleaning in lots of cold water is the only way. But first, remove the tough green tops and save for stock (see right). Then slice part way down two sides of the leek and gently swill away any grit beneath the layers before chopping. Once chopped, wash well again under cold running water. If you want thinner slices, once shredded, leave to stand in a large bowl of water for five minutes to let debris settle, then rinse again; drain well before using.

Leeks marry well with potatoes in a soup; once caramelised they add subtle depth to a savoury custard tart; they lend themselves to be baked or gratinated with cheese; they really stand out in a simple dish of leeks poached in stock, served chilled with grated boiled egg and a vinaigrette.

Sweating Vegetables

Recipes often call for vegetables to be sweated, but what does that mean? It's usually called for when working with leeks, onions, celery and carrots. The idea is that you cook the vegetables gently in a small amount of oil or butter in order to get them to release their moisture and become soft. If they're starting to brown or caramelise, the pan is too hot. A pinch of salt will help draw out the water, too.

M

Vegetable Stock

•••

A simple vegetable stock can be the basis for a quick and easy meal such as soup, broth, stew or risotto, or even used to add flavour to cooking grains before making a salad from them. Getting a good flavour balance in your stock is key: sweetness from carrots, acidity from fennel and celery and depth from onions and leeks, with a bouquet garni to bring it all alive.

We make all our vegetable soups with fresh stock, using up the trimmings from leeks, fennel and carrots. We also ask our chefs to save parsley stalks for the pot, as these can bring a surprising amount of flavour. Only use fresh vegetables for stock, as old vegetables will impair the taste. Be sure to slice the vegetables as they will give up their flavours more readily than if they are whole or merely halved.

Makes 1.5 litres

Ingredients

3 onions
3 carrots
2 celery sticks
1 leek, or the green tops of 2
1 fennel bulb
1 bouquet garni (see page 236)
a few parsley stalks
1 tsp white or black peppercorns
1 tsp fennel seeds

Equipment

sharp knife and chopping board
large saucepan
sieve

Preparation

Wash and slice all the vegetables.

Method

Place the vegetables in your largest pan with the herbs and spices. Cover the vegetables with cold water (you should use about 2.5 litres) and bring to a very slow boil. Partly cover and cook gently – so the water is just moving – for 1½ hours. Cool and pass through a sieve.

If not using straight away, store covered in your fridge for up to four days, or freeze in useful quantities rather than one big container. Using an ice cube tray to freeze is also a handy way to store this or any stock, so that you can use just the small amount you require.

Know Your Onions

Onions and their close allium relatives leeks, shallots, garlic and chives have been a staple of most cuisines around the world for thousands of years. During the Middle Ages, onions were such an important food to the Europeans that they were used as currency to pay for essentials such as rent and were even given as gifts. They are equally at home as the base of a soup or stew, as an element in a salad or omelette, or to be enjoyed in their own right, pickled or baked.

Onion Varieties

Electric

Jetset

Red Baron

Setton

Troy

Which Allium When?

Brown Onion The most familiar and most used of the cooking onions, unlikely to be used raw

Red Onion The red colour is a sign of lots of antioxidants. Milder than its brown brother, it can be cooked or used raw in salads

White Onion The strongest of them all

Shallot Milder and finer in flavour than onions, shallots can be used raw in dressings and salads. They can also be roasted whole, or pickled

Spring or Salad Onion A baby onion that has not been allowed to grow fully, these are used raw in salads and often to garnish Asian dishes. They can also be grilled, when they are sweet and strong

Buying and Storing

Choose onions which are firm with paper-like skins and discard any with green shoots. Store in a cool dark cupboard, ideally in a paper bag. Don't keep onions (except spring onions) in the fridge.

Caramelised Onions

Thinly slice onions and cook over a low heat with a little oil and unsalted butter, allowing them to colour slightly before stirring. Repeat until all are soft and golden. These can be used as the base of savoury tarts or in stews.

M

Five Ways to Stop the Tears

When Preparing Onions

Place a spoon in your mouth

Wear swimming goggles

Chill in the fridge, to slow the release of the sulphurous oil

Leave the roots on until the very end

Chew on a piece of bread

If all else fails, try all five together

Blood Oranges

Grown predominately in Italy, the flesh of these sweet oranges develops its characteristic maroon colour when the fruit experiences low night temperatures and mild days. The season runs from December to April, but the oranges are usually at their flavour peak in March. Sweet, juicy and flavourful, they make a powerful and wonderfully coloured juice, can be made into marmalade, caramelised or even candied (see right).

. . . .

Candied Fruits

Through soaking in increasingly strong sugar syrups, fruit is candied. Most often seen as

Apricots	**Mandarins**
Cherries	**Orange**
Citrus Peel	**Peaches**
Kiwi	**Pears**
Lemon	**Pineapples**

The French marrons glacé (candied chestnuts) are traditionally given as a treat at Christmas, as are Elvas plums from Portugal, candied greengages which manage to retain some of their original flavour. If considering candying fruits at home, candying orange peel and dipping it in chocolate is probably as far as you need to go (see right).

Candied Blood Oranges

•••

This process of candying involves heating and cooling the fruit in intervals, so requires a little bit of commitment and is best started early in the day to allow for cooling time. This technique of cooking in sugar syrup has been around for thousands of years; effectively when the process is completed the fruit has mostly been converted to sugar, so will keep for months. They are a delight to eat for a sweet treat from time to time, especially after supper, or chop them into puddings or cakes.

Makes about 500 g, depending on the size of the oranges

Ingredients

4 blood oranges
1.2 kg golden granulated sugar, plus more to coat
Tempered chocolate, to coat (optional, see page 71)

Equipment

sharp knife and chopping board
mandolin (optional)
large mixing bowl
large saucepan

Preparation

Wash and slice the fruit into discs no thicker than 5 mm, using a mandolin if you have one. Place in a large bowl.

Method

Boil 1 litre of water with 600 g of the sugar, pour over the sliced fruit and set aside to cool overnight.

The following day, pour into a large saucepan with 200 g more of the sugar, cook the fruit for 10 minutes, then allow to cool once more.

Repeat for two more doses, adding 200 g of sugar for each and cooking for 10 minutes before cooling the fruit completely. Stretch this process over two days if timings are an issue. Leave the fruit in the syrup to steep overnight. Then remove and drain on wire racks.

Preheat the oven to 100°C/212°F/gas mark ¼. Dip the orange slices in sugar and place on a rack in a single layer. Dry out in the low oven for two hours, or until they firm up slightly. Leave to cool. Store between sheets of greaseproof paper in an airtight container for up to six months. Dip them in Tempered chocolate for a note of luxury.

April

•••

Asparagus

April is marked by the arrival of asparagus, known to some as 'sparrow grass'. It's only around until June and is weather dependent, so make the most of it. It tastes so different from anything else you'll eat all year.

Asparagus grows in light and sandy soils, so give it a good wash first, then take your spear and hold between both hands, pulling the tip down while holding the base firm until SNAP!, the spear breaks, leaving you hopefully with a short stubby end in one hand and a long, elegant spear in the other.

(Don't discard the stubby ends, keep them in the fridge until you have enough to make a soup.) The long and elegant spear is at its best when boiled for a matter of minutes, before being served in any of these ways:

With hollandaise, a poached egg and lots of freshly ground black pepper

With grated Parmesan, extra virgin olive oil and basil

Chopped in chunks and dropped in a bowl of pasta with creamy goat's cheese

Chargrilled and popped into an egg mayo sandwich

Wrapped in Parma ham and dipped, as if they were toast soldiers, in a boiled duck egg

Made into a salad with peas, broad beans and Baby Gem lettuce

Slipped into a savoury tart with nutty Berkswell cheese

As the main player in a spring risotto

A warning: asparagus is only here for a short time. If you see it in a shop and it's not spring, keep walking; it'll have been flown in and taste of little.

Caesar Salad

Romaine or Cos

Soft and Floppy

Butterhead
Escarole
Lollo Rosso
Oak Leaf
Radicchio

Firm and Crisp

Cos
Frisée
Iceberg
Little Gem
Romaine
Webb's Wonder

For the quintessential English salad, choose Butterhead, cress and cucumber with Salad cream (see page 328)

Prawn Cocktail

Iceberg

Braised Lettuce and Peas

Little Gem

Types of Salad Greens

Chard (swiss chard, rainbow chard) Similar to spinach, but with a more pronounced flavour. Young leaves are excellent in the salad bowl, and coloured varieties are especially welcome. To cook more mature chard, separate the stalks from the leaves, as they take longer to cook.

Chicory A firm, crisp and pointy head of pale cream or red-tinged leaves grown either underground or indoors with no sunlight, to prevent it from turning green. It can also be cooked (braised or roasted) or eaten raw.

Lamb's Lettuce (mâche) So-called due to the similarity in shape of the small, tender leaves and a lamb's tongue, the leaves have a distinctive and tangy flavour.

Mizuna Spiky both in appearance and flavour, this leaf adds texture and flavour to your salad bowl.

Rocket A leaf with a bit of a kick to it – peppery and firm, it stands up well to being dressed – rocket has become slightly ubiquitous as the salad of choice in any number of eating establishments. It can be the basis for a great-tasting pesto instead of using basil.

Sorrel A small, tender green leaf, but this time with a lemony flavour, that brings a lovely freshness to salad bowls.

Spinach Always choose the perkiest leaves and rinse really well as grit has a habit of clinging to the leaves. Spinach can be eaten young and raw in salads or wilted with some hot oil or water. Fully grown leaves can be steamed, boiled or added to stews and soups; for a slightly less mineral feel in the mouth, cook it with butter. It's related to beetroot and quinoa.

Tatsoi A relative newcomer to the salad bowl and a baby brother to pak choi, these small round leaves have a mild mustard-like flavour. Similar in texture to baby spinach. Once fully grown, cook in Asian-style dishes.

Watercress Once called poor man's bread as it was plentiful and cheap in Victorian England. Cultivated in the fresh running rivers of southern England, it's crunchy and has a peppery kick. Don't be afraid to enjoy the stalks, too. It can be made into a tasty soup or is great in a sandwich with egg mayo or roast beef and horseradish.

Buying, Using and Storing

Some shop-bought salad leaves are washed in a chlorine solution before packing and the bags are often sealed using a system which removes the oxygen to help extend their shelf life. We think it's better to search out heads of lettuce, or untreated bags, at a farmer's market or a greengrocer.

Mix it up with your own salad leaf combinations. Take a head of lettuce, some herb leaves, spinach or watercress and dress. It's a meal in itself.

A good salad spinner is a valuable kitchen tool, as wet leaves make for a soggy salad and a diluted dressing. If you don't have a spinner, dry the leaves well with a clean tea towel or kitchen paper.

You can quickly revive tired and limp salad leaves by soaking in a big bowl of cold water just before you need them; it will soon perk them up.

Once bought, keep all lettuces and leaves in the refrigerator salad drawer. Keep picked leaves in a perforated plastic bag. Don't put wet leaves in the fridge, instead remove as much water as possible if you've washed them. Wrap whole lettuces in paper. Most leaves will only keep for a few days.

Grow Your Own

Salad leaves are so easy to grow – even a window box or container will give you a summer plateful – choose a 'cut-and-come-again' variety.

Lemons

There is a certain point each spring when lemons from the Amalfi coast of Italy are at their peak. Amalfi lemons are unusually heavy, knobbly, unwaxed and have an intense aroma and flavour as well as plenty of juice. Use them in baking when zest is called for, as the essential oils released are so heady; preserve them in salt (see page 396), make the most English of puddings, a Sussex pond, with a whole lemon baked at its centre, go for nostalgic lemon curd to serve at tea, or a posset for pudding.

Lemon Posset

•••

A sharp little set pudding dating back to medieval times. The acid from the lemon curdles and sets the sweetened cream. Possets are quite rich, so set them in little espresso cups or ramekins and serve with vanilla shortbread. They can be made the day before.

Serves 4

Ingredients

2 unwaxed lemons
425 ml double cream
125 g caster sugar

Equipment

zester
juicer
4 ramekins or espresso cups
saucepan
sieve

Preparation

Wash and zest the lemons and squeeze their juice.

Chill four cups or ramekins in the fridge.

Method

Boil the cream with the sugar and zest, then reduce the heat and simmer gently for 10 minutes.

Remove from the heat, add the lemon juice and stir.

Pass through a sieve and divide between the cups or ramekins. Allow to cool, cover and leave to set for a few hours in the fridge.

May

...

Jersey Royal Potatoes

Each April the new season's crop arrive in mainland Britain from the island of Jersey off the north-west coast of France. The first of the crop is horrendously expensive, despite their exceptional flavour, but by May, when the harvest is in full swing, they're hard to ignore and we should make the most of them.

These small, sometimes kidney-shaped potatoes are the first of the season due to the location and climate they're grown in. Jersey has a light, fertile soil that the farmers feed with the seaweed that washes up on its shores. The potatoes have been produced on the island since the 1880s and the 20 island farmers grow 30,000–40,000 tonnes a year, most of which are eaten in the UK. They're a lovely seasonal treat and shouldn't be messed with. Boil in salted water and serve with a knob of butter and some mint.

Types of Potato

Potatoes fall into two types – waxy or floury – and have different uses:

Waxy Good for salads, sautéing and gratins
Charlotte, Epicure, Jersey Royals, Pink Fir Apple

Floury Good for roasting, baking, mashing and chips
Desirée, King Edward, Maris Piper, Yukon Gold

Potato crops are classified as being either earlies (the first to crop), mids (the second to crop) and lates or main crop (the last to crop).

Sweet Potatoes Not a potato at all, but a tuber nonetheless, these are quicker to bake than regular potatoes and make an easy and relatively healthy oven-roasted chip (see page 416).

**When You're Bored with
Boiled Potatoes Try**

Mashed with olive oil
and Parmesan

Potato salad dressed with
a Green sauce

(see page 251)

In a vegetable curry

Roasted in goose fat

Potatoes boulangère

Crushed new potatoes with crème
fraîche and lots of fresh herbs

Bubble and Squeak

Our favourite early

Jersey Royal

Potatoes are used to make vodka

Introduced to Europe from the Americas in the 16th century

Potatoes fuelled the population of the UK in the industrial revolution by providing a cheap and plentiful source of calories and nutrients

Keep in paper bags in a cool, dark place

Our favourite main crop

Yukon Gold

They are the world's fourth largest food crop after maize, wheat and rice

175

Gooseberries

These small, green and hairy fruits seem to have found favour on British tables, where in other countries they've had less success. Perhaps that's because they pair well with some other British favourites: elderflowers, cream, roast pork and grilled mackerel. Most gooseberries found in shops are for cooking, being too sour to eat raw, although some 'dessert' varieties, often with a red tinge and usually from the continent, are sweeter and can be enjoyed uncooked. For those who enjoy tart fruit, the gooseberry is a must. Gently poached in a little water, perhaps with elderflowers to add flavour, the sugar which is so desperately needed should only be added at the end of poaching, else the skins will toughen. Early varieties produce the first British summer fruits as early as May. Use in crumbles, compotes, pies and purées, or classically in a fool:

Gooseberry Fool

Choose fruits that are tart and carry acidity to balance with the cream (rhubarb and blackcurrants make perfect fools, too). To make the fool, cook 300 g of fruit with 60 ml of elderflower cordial and 90 g of sugar until softened. Cool, then blitz half to a purée. Whip 500 ml of double cream softly (see page 105) and fold everything together. Serve in 6 chilled glasses.

M

June

•••

Broad Beans

The earliest bean to arrive each summer, they are around just long enough for you to explore their use in a number of different ways. Also known as fava beans, in other countries they're dried to save for winter stews. But in the UK we make the most of them fresh, during their short summer season. If you grow them yourself, when they're very young and a pod is only the size of your little finger, they can be cooked whole. Drop the pods into boiling water for a few minutes, then remove and dress. However, most of us will pick or buy broad beans fully grown, when they need to be removed from their velvety pods, then dropped in boiling water for a matter of minutes. When they're young and fresh you can eat them skin and all. But if they're starting to wrinkle, try removing the grey skins once cooked, to unleash the fluorescent green kernel inside. (It's a bit of a faff but your tastebuds are duly rewarded.)

Broad beans suit all manner of foods and are equally at home alongside some new season's roasted or grilled lamb as they are by themselves, dressed in oil and herbs. They look delightful in a risotto with fresh peas and goat's cheese, or suit being blitzed into a houmous-like dip. However you eat them, they are at their happiest when served with mint.

When buying beans in their pods it can be hard to gauge how much you should buy; it of course depends on how many beans are in each pod, but as a guide allow about 500 g of pods per person.

Garlic

Around this time of year you'll find 'wet' or fresh garlic in the shops. The fleshy bulbs that we most often use are in fact dried in the sun. Wet garlic, or bulbs that have been just harvested in summer (traditionally garlic is planted on the shortest day and harvested on the longest day), are much milder and have a fresher 'greener' flavour.

Garlic is so widely used around the world as an aromatic that it almost deserves a chapter of its own. Marrying incredibly well with so many other herbs, spices and ingredients, we could hardly imagine cooking without it.

Garlic can turn stale quickly, so keep an eye on your bulbs, discarding any that feel soft or empty. Any green shoots should be removed before use.

Garlic can be bought 'ready minced', dried and as garlic salt but, frankly, don't waste your money. Besides, who can't be bothered to smash a garlic clove? It's cleaning the garlic crusher that makes the job boring; we don't own one. Simply cut the root end from a clove of garlic, give it a sharp whack with the side of a heavy knife and the skin will peel away.

• •

British Summer Soft Fruits

Blackberries **Raspberries**

Blackcurrants **Redcurrants**

Blueberries **Strawberries**

Gooseberries **Tayberries**

Loganberries **Whitecurrants**

Strawberries

The one fruit that seems to jar more than any other when seen out of season. Perhaps because it conjures childhood memories of warm summer afternoons spent picking plump berries that you had waited all year to enjoy. A strawberry in a hermetically sealed plastic punnet, in a chilled counter at a supermarket in December, is a poor imitation.

Traditionally at their peak in late June, just in time for Wimbledon, these days, due to improved growing techniques and cultivars, the season can be enjoyed from May to September (but no longer, please).

Look for fresh-picked, vibrant-coloured fruits. As soon as you refrigerate them the flavour starts to alter, so look for shops that sell them un-chilled. Search out specific varieties to enjoy; not all strawberries taste the same. Only wash and de-hull the berries just before eating. Be a purist and enjoy them unadulterated, adding cream if you must or balsamic vinegar to hide those that lack flavour. Rhubarb with strawberries is a perfect summer crumble. Jam that retains essential strawberriness over sugary sweetness is a wistful reminder of the summer gone.

July

...

Peas

Following hot on the heels of the broad bean, the pea is next on the list of fresh summer pulses to arrive. If it weren't for potatoes, peas would probably be the UK's national vegetable, such is its popularity, served up on our plates all year round in its frozen, bagged form.

However, a frozen pea, as sweet as it might be, cannot be compared to a pea fresh out of the pod; if picked freshly from the garden we're talking about a completely different eating experience. Frozen peas all taste the same – sweet and well... sweet – whereas a pea fresh from the pod can have any number of flavour attributes. The point is something happens in the freezing that allows you never to be disappointed but, at the same time, never quite surprised. By the way, beware, a frozen pea cooks more quickly than a fresh pea from the pod.

If you manage to pod enough peas to make a worthwhile-sized portion. without eating more than you save, they can be prepared in lots of ways: why not try a pea purée (posh mushy peas), Potted peas (see page 363), a chilled soup of peas and mint, peas in broth with Baby Gem lettuce, pea risotto, pea fritters, salad with peas, peas with pasta, peas added to curry...

And let's not forget the pea shoot, the tender tips of a growing plant that carry the same flavour as a fully grown pea, that can be used as a garnish or added to your salad bowl.

How to Blanch Vegetables

Blanching kills the enzymes that live on the outside of vegetables. It's an important technique for preparing vegetables for all sort of dishes, from those that are to be preserved to those that will feature in our composite salads. Blanching should be done in your largest pot, as the more water you bring to the boil the less it will drop in temperature when vegetables are added. Add a good handful of salt; the water should taste like sea water. This will retain the colour of the vegetables and season them, too. Depending on the size and type of the vegetable, blanching should take between two and five minutes. Once cooked, vegetables should be placed into an ice bath (a bowl of cold water with ice cubes) to stop the cooking process and keep the vegetable crisp.

Vegetables to Blanch

Asparagus

Bobby Beans

Broad Beans

Carrots

French Beans

Peas

Purple-sprouting Broccoli

Runner Beans

Raspberries

Scotland is renowned for its raspberry growing and that is said to be due to the long, not too hot, summer days. Golden raspberries appear at the end of summer and into autumn. As with strawberries, raspberries should be enjoyed only in season; sun-ripening on the cane allows the natural sugars to form in the fruit. Look for varieties that please your tastebuds and make a note of what they were for next time.

Raspberries can be used in baking and they make an excellent jam, alone or in a mixed jam with the best of all soft summer fruits (see page 415).

Raspberry and Lemon Verbena Cordial

•••

Serve on a hot summer's day, diluting one part of cordial with five parts of sparkling water and serving over ice. If you don't have lemon verbena to hand (though it's easy to grow and very useful), omit it and use a slice or two of lemon instead.

Makes about 300ml

Ingredients

250 g fresh or frozen raspberries
150 g granulated sugar
2 tbsp chopped lemon verbena
  leaves

Equipment

300 ml glass bottle with lid
food processor
saucepan
sieve

Preparation

Sterilise a 300 ml glass bottle (see page 408).

Defrost the raspberries, if using frozen.

Method

Blitz the raspberries and sugar to a purée in a food processor. Bring to the boil in a saucepan with the lemon verbena and simmer for a few minutes to allow the flavours to infuse.

Pass through a sieve, discarding the pips and seeds, then pour into the sterilised bottle.

Keep the cordial in the fridge. Consume within one month.

August

•••

Tomatoes

English tomatoes got themselves some bad press a few years ago, when growers were producing for high yields rather than taste. Luckily, you can now find specialist growers producing a wonderful range of tasty tomatoes; on the vine, plum, cherry, beefsteak and multi-coloured, multi-shaped 'Heritage' types.

As good as a fresh tomato is, there's a lot to be said for canned tomatoes, too. Due to their high acidity the fruits are well suited to canning and we've come to rely on a can or two in our storecupboard at all times. For the cook, they're often easier to use in a sauce than are fresh tomatoes and certainly a quicker option, as they're already peeled.

Cans of tomatoes come in a variety of forms: plum, cherry, whole or chopped, some with added herbs. They are all useful additions to your storecupboard, but we suggest the whole tomatoes rather than the chopped versions and, for sweetness alone, we recommend cherry tomatoes; they are a bit more expensive but a notch up on their bigger brothers. Add them to sauces or stews or use to make a pizza sauce.

Tomato paste or purée is another storecupboard staple, a quick way to add depth and richness to a tomato-based sauce.

Passata, a relatively new storecupboard ingredient in this country, is essentially a tomato concentrate that's made by straining chopped tomatoes to remove the seeds and skins. It can be used as a quick way to get ahead when making a tomato-based sauce.

It's also useful to have both oak-smoked and sun-dried tomatoes in oil. They can be enjoyed with cold meats and added to sandwiches or salads.

Tomatoes

1

Buy in season. The UK season has been extended through improved growing conditions from April to November

2

Pick them up and smell: they should give off a strong tomatoey aroma

3

Remove any plastic packaging once back at home

4

Don't store tomatoes in the fridge; anything below 5°C destroys their cell structure

5

Try a heritage or heirloom variety: Abraham Lincoln, Black Zebra, Banana Legs, Black Prince, Big Boy, Purple Calabash, Tigerella

6

Always slice tomatoes horizontally

7

Slice, sprinkle with sea salt, add a glug of olive oil and torn basil leaves for a taste of the Med

8

Oven-dry tomatoes to intensify their flavour with olive oil, salt and thyme leaves

9

They're officially a fruit not a vegetable; the second part of their Latin name *Solanum lycopersicum* translates as 'wolf peach'

10

La Tomatina is an annual festival in Buñol, Spain, where participants throw an estimated 150,000 tomatoes at each other over a week

Mediterranean Stone Fruits: Peaches, Nectarines and Apricots

The arrival of these from mid-July is most welcome. As with all fruit, they need to be ripe. A hard peach, nectarine or apricot always disappoints. Recently, quality seems to have improved. Their smell will tell you if they're ripe and saves the embarrassment of being caught giving one a squeeze. In addition to eating as nature intended, use in a salad with cured meat and/or soft cheese. Chargrilled, they add another flavour dimension, or preserve in syrup or alcohol for the winter.

September

•••

Apples

In the UK more has been written about apples than probably any other fruit; it's considered our national fruit by many and the merits of one variety's flavour over another can cause heated debate.

In the 19th century, Britain became a hotbed for the development of new apple varieties. Gardeners and nurserymen across the land battled to produce apples to suit their particular growing conditions, to improve the flavour and eating qualities as well as yields and storing capabilities. Today we're still enjoying the fruits of their labours, as many of those horticultural experiments have stood the test of time.

An apple a day? Well, certainly that's possible for nine months of the year, if you want to eat an apple grown in the UK. The first apple of the season arrives in early August, most commonly the Discovery, followed by Spartan, Bramley, Cox, Red Windsor, Egremont Russet and Jonagold, with some varieties that can be kept in store until at least April of the following year. We think it's worth waiting between April and August for the next crop, rather than choosing an imported apple that's probably been flown from the other side of the world and won't taste as good as it should.

English apples have recovered their reputation in recent years, following a couple of decades of decline, which some put down to our entry into the EEC in the 1970s and the resulting influx of apples from other European countries. During this time, many orchards were lost as their perceived value decreased and it's only in the last 10 years that there's been a revival. Thanks in large part to the National Fruit Collection in Brogdale, Kent, which houses some 2,200 different varieties, the apples available now extend beyond the Granny Smith and Golden Delicious that flooded the market back then. Today, farmers and orchards up and down the country are investing in and harvesting cultivars native to or bred for these shores. With a myriad of names that can sometimes defy belief – Bloody Butcher to Sandlin Duchess – there's an apple for everyone's taste. However, in the kitchen, certain apples suit certain occasions: the trick is to know which one to use when.

For cooking we generally prefer a softer apple that collapses to produce a generous mound of purée. The Bramley is our best-known cooking apple and does the job without any fuss.

If baking, you often want an apple that softens sufficiently yet holds its shape on top of or in cakes or tarts – and the drier the apple the better chance it stands – try a James Grieve. If you are looking to place an apple in a salad to serve with cheese, or to put in your lunchbox, choose a Cox's Orange Pippin, or a Worcester Pearmain.

There are books and websites which delve far deeper into the subject of apples than we can hope to do here. Or why not visit the National Fruit Collection one autumn and see and taste the range of apples that have been grown over recent years.

Varieties of Apple

A
ADAM'S PEARMAIN

B
BLENHEIM ORANGE

C
COX'S ORANGE PIPPIN

D
D'ARCY SPICE

E
EGREMONT RUSSET

F
FIESTA

G
GRENADIER

H
HOWGATE WONDER

I
IDARED

J
JAMES GRIEVE

K
KESWICK CODLIN

L
LAXTON'S SUPERB

M
MILLER'S SEEDLING

N
NEWTON WONDER

O
OXFORD HOARD

P
PEASGOOD'S NONSUCH

Q
QUEENBY'S GLORY

R
RED FALSTAFF

S
SPARTAN

T
TYDEMAN'S LATE ORANGE

U
UNDERLEAF

V
VICAR OF BEIGHTON

W
WORCESTER PEARMAIN

Y
YORKSHIRE GREENING

Wild Mushrooms

Not a vegetable but certainly found on vegetable counters at this time of year, wild mushrooms are a seasonal treat that speak of the onset of autumn. There are more than 15,000 varieties to be found in the UK alone; however, deciphering which ones to eat is best left to the experts rather than take the risk yourself. Not all mushrooms taste the same; some can be fairly mild and others very deep in flavour.

When preparing fresh mushrooms it's worth investing in a mushroom brush to remove any unwanted debris, rather than washing them. Remove damaged or tough parts with a sharp knife and slice or quarter before cooking to ensure there are any no bugs hiding underneath or within.

Mushrooms, both wild and cultivated, can be added to soups and stews and make a great risotto or a rich sauce. However, they're best enjoyed at their simplest: fried with butter and herbs and served on hot toast.

Make Your Own Dried Mushrooms

Drying them extends the chance to use wild mushrooms. Wipe or brush the mushrooms clean, but don't submerge in water. Slice and lay out over a rack, not touching each other. Place in a fan-assisted oven at about 75°C/165°F/gas mark ¼. Too high a heat will damage some of the nutrients and impair the flavour. Allow to dry slowly, turning from time to time. Depending on size and thickness, they take four to eight hours. Check for readiness by seeing if they snap when broken. Store in an airtight container away from sunlight; if properly dried they keep for a year.

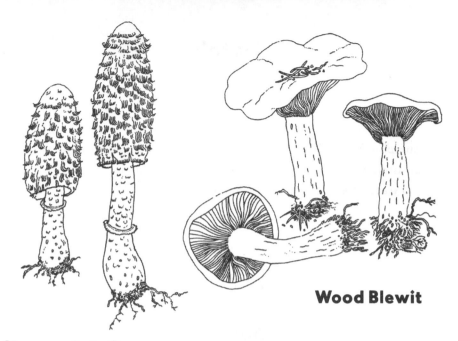

Wood Blewit

Shaggy Ink Cap

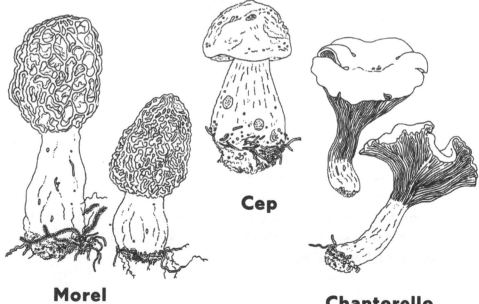

Morel

Cep

Chanterelle

October

•••

Squashes and Pumpkins

If there is one vegetable to really shout that it's autumn, it's got to be pumpkin. A pumpkin is a member of the winter squash family that includes an assortment of different-coloured, shaped and sized vegetables (or more accurately fruits). Some names to note and our favourites include:

Acorn

Blue Hubbard

Butternut

Crown Prince

Munchkin

Onion

Once harvested, most store well and some of the larger squashes may last until the latter days of winter and provide food for plenty, while smaller types provide just enough for one. Their flesh is sweet and is best baked or roasted. It can then be enjoyed in that simple form, or taken to another level in soups, stews and casseroles. Be careful when peeling, as their skins can be tough and challenging.

How to Roast Vegetables

Preheat the oven to 200°C/400°F/gas mark 6. Line a roasting tin with baking parchment. Chop the vegetables into bite-sized pieces and place in a large bowl. Dress in a few tablespoons of light olive oil, just enough to coat. Cover the vegetables with any robust herbs or garlic and season well. Place in the hot oven and reduce the temperature to 180°C/350°F/gas mark 4. Move the vegetables every 10 minutes, until caramelised on the outside and softened on the inside, but holding good shape. Remove and adjust the seasoning. Splashing a tray of roast pumpkin with sherry vinegar halfway through cooking will add to its caramelisation and depth.

M

Vegetables to Roast

Aubergine	**Parsnip**
Beetroot	**Potato**
Carrot	**Squash**
Celeriac	**Swede**
Courgette	**Tomato**
Jerusalem Artichoke	**Turnip**

Pears

Where many would consider the apple an English fruit, a pear to some is more of a French fruit. This is partly because of the names given to the varieties we're now familiar with (Doyenne d'Ete, Marguerite de Marillat) and, if you look back into horticultural history, it was the French who spent more time than most trying to perfect the pear.

The horticulturist Edward Bunyan commented that, while it is 'the duty of an apple to be crisp and crunchable, a pear should have a texture that leads to silent consumption'.

Pears are usually picked in an unripe state, which prevents their soft flesh from being damaged during transit. The trick is to catch them at the ideal point of ripeness and it is inevitable that some will be perfect and others less so. Ensure that, when storing, none are touching each other as this can lead to their early decay.

When it comes to choosing a particular pear, there are luckily not quite as many varieties as apples, but the stars stand out. For us it's the following:

Conference This pear is as good in January as in October. They're longer and thinner than a typical pear and are very popular in the UK. They're firm to touch even when ripe and therefore work well poached whole... and look rather elegant, too.

Doyenne du Comice Translated, this name means 'top of the show' and, once eaten, you can see why. When perfectly ripe they have a smooth texture, lots of flavour and are juicy to boot. Enjoy them on their own, in a salad or – for the perfect flavour combination – with a piece of blue cheese, some oatcakes and walnuts.

William This is a pear that's as good uncooked as it is cooked. It's firm and can have a crunch when eaten raw, but holds well when cooked, rather than softening to a mush. Its appearance is typically pear-like, with a green skin that ripens to yellow with blushes of red. It's the pear you'll also find most commonly in a can.

In the kitchen, pears work well in cakes, puddings and desserts and are particularly good with chocolate, as well as in salads when paired with bitter chicory leaves. A pickled pear is traditionally served with roast goose at Christmas, whilst the addition of pear to our Piccalilli (see page 451) gives a sweet and delicate note to strong mustard flavours.

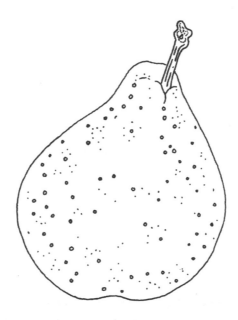

November

•••

Jerusalem Artichoke

These little brown knobbly tubers can be unearthed come late autumn, after the first frosts have taken their toll. Nothing like their globe artichoke namesakes and, surprisingly, related to sunflowers, they are best known by some for their unfortunate side effects that were described by John Goodyer in 1621 as: '...which way soever they be dressed and eaten, they stir and cause a filthy loathsome stinking wind within the body...' We think that's a slight exaggeration and a little unfair. Their subtle nuttiness can be appreciated in a variety of dishes.

You don't need to peel them, a careful scrub with a vegetable brush should suffice. If peeling and slicing, it's worth putting them in a bowl of water acidulated with lemon juice to prevent them from discolouring. They can be roasted, added to stews, even made into little vegetable crisps. They can also be eaten raw and added to salads if sliced thinly enough. A favourite, though, is often a gentle soup made from the tubers.

Quince

Of all the fruits grown in the UK, the quince feels at once exotic and at home and, as predecessor to both the apple and pear, also has an ancient feel. It's not the most popular fruit and can't simply be bitten into; it needs a cook and usually some sugar. As one of the last fruits of autumn (save the medlar), quince can last until Christmas and has the added bonus of easily seducing you with its sweet perfume, which can fill a room.

In its simplest form, it can be baked or roasted in the oven with wine or water, a good handful of sugar or dollop of honey and a sprinkle of spice. It pairs well with roast meats and can be pickled to serve with cold cuts.

When cooking with apples or pears, adding a small amount of quince to a crumble, pie or pudding brings another dimension.

Be prepared though, as their skins and flesh are tough until cooked and the sharpest of knives will be needed. Drop into water acidulated with lemon juice to prevent the peeled fruit from turning brown.

In recent years quince has become best known as the quince paste (membrillo) that is served alongside the Spanish cheese Manchego (the latter can easily be substituted with an English Berkswell).

When buying, look for locally grown fruits rather than imports.

Fruit Cheese When is a cheese not a cheese? When it's a fruit cheese. A fruit cheese is essentially like a very hard-set jam, that you can slice through. It's a lovely way of preserving and it lends itself well to fruits that have lots of pips or stones that would be otherwise hard to remove from a jam; damsons and quince being very good examples.

Quince Cheese

Cover 1 kg of washed, chopped quince (skin on) with water and simmer until tender. Leave to cool. Next day, push through a sieve or pass through a mouli. Weigh the pulp, add an equal amount of golden granulated sugar and bring to the boil. Cook until thickened and dark, keeping an eye that it doesn't catch. Pour into a cling film-lined cake tin and set in the fridge. Serve with cheese, or use as a flavour-enhancer in tagines, or melt into apple crumble for a seasonal twist.

M

Vegetables to Braise

Baby Carrots	**Endive**	**Savoy Cabbages**
Baby Turnips	**Globe Artichokes**	**Spinach**
Cavolo Nero	**Kale**	**Spring Onions**
Chard	**Leeks**	

How to Braise Vegetables

Vegetables are best braised in good-quality vegetable stock in a heavy-based saucepan with a lid. Wash the vegetables, trim them, then cut into the desired lengths. Melt butter or heat olive oil in the saucepan. Add the vegetables, including aromatics such as bay leaf, garlic or thyme and colour them in the fat over a medium-high heat. Pour in enough stock and a splash of wine to create a 5 cm-deep steam bath in which the vegetables can cook, but don't drown them. Cover and reduce the heat. Cook until the vegetables are tender and keep warm. Reduce the braising liquid over a high heat until you have a flavoursome 'sauce' to serve with the vegetables.

Quince Bellini

We use prosecco for this cocktail as it has a more delicate flavour than champagne and allows the quince to shine. Take 100 g of Quince cheese (see previous page) and heat with 125 ml of water until dissolved. Place 1 tsp of purée in a fluted glass, pour over ice-cold prosecco, stir and serve. Makes enough for 6 glasses.

M

December

...

Cranberries

These small round, bright red berries are too tart to eat uncooked and need the addition of sugar to make them palatable in the classic Christmas cranberry sauce that sits alongside your turkey. (When making a cranberry sauce, be sure to add the sugar at the end of cooking to prevent the skins of the berries from toughening.)

Primarily grown in America's New England states, they prosper on low shrub-like bushes in boggy conditions. When it's time to harvest, the fields are flooded with water, then the berries are mechanically removed from the bushes and float on the water ready to be hauled in by the farmer.

One of their remarkable properties is that they contain benzoic acid, a natural preservative that allows them to be kept fresh for months after harvesting. They can of course be dried, too.

When fresh, they make excellent jellies and sauces to go with game and other rich meats and can also be used in baking cakes, crumbles and tarts. In their dried form they are used to add a touch of sharpness to a cake, but they also make an interesting and colourful addition to a winter salad (see page 199).

Dried Fruits

December, with its winter solstice and Christmas celebrations, is a time for feasting and, in the Northern hemisphere – with a lack of fresh fruit around – dried fruits have played an important part in the traditional foods of this point in the year. Our Christmas puddings, cakes and mince pies would be sadly lacking without them.

Probably one of the oldest forms of preserving, fruits of various types can be dried to prolong their use. Originally sun-dried, most dried fruit is now produced with the aid of specialised dryers or dehydrators. By reducing the moisture content, drying allows natural sugars to act as preservatives. Nowadays, some dried fruit has sulphur dioxide added in the drying process, thus preventing both oxidisation of the fruit and colour and flavour loss. When reviewing ingredient labels, don't be put off by the presence of sulphur dioxide (E220); it is harmless in these quantities.

As well as prolonging the shelf life of the fruit, drying also intensifies the flavour and sweetness. Often considered as a handy healthy snack (dried fruits retain most of their nutritional value), they are often used in baking and confectionery as well as added to savoury dishes to add sweetness and moisture.

What's the Difference Between the Vine Fruits?

Currants The smallest of the three, black in colour, these come from a special type of seedless black grape.

Raisins Dried red grapes that can vary in size from moderately small to fairly large. Muscatel grapes are a bit of a luxury and should be enjoyed on their own rather than added to baking or other dishes. Also look out for Flame raisins, which tend to be bigger than others.

Sultanas Often originating in Turkey, these dried white grapes are generally sweeter and plumper than either raisins or currants. They are usually more golden in colour, although this can be due to the addition of sulphur dioxide which helps to retain their original colour.

Brussels Sprouts

Another vegetable that divides opinion, one is either a lover or a hater. It's all down to the cooking; these small and perfectly formed baby cabbages seem to particularly suffer from overcooking. Treated correctly, it's hard to believe that they could drum up such negative emotions. A quick boil in plenty of lightly salted water does the trick (al dente is the way to go) and it's generally agreed now that you don't need to cut a little cross in the bottom of each one, thus saving precious time when preparing them.

They're obligatory with Christmas lunch, even if it's just two or three per plate. Instead of boiling, blanch first, then quickly sauté with butter, some lardons and chestnuts until caramelised. At other times, try them in stir-fries, halved or shredded, or shredded raw into a salad, as below. Sprout tops – the leafy green head to the plant – can be prepared as other cabbage leaves and are particularly sweet and tender during November and December.

Winter Coleslaw with Shredded Brussels Sprouts, Fennel and Dried Cranberries

Shred Brussels sprouts with fennel, white cabbage and red onion on a mandolin. Dress with a classic French dressing to stop discoloration (see page 455). Add tarragon leaves and season well with sea salt. Allow to stand for one hour while the vegetables soften in the dressing, then toss again and serve with some apple juice-soaked dried cranberries and chopped roasted hazelnuts.

M

Plum Pudding

•••

We use butter instead of vegetable suet and this gives a more luxurious texture. The prunes marry well with the brandy. Every Christmas pudding needs a good kick of booze. It's Christmas after all.

Makes 2 x 1-litre puddings

Ingredients

1 orange
1 unwaxed lemon
100 g prunes
1 eating apple
75 g self-raising flour
½ tsp sea salt
2 tsp mixed spice
1 tsp ground nutmeg
¼ tsp ground cloves
175 g unsalted butter, plus more
    for the pudding bowls
200 g sultanas
200 g raisins
100 g currants
75 g mixed peel
50 g glacé cherries
100 ml each stout and brandy
200 g dark muscovado sugar
25 g black treacle
3 eggs, lightly beaten
75 g fresh breadcrumbs

Equipment

zester and juicer
box grater and sieve
2 x 1-litre ceramic or plastic
    pudding bowls

Preparation

Zest and juice the orange and zest the lemon.

Chop the prunes.

Grate the apple.

Sift the flour, salt and spices together.

Butter 2 x 1-litre pudding bowls.

Method

Soak the dried fruit, peel, cherries, apple and zests in the orange juice, stout and brandy overnight, with sugar and treacle.

Next day, stir in the eggs and fold in the bread-crumbs. Melt the butter in a pan and add, then gently fold in the flour mixture. Divide between the basins and cover each with a disc of baking parchment. If you are using ceramic pudding basins, tie a larger circle of baking parchment around with string, to cover the lips. If using a plastic basin, just pop the lid on that it came with.

Steam over a low heat for six hours, keeping an eye on the water level so that it doesn't run dry, then remove and cool. Wrap in cling film and store until Christmas Day in a cool spot. Give one away before Christmas. Your pudding will need a two-hour steam to heat through properly. Serve with brandy custard or double cream, not forgetting to ignite the pudding before you bring it to the table (warm the brandy first).

GRAINS

An Introduction to Grains

Probably the very oldest cultivated crops, grains play a crucial role in the kitchen. Without them there would be no bread, no pasta (and no bolognese sauce) and no rice (or curry). That's because civilisations and food cultures grew up around the need to care for grains. With the farming of grains, gone were the days of hunting and foraging for our supper. The Egyptians, Romans and Greeks based their communities around the propagation and cultivation of barley, wheat and rye; in the East it was millet and rice; in the Americas maize, quinoa and amaranth.

Today grains, whole and processed, are eaten by most of the world's population every day. They form the foundation of everything that we eat. Yet many people don't know much about them. With luck, this chapter will help you to learn more. We all want to eat more healthily. We want our food to do us good – or at least to do us no harm – and including more whole grains (and less meat) could be the way to go.

Whole Grains Used in soups, stews and salads, or cooked in their own right as an accompaniment.

Processed Grains Flaked, rolled or puffed.

Flours Produced by milling grains: for bread, pasta, noodles and for thickening sauces.

Barley

•••

Considered to be the first cultivated cereal. Up to the end of the 18th century it was the main grain used to make bread, until wheat took over. Now, with more than half the world's production of barley used as animal feed, it does not feature very highly – in its whole grain form – in our storecupboards. But it is there, still, lurking in malt whisky, beer, stout, Maltesers and Rich Tea biscuits.

Barley Couscous In North Africa, barley couscous is used for the family, while wheat couscous is served at special occasions and to visitors.

Flaked Barley Add to muesli, or use to make a porridge. Barley is low in gluten and a good option for those seeking to reduce gluten in their diets.

Pearl Barley The barley grain in its hulled, steamed and polished form. Use in winter stews and soups and barley 'risottos'. It can also be used to make Lemon barley water (see page 213), the drink that was synonymous with Wimbledon Centre Court until highly processed 'energy' drinks became required drinking there.

Pot Barley Sometimes called Scotch barley. It only has the indigestible part of the husk removed and is therefore highly nutritious. We have been adding it to casseroles for years.

Buckwheat

•••

The seeds from a plant related to sorrel and rhubarb but not, despite its name, to wheat. These small triangular-shaped 'grains' perform in a similar way to wheat, hence the name. Gluten-free buckwheat is best known in the forms of soba noodles (see page 334) and blinis.

Grains Roast these to develop their flavour (heat in a frying pan with a little oil, stirring constantly), then use them in soups, stews and salads.

Groats These cracked grains should be roasted (as above) before being soaked and used in baking.

Corn (Maize)

Corn was once used as a collective name for most grains; these days maize is often introduced to young mouths from inside a can.

Cornmeal Most usually eaten in the UK as polenta, cooked with water and served like mashed potato, or left to go cold and form a block, then sliced and fried. It can also be used in cornbread, an American staple.

Popcorn A particular type of corn which, when heat and oil are applied in a pan, 'pops'. Not particularly nutritious, but the grain can be used to carry savoury and sweet flavour combinations (see page 216), rather than the dubious artificial flavourings found in cinema foyers.

Oats

Oats come in a variety of sizes or grades, that dictate how they should be used. They've a fond place in the hearts of many Scots.

Groats Best for thickening stews and soups.

Oatmeal Once the grain has been ground coarse or fine, it can be mixed with flours to make scones and oatcakes, or in porridge.

Rolled Oats Rolled into whole or cut flakes for baking and porridge.

Quinoa

•••

An ancient seed cultivated by the Incas and referred to as the 'mother of all grains'. It's considered a 'superfood' for its high level of amino acids and protein content similar to that of meat. The burgeoning interest has led to its three-fold price increase in the last decade. We like to fry it before simmering for a nutty flavour and to use mixed colours: white, red and brown or black. It's worth noting that it is gluten-free.

Rice

•••

It's said there are more than 40,000 varieties of cultivated rice, though the number on our supermarket shelves is considerably fewer. Knowing which rice to use for what dish can still be a challenge. Here's some help:

Basmati A long-grain rice from the Himalayas with a distinctive aroma. Cook this in a biryani or pilaf. You can buy brown basmati rice, but it doesn't have the same potent fragrance.

Camargue France's answer to Italy's arborio (see page 207) and Spain's calasparra is a red-coloured short-grain whole-grain rice with a nutty taste. It can be cooked in a similar way to risotto and paella rices.

Easy-cook It's often thought the name means this is quicker to cook, but it takes longer. It has been par-boiled with the husk on, so when the rice is boiled again it has a better chance of holding its shape and staying fluffy.

Paella Calasparra is a Spanish rice grown around Valencia and the vital ingredient in paella. The medium-grain rice perfectly soaks up the flavours of stock, saffron and anything else the cook cares to throw into the pan.

BASMATI PAELLA RISOTTO

Rice can be divided into three simple types: long-, medium- and short-grain, and all three types can be either brown or white.

Brown rice is the whole grain, with only the husk removed. White rice has been milled to remove the bran, then polished with a mix of talcum and glucose! Of course, it lacks the nutritional benefits of the whole grain.

When cooked, the grains of long-grain rice should stay separate and fluffy. Shorter, plumper medium-grain rice is more likely to stick together when cooked and therefore works well in risottos and paellas. Short-grain rice is generally round, contains the most starch and easily sticks together.

Pudding Any short-grain white rice that can be cooked in milk to create a comforting pudding. It is not a specific variety.

Risotto Arborio is the classic risotto rice from Piedmont in Northern Italy. It's a great all-rounder, a medium- to long-grain rice that absorbs plenty of liquid, yet remains firm. Carnaroli is considered by some as a better risotto rice due to its higher starch content, firmer texture and longer grain.

Wild The long black grains from a North American aquatic grass are hulled and polished and considered an expensive delicacy. It maintains a firm 'bite' and nutty flavour once cooked.

Rye

•••

Predominantly used to make flour, to be used on its own or mixed with others, such as barley and wheat. Rye may be processed into flakes to add to porridges or mueslis, or to doughs when baking, to give texture.

Spelt

•••

Often mistaken for being gluten-free, in fact this is an ancient wheat that has regained popularity in recent years. Its molecular structure is thought to make its gluten easier to digest. It can be bought as 'pearled' spelt and added to soups and stews or used to make risotto. It also comes as flakes to add to breakfast cereals, or to make into porridge.

Wheat

•••

Varieties include emmer, einkorn, durum, spelt.

Bulgar Wheat Wheat berries cooked to a pulp, then dried and broken into grain-like particles. To serve, soak in twice their volume of hot liquid. They form a great base for a salad such as tabbouleh, with lots of herbs.

Cracked Wheat Wheat grains are cracked or crushed, allowing a much faster cooking time than if they were whole. It can be cooked and served as a side dish, added to bread, or made into a stuffing for meats.

Farro Used in Italian cooking, in salads and soups, this is essentially the same as a wheat berry, except that it can be found in three sizes: *grande*, *medio* and *piccolo*. Each size usually denotes a different variety of wheat.

Freekeh Green wheat that is sun-dried, then carefully set on fire so only the stems and chaff burn (the berries don't burn due to their high moisture content). The roasted, nutty flavour is great in pilafs, salads and stews.

Semolina Durum wheat cracked into coarse pieces and sifted from the bran. Used to bake bread, to roll into couscous, or milled into fine '00' flour to make pasta. Many will remember semolina with a certain fondness (or not) as comforting nursery food, cooked in milk with a blob of jam.

Wheat Berry The whole grain of wheat. Reddish-brown in colour, they form the entire wheat kernel, excepting the hull. They are added to breads to give a nutty texture but also make a great base for salad. In Poland they are made into a porridge with honey, seeds and nuts at Christmas time.

Wheat Flakes Steamed and rolled wheat berries that have been flattened and dried. Add them to muesli, or combine them with oats to make a porridge. Some can be bought in a malted version.

Porridge Rules

•••

Porridge aficionados will want to equip themselves with a 'spurtle', a 15th-century kitchen tool that looks like a piece of wooden dowel; the rod-like shape is perfect for stirring porridge.

Traditionalists are firm on what makes porridge: only untreated pinhead oatmeal – coarse-, medium- or fine-textured – water and salt. We are all for tradition, but also happy to experiment so our morning porridge keeps our taste buds on their metaphorical toes.

Whether traditional or a little left-field, here are a few simple rules to help you make your porridge memorable every morning:

1

Slow, even cooking is required, so porridge must be made in a pan; please no microwaves that can create uneven heat spots.

2

Stir continuously for up to 10 minutes, watching for the texture to become thick, but still pourable (spurtles at the ready).

3

Add salt halfway through cooking: adding it too early can toughen the oats; too late can result in a thin 'afterthought' taste.

4

For a truly authentic porridge, only pinhead oats will do. But we quite like a mixture of equal parts of coarse pinhead with jumbo rolled oats: toothsome but not a grind. Standard rolled oats give a very sloppy, poor relation to the real thing.

5

Use water as your main liquid and add whole milk, soya, coconut or nut milk – milk should make up somewhere between one-third and one-half of the total liquid – to give you something satisfying and flavoursome without being overly rich.

6

Soak your oats overnight if you want to cut down on cooking time in the morning; this will probably save you five minutes or so. We sometimes soak our oats with some whole nuts in the water. These give off their milk overnight, creating light nut milk to add a subtle richness to porridge.

Argan Oil, Toasted Pumpkin Seeds and Dark Dried Apricots

Date Syrup and Walnuts

Chopped Toasted Almonds with Sour Cherries

Honey Poached Apricots and Crushed Pistachios

Crumbled Jaggery and Cardamom Infused Milk

Sliced White Peaches and Blueberries, Live Yogurt

Sliced Banana Fried in Butter, Coconut Milk, Toasted Coconut

Grated Apple, Roasted Hazelnuts and Cinnamon

Summer Berries and Wildflower Honey

Pink Grapefruit, Chopped Pecans, Agave Syrup

Smoked Streaky Bacon and Maple Syrup

If it's

Pedro Ximenez Soaked Sultanas and Single Cream

Christmas Morning

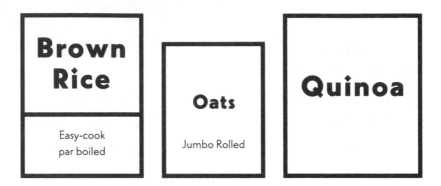

Storage

Always check the packet before you buy, to ensure the grain you choose has a reasonable shelf life left.

Whole Grains If stored in dry, airtight conditions, whole grains should last for around six months in your pantry or storecupboard. You can keep them for up to a year in the freezer.

Flours and Processed Grains Generally keep for one to three months in dry, airtight conditions.

Cooked Grains Most will keep safely for four to five days when kept refrigerated below 5°C. Always chill cooked grains, particularly rice, if you wish to store it. You can quickly chill them by placing in a sieve and running under the cold tap, allowing to drain well. The cold grains can then be covered and stored in the refrigerator. The cooked grain doesn't need to be reheated, if you are using it in a salad. It's generally thought to be best practice not to reheat previously cooked rice, but use your own judgement and common sense and always ensure reheated food is piping hot before eating.

Lemon Barley Water

Rinse 225 g of pearl barley, cover with 2.5 litres of water and bring to the boil, then reduce the heat and cook gently for up to 1 hour or until the barley is tender. Meanwhile, take 5 unwaxed lemons and remove the zest, taking care not to remove too much of the white pith at the same time. Place the zest in a bowl with 200 g of caster sugar. Squeeze the 5 lemons and set the juice aside. Take the cooked barley and strain, pouring the liquid over the lemon zest and sugar, stirring so all the sugar dissolves. (By the way, you can reserve the cooked barley to add to a winter hotpot or a bowl of chicken broth.) Let the liquid and lemon zest steep for an hour, or until cooled. Then add the lemon juice and some sprigs of mint. Store in the fridge and either drink neat or add water to taste. This will keep in the fridge, covered, for a day or so. Makes about 2 litres.

A Bowl of Bircher Muesli

The night before, mix 75 g of jumbo rolled oats, 75 g of dried fruit and 75 g of toasted nuts and seeds together in a bowl. Grate an apple into the mixture and pour over 250 ml of milk or apple juice. Mix, cover with cling film and place in the fridge. The muesli will be ready to serve the next morning. You can add more milk or juice if required and fresh berries or other fruit. Makes 2 generous servings.

M

Pinhead Oatmeal

Serves 1

A ratio of 3:1 liquid to oatmeal
gives you a porridge that is pourable
and never gloopy

Heat 1½ cups of liquid (we find 1 cup of water and ½ cup
of whole milk is luxurious without being overly rich) and
sprinkle in ½ cup of coarse pinhead oatmeal (or a mixture of
coarse and medium or jumbo oats, depending on the texture
you want). Cook over a medium heat, stirring constantly,
for 5 to 10 minutes, adding a small pinch of salt halfway.
Allow to stand for a few minutes, covered, so the porridge
can cool and thicken a little. Pour over a little more whole milk
and sprinkle with dark sugar to serve. If you want a nuttier
porridge, gently toast the oats in a dry pan before you start.

Three Grain

Serves 2

A combination of jumbo oats,
barley and quinoa flakes

Take ⅓ cup of jumbo oats, ⅓ cup of barley and ⅓ cup
of quinoa flakes. Heat 3 cups of liquid (milk and water
combined) until boiling, then add the oats and barley. Reduce
the heat and stir until cooked (5 to 10 minutes). Remove from
the heat, add the quinoa flakes and stir, adding a splash more
liquid if needed. Leave to stand for 3 minutes before serving.

Quinoa Flakes

Serves 1

These cook in a fraction of the time of oats, so make a quick breakfast

Heat ½ cup of milk and ½ cup of water. Bring to the boil slowly. Remove from the heat, add ⅓ cup of quinoa flakes and stir. Leave for 3 minutes, then add sliced dates, pecans and maple syrup, with milk if you wish.

Jumbo Rolled Oats

Serves 1

This is our default porridge recipe. Easy, quick and delicious. Bring to the boil 1 small cup of whole milk and 1 small cup of water. Add 1 cup of jumbo oats into the simmering liquid. Season with a tiny pinch of salt. Reduce the heat and cook very slowly, stirring from time to time, until thickened but still pourable. Pour into a warm bowl and sprinkle with dark muscovado sugar and toasted seeds.

Barley Flakes

Serves 1

Barley flakes swell up more than oats, so give a different texture (and arguably more flavour) to your porridge.

Heat 1½ cups of mixed milk and water until almost boiling, add the barley flakes and stir. Reduce the heat, stirring, until the liquid has been absorbed (5 to 10 minutes). Leave to rest for a few minutes and serve with honey or sugar.

Rosemary Popcorn

Preheat the oven to 100°C / 210°F / gas mark ¼. Pop 100 g of popcorn in 2 tbsp of hot sunflower oil in your largest lidded saucepan. Keep the lid on the pan and give it a good shake from time to time. Set aside. Chop 3–4 sprigs of rosemary finely and mix with 2 tsp of Dijon mustard and 3 tbsp of honey. Cover the popped corn with this honey mixture over a gentle heat. Season generously with 1 tsp of sea salt and freshly ground black pepper and spread out on a baking sheet lined with baking parchment. Dry the corn in the low oven until crisp (15–20 minutes), stirring from time to time. This is best eaten on the day it is made. Makes enough for 4.

Sea Salt Honey Caramel Popcorn

Pop 100 g of popcorn in 2 tbsp of hot sunflower oil in your largest lidded saucepan. Keep the lid on the pan and give it a good shake from time to time. Set aside. Heat 4 tbsp of honey and 4 tbsp of unsalted butter in a clean saucepan. Allow them to combine, shaking the pan carefully, but do not stir. Once they've started to turn a golden caramel colour, remove from the heat and add a pinch or two of sea salt flakes to taste. Now pour the caramel over the popped corn and stir until well coated. Spread the mixture on baking parchment to cool. The caramel will harden. This will keep for 3–4 days in an airtight container. Makes enough for 4.

M

Store for long periods

GLUTEN FREE GRAINS

...

Amaranth
Buckwheat
Corn
Oats
Quinoa
Rice

Contains gluten

Barley
Rye
Semolina
Spelt
Wheat

The backbone of most global cuisines

SPELT

Contains gluten

(commonly thought

not to do so)

Flours

•••

When crushed, whole grains usually give up flour. A little bit of science:

The higher the protein content, the harder and stronger the flour will be and so the more likely it will be to produce crusty or chewy breads.

The lower the protein content, the softer the flour and the better it will be for baking cakes, biscuits and pastry. So it's more important than you might think to take a look at the percentages on the label:

- 9 per cent for light cakes and sponges
- 10 per cent good all-rounder
- 11 per cent pastry flour
- 12 per cent + for bread making

Today, most grocers and supermarkets carry a plethora of varieties and styles of flours. It wasn't long ago that the choice was simple: wheat flour, plain or self-raising. Plain was used for pastry, yeasted breads and to add to sauces, while self-raising had a leavening agent added – usually baking powder – to give a rise to cakes, biscuits and scones.

Most of us just want to know what flour to use when:

Flours and their Uses

	Bread	Baking	Pasta	Noodles	Thickener	Desserts
Strong	●	●		●		
Durum			○			
Plain	●	●			●	
Self-raising		○				
Spelt	●	●	●			
Buckwheat	○			○		
Cornflour		●			●	●
Rice	○	○		○	○	○
Rye	●					
Nut Flours		○			○	○

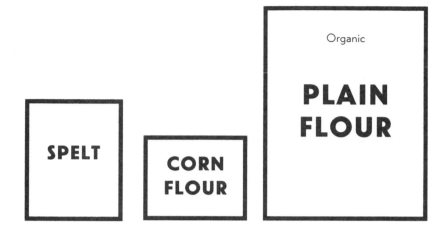

Crumble Mix for the Fridge

Preheat the oven to 180°C / 350°F / gas mark 4. Pulse in a food processor: 150 g of chilled unsalted butter, 200 g of plain flour, 100 g of caster sugar and 125 g of jumbo oats to make a crumb. Stir in 2 tbsp of runny honey, a handful of chopped almonds and a pinch of salt. Spread out on a baking sheet and bake for 20 minutes. Cool and store in an airtight container in the fridge for up to a week, to bake over fruit compotes (be careful, as it has been par-baked so can scorch), or as a cold topping for ice creams or curd tarts. Or freeze it for up to six months. Makes enough for a family-sized crumble.

M

	Rinse	Grain to Water Ratio	Cooking Notes
Amaranth	Y	O ≈	
Pearl Barley	Y	O ≈	**Add directly to soups and stews for the last 20 minutes**
Buckwheat	Y	O ≈	
Bulgar Wheat	Y x3	O ≈	
Couscous	N	O ≈	
Cracked Wheat	Y x3	O ≈	**Add directly to soups and stews for the last 20 minutes**
Farro (pearled)	Y	O ≈	Add directly to soups and stews for the last 20 minutes
Freekeh	Y	O ≈	
Quinoa	Y	O ≈	Add directly to soups and stews for the last 10 minutes
Rice, White Long Grain	Y x2	O ≈	
Rice, Brown Long Grain	Y x2	O ≈	
Spelt (pearled)	Y	O ≈	
Teff	Y	O ≈	
Wheat Berries	Y	O ≈	
Wild Rice	Y	O ≈	

Cooking Stage 1	Cooking Stage 2	To Serve
Bring to the boil	Simmer for 25 minutes	Drain
Bring to the boil	**Simmer for 20–30 minutes**	**Drain**
Bring to the boil	Simmer for 10 minutes	Drain
Bring to the boil	**Simmer for 12 minutes**	**Leave for 10 minutes, covered, then fluff up with a fork**
Place in a bowl and pour over boiled water	Leave for 5–10 minutes	Add some olive oil and fluff up with a fork
Place in a pan and pour over boiled water	**Bring to the boil, then simmer for 10–12 minutes**	**Drain and leave for 5 minutes**
Bring to the boil	Simmer for 20–30 minutes	Drain
Bring to the boil	**Simmer for 20–30 minutes**	**Drain**
Fry in a little oil for 2–3 minutes	Cover with water in a pan, bring to the boil, then simmer for 10 minutes	Drain
Place the rice in a pan and pour over boiled water	**Bring to the boil, cover and cook for 10 minutes**	**Spread a tea towel under the lid and stand for 5 minutes**
Place the rice in a pan and pour over boiled water	Bring to the boil, cover with a tight-fitting lid and cook for 35 minutes	Spread a tea towel under the lid and stand for 10 minutes
Bring to the boil	**Simmer for 20–30 minutes**	**Drain**
Bring to the boil	Simmer for 15–20 minutes	Drain
Bring to the boil	**Cook for 50–60 minutes**	**Drain**
Bring to the boil	Cook for 25–35 minutes	Drain

Wild Rice, Wheat Berry, Pea and Ticklemore Salad

•••

The nutty rice and earthy wheat berries support the flavours of the goat's cheese and toasted almonds successfully. Use fresh peas and broad beans where possible for a burst of summer goodness and add lots of herbs.

Serves 6

Ingredients

150 g wheat berries
150 g broad beans, podded
   and shelled weight
150 g peas, podded weight
150 g wild rice
bunch of mint
bunch of parsley
100 g whole almonds
100 g Ticklemore goat's cheese,
   or another crumbly goat's
cheese sea salt and freshly ground
   black pepper
100 ml Classic French Dressing
   (see page 455)

Equipment

mixing bowl
sieve
sharp knife and chopping board
baking sheet
serving bowl

Preparation

Soak the wheat berries overnight in a mixing bowl in plenty of water. Drain.

Pod and shell the broad beans and shell the peas.

Wash the rice in a sieve.

Wash, pick and chop the herbs.

Preheat the oven to 140°C/275°F/gas mark 1.

Spread the almonds on a baking sheet and roast them for 20 minutes. Cool and chop roughly.

Crumble the cheese.

Method

Cook the wheat berries in clean water for one hour, until softened. Add salt and leave to cool in the liquid.

Meanwhile, cook the rice in planty of salted water for 45 minutes, or until the grains open slightly but still have a good bite. Drain and dress in half the dressing as it cools.

Blanch the peas and beans in a pan of salted water for three minutes until tender, then refresh in cold water.

Drain the wheat and mix with the rice. Add the peas and beans and the herbs. Mix through the almonds and the remaining dressing. Taste for seasoning before scattering with the cheese. Serve.

Wholemeal Soda Bread

•••

This is a very quick, tasty bread and there's no fuss or waiting around for doughs to rise. The quality of the bread will rely on the flour you buy, so go for stoneground versions. This is always best eaten on the day it's made, but will keep for two days under wraps. Serve with soups and cured fish.

Makes 1 loaf

Ingredients

225 g plain flour, plus more to dust
225 g wholemeal flour
1 tsp bicarbonate of soda
1 tsp sea salt
50 g oats
1 tbsp honey
1 tbsp sunflower oil
400 ml buttermilk

Equipment

sieve
large mixing bowl
baking sheet
sharp knife
wire rack

Preparation

Sift the flours, bicarbonate of soda and salt into a large mixing bowl. Stir in the oats.

Method

Preheat the oven to 220°C/425°F/gas mark 7.

Stir together the honey, oil and buttermilk, add the oats into the flour mixture. Make a well in the centre of the flours and pour in the honey mixture. Start to bring the flour mixture gently into the well. Now make a claw shape with your hand and, in firm circular motions, bring the dough together quickly and briskly (the less handling the better for this style of loaf). Place on a floured surface and, without kneading, shape the dough into a neat round. Lift it on to a floured baking sheet. Cut a deep cross into the dough, across the whole diameter to help with an even bake and insert a sharp knife into each quarter for the same purpose.

Bake in the centre of the oven for 15 minutes, then reduce the oven temperature to 200°C/400°F/gas mark 6 and bake for a further 20 minutes. Tap the bottom of the loaf: it should sound hollow. Return to the oven upside down to bake for a final five minutes. Remove to a wire rack to cool. Eat as soon as possible.

Oat Shards

•••

This is a wheat-free treat that can be stored in the freezer, uncooked, in
sheets once rolled, ready to pop into a hot oven when the biscuit barrel
is unexpectedly empty. No need to cut these biscuits before baking,
just break up into pieces once cooled.

Makes 400 g

Ingredients

120 g golden caster sugar
160 g unsalted butter
220 g rolled oats
½ tsp baking powder
1 tbsp sunflower seeds

Equipment

2 baking sheets
baking parchment
food mixer
rolling pin

Preparation

Line two baking sheets with baking parchment.

Method

Beat the sugar and butter in a food mixer until pale.
Mix the oats, baking powder and seeds together,
then stir into the butter mixture to form a dough.
Wrap in cling film and chill for one hour.

Preheat the oven to 180°C/350°F/gas mark 4.

Roll out the dough between two pieces of baking
parchment as thin as you can make it. Lay the sheets
of biscuit dough on the prepared baking trays.

Bake for 15 minutes, or until golden brown. Cool
and break up into long triangles to form 'shards'.
Store in the biscuit barrel... if they last long enough.

10

HERBS

An Introduction to Herbs

For us, cooking without herbs is inconceivable. We can barely remember the last time when herbs were not essential to what we were making, whether plucking a few leaves to add depth to a bubbling casserole, or dotting them in among salad leaves. Whatever we are cooking, it will nearly always benefit from a herb or two; even the English breakfast doesn't escape, as we sneak in thyme leaves with the grilled tomatoes.

Herbs have been used since human life began, firstly as medicines and probably insect repellents, but also in perfumes and, of course, cooking.

The English herb garden is part of our national identity. The traditional cottage garden – very much a medieval English invention – was designed partly to sustain the cottage dwellers, with its fragrant, medicinal and edible flowers, fruit trees, vegetables and herbs, possibly with a bee hive.

The Elizabethan knot garden – formally arranged and bordered beds of aromatic plants and culinary herbs – replaced the more ramshackle cottage garden, but still championed the same herbs.

Herbs form part of so many of the dishes that we grew up with and make us feel rooted culturally: sharp mint sauce complementing roast lamb; sage and onions with pork; tarragon scenting a roast chicken; chives lending their soft onioniness to egg mayonnaise or buttery new potatoes.

Herbs enhance the flavours of other ingredients. Consider the earthiness wild oregano lends to lamb, or the flavour of summer that basil brings to ripe tomatoes and oozing mozzarella, miraculously making the tomato more tomato-ey and the mozzarella more creamy. And it's not just their incredible hit of flavour, it's the effect herbs have on our nostrils, taking us to an English meadow; a holiday in Provence, the whiff of thyme in the air; or a beach in Thailand, with one deep inhalation of a bunch of holy basil.

Honestly, we couldn't live without herbs and we strongly urge you not to either. And don't just use them as a garnish: poking a sprig of parsley into the top of a vol-au-vent is not cooking with herbs. Start using them liberally and be bold and extravagant.

Married with spices, herbs make up the most powerful weapons in your cooking armoury. Luckily they are incredibly easy to grow, even in a window box, and can be bought very reasonably if you shop carefully.

Herbs Go With

•••

Basil Avocados, capers, courgettes, mozzarella, olives, Parmesan, salmon, strawberries, tomatoes

Bay Beef, blackberries, custard, lemons, pears, peppercorns, rabbit, red cabbages, rice pudding, venison, white sauce

Chives Crème fraîche, mayonnaise, omelettes, oysters, potatoes, sea bass, soft cheeses

Coriander Black beans, chilli, coconuts, crab, limes, pork, red peppers

Dill Carrots, cucumbers, eggs, fennel, goat's cheese, potatoes, sea trout

Marjoram Aubergines, oranges, poultry, sheep's cheeses, tomatoes

Mint Broad beans, chocolate, lamb, lemons, mangoes, peas, pineapples, potatoes, yogurt

Oregano Cumin, feta, garlic, lamb, rice, tomatoes, yogurt

Parsley Capers, chicken, chorizo, citrus, cracked wheat, mushrooms, olives

Rosemary Bacon, beef, chicken, garlic, lamb, lemons, rhubarb, scallops, shallots, venison

Sage Beetroots, butter, calf's liver, chestnuts, onions, pork, prosciutto, pumpkins

Tarragon Asparagus, butter, chicken, cream, crème fraîche, Dijon mustard, eggs, pork, shellfish, yogurt

Thyme Coriander seeds, goat's cheeses, lemons, oranges, pink peppercorns, red onions

Unusual Herbs

•••

Here are some of our favourite unusual herbs. Most can quite easily be grown at home with a little care and more are becoming available in supermarkets, ethnic shops and farmer's markets. Seeds and small plants can be bought for home growing online, at most larger garden centres and, these days, in supermarkets as well.

Bergamot Not to be confused with bergamot the fruit, which flavours Earl Grey tea, this flowering herb does share the fruit's citrus aroma. This leaf makes a lovely aromatic tea infusion and works well with fruit. Also known as bee balm.

Chervil Resembling a tiny, fine flat-leaf parsley, chervil is mildly anise in flavour with a subtle sweetness that makes an ideal companion to delicate fish and cream sauces.

Curry Leaves The leaves of a tree in the citrus family. Shiny and black-green, they are fried in South Indian cooking to release a nutty fragrance. If you find them, snap them up and store in the freezer (see page 244). Look for fresh leaves in ethnic grocers and dried in supermarkets.

Fennel (Bronze, or Green) Not to be confused with fennel bulb, the herb grows into tall frond-like spears if left untended. Softly liquorice in flavour, it works well with dill and chervil to create an intense anise hit.

Kaffir Lime Leaves Intensely citrussy, but quite unlike any other citrus, being highly fragrant and aromatic. Most commonly associated with Thai and Indonesian cooking. Look out for fresh leaves in ethnic grocers and dried in most supermarkets.

Lemon Balm An old-fashioned kitchen garden herb with furry oval spiked leaves and a soft lemon sherbet flavour. It is best used in teas and tisanes and to flavour cakes and ice creams.

Lemon Grass A tropical grass with an aromatic lemony fragrance. Used in Thai, Malaysian and South East Asian cooking, it also works in puddings, ices and drinks. Look for it in ethnic grocers and most supermarkets.

Lemon Verbena Small spear-shaped green leaves from a bush that grows easily as a pot plant or in the garden. Fresh or dried, it adds a herbal lemony fragrance to desserts and tisanes.

Lovage This is also sometimes known as 'sea parsley'. It has largish, softly spiked leaves, which impart a strong celery-like flavour. Very good with poultry and surprisingly also enhances the flavour of potatoes or tomatoes.

Myrtle Used much like bay, these shiny spear-shaped leaves impart a spicy, slightly bitter citrussy flavour. Prized for its flowers and berries, it is in fact a great addition to slow-cooked meat dishes, puddings and cakes.

Sorrel With a name derived from the French for 'sour', use these acidic leaves sparingly with fish and in cream sauces where they bring a lovely sharpness. French, wild and buckler leaf sorrel have different-shaped leaves but share a lemony acidity. Lovely in a salad, too.

Summer Savory An annual plant related to winter savory but with a more peppery taste. Works with other herbs such as thyme, marjoram and rosemary, uniting the disparate flavours in a way few other herbs can.

Sweet Cicely Another feathery anise-flavoured herb related to caraway and fennel. Used in German and Scandinavian cuisine, it is a key flavour in bottles of aquavit.

Thai Basil More sturdy-looking than regular basil, with slightly tougher pointed green leaves and purple stems, this is used across South East Asia and most famously in Thai green and red curries. Another herb that has hints of liquorice.

Wild Celery Leaf With a stronger, more herbal aroma than its salad cousin, this is best used in cooked dishes rather than as a raw leaf. Similar in appearance to flat-leaf parsley but, when crushed, these leaves give off a deep celery aroma.

Wild Garlic Growing in many a hedgerow and roadside across the UK during spring, wild garlic has long spear-shaped leaves and soft white flowers that are also delicious to eat. Often with quite a pungent garlic flavour, it is useful both in cooking and as a salad leaf. Pick your own when you see it.

Winter Savory Unlike its cousin summer savory, this is a perennial, dying back each year and growing anew in spring. More piney in flavour, it works well with game.

Herby Leaves

Many soft leafy vegetables seem to stray into herb territory, in part because of their aromatic qualities and also because of the way we like to use them in the kitchen. We encourage you to think about the way you use these other leaves, to broaden your cooking repertoire and get the benefit of these nutritious and delicious vegetables in a whole variety of new and exciting ways.

Consider for example a peppery rocket and watercress (or land cress) pesto: just replace the basil with the leaves and use walnuts instead of pine nuts. Imagine also adding some blitzed or finely sliced mustard greens to a mustard or horseradish crème fraîche, for an added burst of flavour. They are easily available at most supermarkets and very simple to grow at home.

Don't discount Swiss or colourful rainbow chard as salad leaves: finely chopped, they work very well in a sort of rough tabbouleh, adding an iron-rich quality, or just alongside some sturdy lettuce leaves such as Romaine for a burst of colour and unusual flavour. Often available from farmer's markets, chard also makes a very ornamental plant for home growing (and it is easy to grow, too).

Probably one of the most under-used leaves is the hugely nutritious winter purslane (sometimes known as miner's lettuce), a succulent heart-shaped leaf with a lovely lemoniness that works brilliantly well in salads. Its equally succulent cousin, summer purslane (often called pigweed) also has a pleasing sourness and can be used in the same way. Some farmer's markets may stock it, but you can easily grow it at home (though you'll probably have to find the seeds online).

Primrose

Pea Flower

Edible Flowers

Edible flowers not only look beautiful, they have a wide range of culinary uses. They are highly decorative used fresh in salads, floating on summer soups, or frozen in ice cubes to create summer drinks and cocktails, or sugared or fresh to top cakes and desserts.

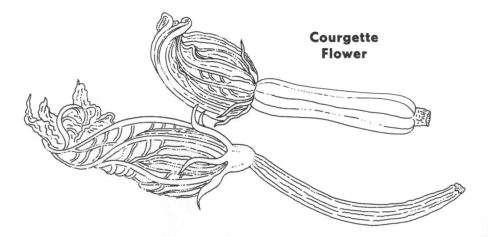

Courgette Flower

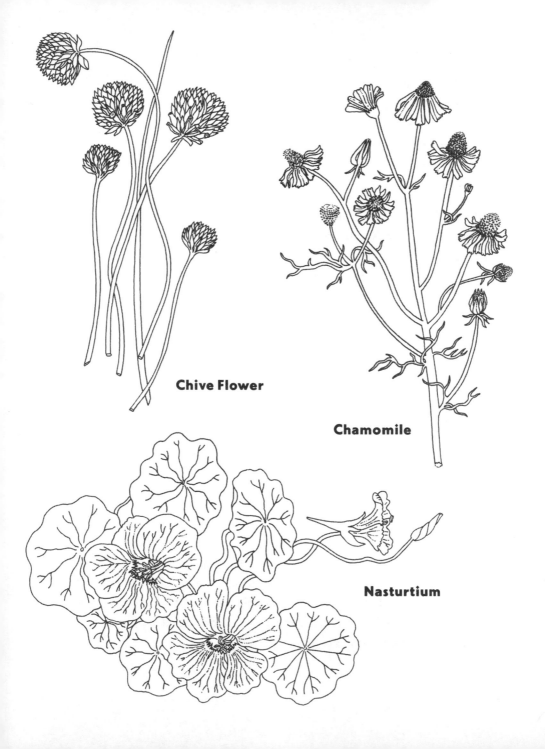

Chive Flower

Chamomile

Nasturtium

Buyer's Guide: Fresh vs Dry

There are very few herbs that are better dried than when fresh. That's not to say that dried herbs don't have their place in the larder. Oregano, when dried, gains a new, deeper tone that can enhance dishes beautifully. Used sensibly and in moderation, dried herbs can offer a greater intensity of flavour – rather more earthy and concentrated – countering the zingy herbal hit of fresh herbs when the two are used together.

Most fresh soft herbs can be used in abundance, ideally in great handfuls that fill your lungs with their scent, liberally scattering your food. The woodier herbs such as sage and rosemary need a lighter touch: use them a little more sparingly to ensure they don't completely overpower a dish.

It's important to chop fresh herbs properly and only at the last minute before using, both because it releases their flavour-giving essential oils and because no one wants a great stalk of parsley in their mouth. Their flavours should accent and intermingle with each mouthful, not appear in large clumps that confuse the palate.

Because of their more intense concentrated flavour, dried herbs need to be used more sparingly. We recommend substituting fresh for dried herbs in a ratio of 3:1, so 1 tbsp of fresh equates to 1 tsp of dried (3 tsp = 1 tbsp). However, if in doubt, err on the side of caution and add small amounts at a time. You can always add more, but you can't take it away.

Dried herbs are at their best used at the beginning of cooking, giving them a chance to mellow and mingle with the other ingredients. As a general rule, the softer the fresh herb, the later you should add it to your cooking. Chervil and basil are very delicate and should be added at the last minute or – ideally – not actually cooked at all. Woodier herbs such as bay and rosemary can take quite a lot of cooking and are safe to add early on in the cooking process.

Sourcing and Spotting Quality

Forget the supermarkets with their mean, overpriced little plastic packets of herbs. Look out for ethnic grocers and farmer's markets, where you are likely to find larger bunches of (often much fresher) herbs. The price will tend to be a lot more pleasing as well. It goes without saying that any fresh herbs you buy should be perky and robust-looking; anything yellowing or limp won't last the journey home, let alone make it into the pot.

When buying dried herbs and herb blends, you need to look carefully to guarantee quality, as the signs may not be so obvious. Wherever possible, look for whole dried herb branches, without too much in the way of dust and broken particles. If that is not an option, then pay close attention to the provenance of the herb and the packing and sell-by dates. Purchase from quality merchants whom you know to have a high turnover of stock.

Storing Herbs

Fresh herbs perish quickly. We find the best way to keep them in the fridge is to wrap them in a couple of layers of kitchen paper, then place in resealable plastic bags and store towards the front of the fridge. If they are touching the back, they can become part-frozen and turn to mush.

Proper freezing of herbs can be a great way to preserve them for longer (see page 244 for more detail).

Dried herbs benefit from being kept cool, dry and out of direct light. A jar with a tight-fitting lid is a must and, if you are decanting them, keep the packing and use-by dates so you can discard anything past its best.

If in doubt, take a pinch of dried herbs and crush them between finger and thumb: the aroma should be strong with no hint of mustiness. Colour is also a good sign; herbs lose some colour during the drying process, but anything really sad-looking will be as grey in flavour as it is in appearance.

Classic Herb Blends

...

Bouquet Garni

Bay
Parsley
Sage
Thyme

Tied together and used to flavour anything from stocks to soups and casseroles, then fished out before the dish is served. Also available to buy as a dry blend to sprinkle into dishes, but that won't have the same resonance as fresh and we wouldn't recommend it.

Fines Herbes

Chervil
Chives
Parsley
Tarragon

Soft and delicate, these herbs are a mainstay of French cooking and are used in anything from vinaigrettes and omelettes to poultry dishes where a soft fragrance is required. Sometimes sold as dried blends, which in our opinion should be avoided. (Soft herbs don't dry well.)

Herbes de Provençe

Marjoram
Oregano
Rosemary
Savory
Thyme

Strongly aromatic herbs prized for the resinous
quality they impart to slow-cooked meat dishes.
Often sold as a dried blend, which can work
well added to a slow-cooked dish giving a more
intense flavour, but we prefer to use fresh,
giving a 'greener' fragrance to food.

Flavour Bomb

Sometimes there is just no time to make a stuffing (especially
on Christmas Day). Instead, core a cooking apple and stuff it with
a mixture of woody herbs such as rosemary, thyme, marjoram
or oregano. Peel 4 strips of zest from an orange with a vegetable
peeler and fix them on to the apple using 3 cloves to stud
each strip. Pop into the cavity of a bird or under a leg of pork
before roasting.

M

Sun-loving Herbs

Basil

Bergamot

Borage

Chamomile

Chives

Coriander

Fennel

Lavender

Lemon Verbena

Marigolds

Marjoram

Nasturtiums

Oregano

Pansies

Purslane

Rosemary

Sage

Savory

Thyme

Do Well in Sun or Shade

Bay

Chard

Dill

Land Cress

Lemon Balm

Lovage

Parsley

Sorrel

Tarragon

Partial Shade-loving Herbs

Chervil

Mint

Mustard Greens

Primroses

Rocket

Violets

Grow Your Own

•••

Herbs are perfect pot or window-box plants. Boxes on a kitchen window ledge are easily accessible in the midst of a culinary conjuring act. You only need to think about how much sun or shade your herbs will get (see previous page).

Beyond that, make sure you use a good soil compost – herbs hate peaty soils – and water regularly, preferably in the morning to give the leaves a douse before the heat of the day gets to work and causes them to wilt.

An occasional feed with a good all-round plant food in spring and summer and you will have healthy and abundant stock to pick from time and again.

Growing Indoors

Herbs can grow very successfully indoors, particularly during the winter. Ornamental as well as fragrant, they can be very welcome house guests.

Soft herbs do well indoors: basil, chives, coriander, dill, marjoram, mint and parsley. Sow seeds on to damp soil in a well-drained pot. Seeds germinate at 18–20°C, so use a plastic bag to create a mini greenhouse to get them going. All they need is a spot near a sunny window and regular watering.

Micro Herbs

The darlings of Michelin-starred restaurant tables in recent years, these are the first shoots, picked from six days after germination. They impart an intense burst of flavour and also look pretty. Sold to the restaurant industry at a high price, they are easy to grow. Try coriander, basil, chervil, rainbow chard, fennel, mustard, beetroot or radish. Plant seeds close together over lightly packed compost, then water via the tray it sits in so the compost absorbs water from below. Harvest with scissors.

Herbs and the Larder

•••

Of course nothing beats fresh herbs. However, if you are buying large bunches of herbs from markets or ethnic grocers, or you are growing your own, there will inevitably be the odd glut: armfuls of parsley and mint that, unless picked and used, will be gone come the end of summer when they die back. For those occasions, here are a range of techniques to preserve delicate leaves and flowers.

Preparing Herbs for Preservation

1

Whichever herbs you are harvesting, or preservation method you are choosing, you will need to ensure they are perfectly clean and dry.

2

Pick herbs mid-morning after the dew has dried but before the sun has had a chance to deplete the leaves of their delicate essential oils: this is where the flavour comes from.

3

Wherever possible, pick whole stalks, leaving 2.5 cm or so of growth on the plant, ideally with a new shoot left intact at the base.

4

Pick over your herbs, removing any blemished or rotting leaves, weeds, cobwebs and so on.

5

Carefully rinse or wash the herb branches in as little water as possible to prevent any bruising.

6

Shake herbs dry, lay them on a couple of layers of kitchen paper and allow any excess moisture to dry off.

7

Once picked, herbs will start to wilt and deteriorate in flavour, so try to preserve them as soon as they are clean and dry.

Dried Herbs

•••

Air-drying summer herbs for winter use is a time-honoured tradition. But not all herbs, in our opinion, are suitable for drying. Resinous, hardy and low-water-content herbs definitely work best and we tend to keep the list of suspects fairly short.

Herbs Best Suited

Bay

Marjoram

Oregano

Rosemary

Sage

Thyme

Storing Dried Herbs

Once dried, herb branches may be slightly unwieldy kitchen companions. They are better stored in a sealed jar to keep them at their best. We tend to carefully strip the branches of their dried leaves and transfer them, as intact as possible, to glass jars with proper lids. We only crush them as we need to use them, to retain their volatile oils.

Air-drying

1
Slow air-drying retains the essential oils better than other methods.

2
Choose a warm (but not humid) space with good air circulation and no direct sunlight; the ideal temperature is around 20°C.

3
Remove the bottom one-quarter of leaves from the herb branches and tie them in bunches of six to eight to give enough air circulation around each branch (elastic bands are useful here as they will grip the herbs as they dry and contract).

4
Hang your herb branches upside down and wait for a couple of weeks.

5
Test to see if your herbs are dry by pinching and rubbing a couple of leaves between finger and thumb.

6
If the leaves crumble easily and feel dry then they are ready; if not, leave them for another week and check again.

7
Thicker-stemmed herbs will take longer, as will larger bunches of herbs.

8
If you are concerned about dust while your herbs are drying, then punch a few holes in a paper bag and tie this around the base of the branches with another elastic band so the herbs hang loosely inside.

9
If you are drying multiple herbs, write the name of each on the paper bag so you can easily identify them.

Frozen Herbs

•••

Freezing herbs will retain a lot of their flavour but it's worth noting that, once frozen, herbs will not be fully restored to their former life when defrosted. Freezing alters the composition of the leaves, so it's better to use them in cooked dishes than raw, as they won't be as perky or fresh.

Many herbs can be frozen, but soft-leaved and high-water-content herbs such as chervil, tarragon, chives and fennel are better frozen than dried:

Basil	**Dill**	**Oregano**
Chervil	**Fennel**	**Sage**
Chives	**Lemon Grass**	**Savory**
Coriander	**Marjoram**	**Tarragon**
Curry Leaves	**Mint**	**Thyme**

Frozen Herb Branches

If you want to preserve the herb intact, then freeze whole, fresh, clean branches flat on a baking sheet covered with a plastic bag or cling film; decant into a freezer bag once frozen. No need to defrost, just crumble the herbs straight into whatever you are cooking.

Chopped and Ready to Use

If your freezer is small, then this is a space-saving technique. Chop the herbs, then place in ziplock freezer bags. Remove as much air as you can from the bags, being careful not to pack the herbs too tightly together, before freezing. Again there's no need to defrost these, just crumble or chip a piece off the frozen block.

Herb Ice Cubes

Another way to freeze herbs is to suspend whole leaves in ice cube trays. Place two or three nice leaves in each hollow and fill two-thirds full with water, cover with cling film and freeze. Once frozen, fill the top of each hollow with water and refreeze (this prevents the delicate leaves from 'burning' in the icy air). Once frozen, decant into freezer bags, ready to pull out when you need a herby hit for your cooking or to add to drinks.

This is also the best way to preserve edible flowers. Suspending single flowers in ice creates a beautiful glassy effect, lovely in summer drinks and cocktails. (The exception is chamomile, for which drying brings out a strong earthiness that makes it ideal for teas and infusions.)

Herb Oil Ice Cubes

Some herbs are better mixed with oil before freezing, to stop oxidisation. Most soft herbs are suited to this, as their delicate leaves deteriorate very easily, but nearly all herbs work well, giving up their flavour to the oil which you can quickly add to your cooking (though don't bother with bay leaves as those dry so well). Simply chop your herbs or blitz in a food processor, adding enough olive oil to make a paste. Then transfer to ice cube trays to freeze. Once frozen, decant into a freezer bag.

Basil, Coriander, Mint

These are very volatile soft herbs that decompose quickly. Even in the freezer, the decomposing plant enzymes they contain can turn the herbs black and mushy, making them a rather less enticing ingredient than you probably hoped. To scotch the enzymes, blanch the leaves in boiling water – just a few seconds will kill them – then plunge into ice water to stop them cooking. Pat dry and continue with your chosen freezing method.

Herb-infused Honey

...

The flavour of herbs can also be wonderfully preserved in honey. A natural healer, honey (particularly raw and unfiltered) marries really well with many herbs, creating delicate flavours to use in your cooking... with the added benefit of the herb ramping up the honey's healing properties. Sage honey is brilliant for easing a sore throat or cough, while lavender honey helps relaxation and promotes sleep, for example.

Incredibly versatile, we like to use herb honeys to add another dimension to simple buttered toast, to sweeten a tea or tisane, to add to baking and bread making, to create killer cocktails, as an interesting addition to a cheese board and to marinate or baste meat and sausages, to name a few.

Herbs That Work Well with Honey

Bergamot	Lemon Balm	Rosemary
Fennel	Lemon Grass	Rose Petals
Ginger	Lemon Verbena	Sage
Lavender	Mint	Thyme

Other Flavours You Can Experiment with in Honey Alongside Herbs

Black Peppercorns

Chillies

Citrus Zests

Pink Peppercorns

Vanilla Beans

Making Infused Honey

Use dried or fresh herbs that you have blanched for a few seconds to kill bacteria and enzymes (honey won't support the growth of bacteria, but anything you add might). Keeping herbs whole will stop the flavour penetrating as quickly, but make it easier to strain them out once infused. Use a lightly flavoured honey to allow the herb to shine through (local, raw honeys retain the most flavour and nutrients, while also supporting local bees). Be sparing with strong flavoured herbs, such as lavender, sage and rosemary; be more generous with delicate flavours.

We like to use single herb varieties to create honeys with a clear flavour, but experiment with herbs that you like to use together in other cooking to find flavour combinations that you really love.

1

Use sterilised Kilner or other jars (see page 408) with tight-fitting lids (a wide neck is preferable so you can fill it easily with your ingredients).

2

Place the herbs in the jar, then fill three-quarters full with the honey.

3

Stir the honey and herbs, then fill the last quarter of the jar with the rest of the honey, ensuring the herbs are completely covered.

4

Leave in a cool, dark place for at least five days to allow flavours to infuse.

5

Taste the honey and check if the flavour has developed enough. If not, leave for another few days.

6

Once you're happy with the flavour, fish out the herbs, or strain out with a fine sieve or muslin (warm honey will be much easier to strain than cold).

7

Make sure you label your jars with the herb and date of infusion.

8

Herb-infused honey will last in your storecupboard for at least a year.

Other Ways with Herbs

...

Preserving Herbs in Oil

Preserving the flavours of herbs in bottles of oil is a great way to use up herbs and give you the taste of spring and summer all year round. For ideas and flavour combinations, see page 249 and 250.

Herb Salts

A great way to preserve a glut of garden herbs is to preserve them in salt. First wash and dry the herbs with kitchen paper or a clean tea towel (try parsley, oregano, thyme, dill, basil or chives). Line a baking tray with baking parchment and pour over a layer of flaky sea salt, then lay on the herbs. Sprinkle over more salt and lay down another layer of herbs, then cover with more salt. Dry out overnight in an oven at its lowest temperature. Once all the moisture has been removed from the herbs, blitz them with the salt in a food processor in batches until the salt is fine. Store in a jar away from direct sunlight.

Herb Butters

Herb or 'compound' butters, as they are often called, are another brilliant way to keep the flavour of fresh herbs alive for longer. Much like using oil to preserve herbs, butter seals the herbs from the air, which helps prevent oxidisation and spoiling.

Herb butters are also an excellent way to add flavour to your cooking in an instant; a great fridge or freezer standby which can transform humdrum ingredients into something special in a flash. For more ideas and recipes, see page 250.

Herbed Goat's Cheese, Ricotta or Cream Cheese

Herb butters need only be the start of the dairy journey. Another way to give your herbs a little extra shelf life and add hugely to your cooking repertoire is to experiment with running fresh herbs and edible flowers through soft goat's cheeses, ricotta or mascarpone. Even cream cheese works very well.

These herby concoctions work brilliantly as dips with crunchy summer vegetables, are lovely stirred through simple risottos, as fillings for jacket potatoes, as toppings for open sandwiches, or just spread on toast. Really, the possibilities are endless once you get started.

They keep for a few days in the fridge, but are better used up fairly quickly, which shouldn't be a problem as they don't tend to hang around for long. Here are some ideas to mull over and experiment with:

Soft Goat's Cheese

spiked with chervil, dill, finely grated lemon zest and freshly ground black pepper.

Cream Cheese or Labneh

swirled with extra virgin olive oil, thyme leaves and a sprinkle of sumac.

Ricotta

marbled with chives, pea shoots, broad bean flowers, nasturtium and borage flowers.

Mascarpone

dotted with oregano, marjoram and a little finely grated orange zest.

Four Herb Butters

For every variety, beat the butter in an electric mixer until soft. Add herbs as directed. Season each batch with a good twist of freshly ground black pepper. Form into logs, wrap in cling film and freeze.

Garden Herb

serve with asparagus,
use to cook an omelette
or enrich a sauce

125 g salted butter, softened

1 tbsp finely chopped
parsley leaves

1 tbsp finely chopped dill

1 tbsp finely chopped
chervil leaves

Tarragon

serve with fish or put inside
a roasting chicken

125 g salted butter, softened

3 tbsp finely chopped
tarragon leaves

finely grated zest of
1 unwaxed lemon

Sage and Garlic

serve with turkey or
pumpkin ravioli

125 g salted butter, softened

2 tbsp finely chopped
sage leaves

1 garlic clove,
finely chopped

Chive and Nasturtium Flower

serve over
hot new potatoes or
poached salmon

125 g salted butter, softened

1 tbsp finely chopped chives

2 tbsp chopped
nasturtium flowers

Green Sauce

•••

We serve this salty, versatile sauce with our breaded chicken. It's also a fine accompaniment to fish or lamb, or a dressing for potatoes. It will keep in the fridge for a week and, once you see how it makes or breaks a meal, you'll use it for all sorts of dishes. Try it to dress a purple-sprouting broccoli salad, or serve it over braised beans and marinated feta. We have omitted garlic for a smoother flavour, but feel free to include a couple of cloves.

Makes 150 g

Ingredients

50 g flat-leaf parsley
25 g mint leaves
1 tsp salted capers
2 spring onions
1 lemon
5 tbsp extra virgin olive oil,
  plus more if needed
½ green chilli
1 tsp anchovy paste,
  or 3 anchovy fillets
½ tsp sea salt, plus more if needed

Equipment

sharp knife and chopping board
zester
juicer
food processor

Preparation

Pick and wash the herbs and rinse the capers.

Chop the spring onions.

Zest and juice the lemon.

Method

Put all the ingredients into a food processor and pulse until smooth. Taste and adjust the seasoning, using salt and more oil if necessary.

Store the sauce in an airtight container for up to one week in the fridge.

Crabapple and Thyme Jelly

•••

Crabapples can't be eaten raw and require cooking. This is an excellent way to use them as their high pectin content makes a great jelly that sets beautifully. If you don't have crabapples, use cooking apples. Good with game terrine, duck, slow-roast pork belly and soft, sharp goat's cheese.

Makes 8 x 220 ml jars

Ingredients

2 kg crabapples or cooking apples
1 unwaxed lemon
20 g thyme
white granulated sugar (about
   1.8 kg, depending on yield)
150 ml cider vinegar or white
   wine vinegar

Equipment

sharp knife and chopping board
jelly bag or muslin measuring
   60 x 60 cm
8 x 220 ml jars with lids
large saucepan
sugar thermometer
slotted spoon

Preparation

Place a small plate in the freezer.

Wash and cut up the apples, leaving on the skins and cores. Wash and slice the lemon.

Scald the jelly bag or muslin in a kettle of hot water to sterilise it. Sterilise the jars (see page 408).

Wash the thyme and pick the leaves from one sprig.

Method

Place the crabapples in a large saucepan, lay on the lemon and sprigs of thyme and cover with water. Bring to the boil, then reduce the heat and gently cook for one hour, until completely soft. Strain through the bag or muslin into a clean pot and leave overnight to drip. Don't squeeze the bag or the jelly will be cloudy. Next day, measure the liquid and discard the bits left in the bag.

For every 600 ml of liquid, add 450 g of sugar. Add the vinegar and bring slowly to the boil. Once the sugar dissolves, increase the heat and take the jelly to 104.5°C/220°F on a sugar thermometer. Skim the scum with a slotted spoon, to give a clear jelly.

Once setting point is reached, check the set (see page 415), using the cold plate. Add the thyme leaves, allow to cool for 10 minutes, then pour into the sterilised jars. Seal the jars while hot, then allow to cool. This keeps for 12 months in a cool spot.

Garden Herb Tart

•••

This tart appears on our menu in early spring when the herbs from our suppliers take on a new vivid shade of green. Add roasted vegetables such as courgettes or peppers if you want something more substantial.

Serves 8

Ingredients

1 leek
3 tbsp chopped mixed thyme, oregano and marjoram leaves
6 tbsp chopped mixed parsley, chives and basil leaves
4 spring onions
100 g crumbly goat's cheese
300 g shortcrust pastry
plain flour, to dust
6 eggs
350 g double cream
100 ml whole milk
sea salt and freshly ground black pepper
1 tbsp olive oil

Equipment

sharp knife and chopping board
rolling pin
23 cm diameter deep loose-bottomed tart tin
baking parchment and baking beans
mixing bowl
frying pan

Preparation

Wash and chop the leek, discarding the very tough dark green parts.

Wash, pick and chop the herbs.

Wash and chop the spring onions as finely as possible.

Crumble the cheese.

Method

Preheat the oven to 160°C/325°F/gas mark 3. Roll out the pastry as thinly as possible on a lightly floured surface to the thickness of a pound coin and use it to line the tart tin. Line with baking parchment, weigh down with baking beans and blind-bake for 20 minutes, until the pastry is cooked through.

Beat the eggs with the cream and milk, season with salt and pepper and set aside.

Fry the leek in the olive oil with the thyme, oregano and marjoram until the leek is softened. Season with salt and pepper.

Arrange the cooked leek, parsley, chives and basil, spring onions and goat's cheese in the tart and cover with the custard.

Bake in the oven for about 45 minutes, or until set in the middle and coloured on top.

Serve at room temperature.

RECIPE
253

Tomato and Oregano Sauce

•••

This is a basic sauce but an important one with endless applications. We use a good-quality dried oregano as it has a robust flavour that we think holds well here. The longer this sauce cooks, the better the flavour. Use it with pasta, or make baked beans by stirring through Braised beans (see page 364) with a sprinkling of paprika and a pinch of muscovado sugar.

Makes 600 g

Ingredients

200 g shallots
6 garlic cloves
400 g can plum or cherry
  tomatoes
400 g fresh tomatoes
2 tsp dried oregano
3 tbsp olive oil
½ tsp sea salt
200 g passata
shot of virgin olive oil
pinch of caster sugar (optional)

Equipment

sharp knife and chopping board
potato masher (optional)
saucepan

Preparation

Peel and chop the shallots. Mince the garlic cloves.

Crush the canned tomatoes with clean hands or a potato masher.

Chop the fresh tomatoes and remove the hard white core.

Method

Sweat the shallots and oregano over a medium heat in the olive oil and salt until softened but not coloured. Add the garlic and cook for a few minutes more, being careful not to let it scorch or it will impart a bitter flavour to the sauce.

Add the canned tomatoes, fresh tomatoes and passata and cook, uncovered, on a very low heat for about an hour, stirring from time to time until the sauce has reduced by about half. Taste as you go and remove when you are happy with the flavour.

The sauce should be glossy and rich. Add a shot of virgin olive oil at the end of cooking for pepperiness or maybe a pinch of sugar if it requires sweetening, or salt if you want more flavour. Once cooled, you can blitz it in a food processor for a smooth finish, depending on what you are using it for.

11

An Introduction to Meat

For some – if not most – of us, meat is a product we take for granted more than any of the others that we have written about in this book. We've been brought up in a country where meat-and-two-veg has been the diet for decades. Our issue around the meat part of that phrase is that it's certainly not an essential part of a healthy and balanced diet, especially every day.

We were brought up in homes where our parents worked hard to ensure that meat was regularly on the table, and there was no Sunday without a Sunday roast. The pleasure that meat brought and the role it played in the customs of the home is unquestioned. But our world has changed and our dietary needs are now known to be different.

However, meat is still such an integral part of our weekly shopping habits that we'll take a look in this chapter at its place in our kitchens. We'll do so with two provisos:

There are very strong ethical arguments to reduce the amount of meat we eat and we subscribe to those.

When you do buy meat, try to ensure it has been brought to you with the welfare of the animal at the forefront of its production. If it has, it's likely that it will be very tasty meat.

There are various schemes and certifications available to meat producers in this country that guarantee certain standards in the farming of animals. No scheme is perfect and standards are hopefully changing for the better all the time. At the point at which we write, we suggest looking out for:

A The Soil Association's Organic Certification.

B The RSPCA's Freedom Food Scheme. This aims to ensure good practice in the welfare of animals reared for food.

Not all 'good' meat will necessarily be accredited under these schemes, but this is when it pays to get to know your butcher so you can ask him or her the important questions.

Undeniably, there are cost implications in making these choices, certainly when choosing organic. Perhaps if we ate meat less regularly, we could afford to pay a little more for it when we did. As we hope this book shows in the other chapters, your storecupboard can provide so many options for a varied diet without relying on meat.

Eating All the Animal

We've long been fans of the 'nose-to-tail' eating philosophy and have tried to apply it whenever possible in our kitchens. Apart from yielding some great-tasting foods (have you ever tried chitterlings or pig's cheeks?), it also harks back to the idea of craftsmanship being applied to the meat we butcher for food. Getting the most out of the carcass of an animal makes perfect sense and – by necessity because it can't all be eaten at once – the ways of preserving it or extending its life make for all manner of different foods. We'll revisit this later in the chapter when we look at the various ways of preserving meat.

Fresh Meat

...

Use your local butcher, if you have one. He or she will happily advise you and help you buy what you need, which in turn will bring rewards in your kitchen. Explore all types of cuts; some work better cooked long and slow; others benefit from just a few minutes in a hot pan.

Buying Chicken

In our opinion there are
only two options: free-range or organic.
It's as simple as that

Rare Breeds of Chicken

BUFF ORPINGTON

JERSEY GIANT

BOOTED BANTAM

NORFOLK GREY

SICILIAN BUTTERCUP

Buying Beef

Buy British

Hanging gives the meat time to become tender

Meat should be dry-hung for a minimum of two weeks (some like it as much as 60 days)

Buy grass-fed where possible

Avoid meat that has been wet aged

Meat should be deep red in colour and look dry

It should be firm to the touch

Look out for marbling – the fat running through the muscle – which helps in the cooking

Rare Breeds of Beef

Longhorn

Red Poll

Black Galloway

Gloucester

Red Ruby Devon

Hereford

Buying Lamb

Buy British; it is mainly
outdoor-reared and grass-fed

'Spring' lamb is only ready to eat from
early summer and into late autumn

Meat should look moist and pink
when young, and brownish-pink,
not red or bloody, when older

It is best hung for around a week

Hogget or mutton are richer
than lamb, but not as tender

When Does Lamb
Become Hogget and then Mutton?

Lamb up to one year old
Hogget up to two years old
Mutton two or more years

Rare Breeds of Lamb

Hebridean   Dorset Down

Norfolk Horn   Jacob

Radnor   Shetland

Buying Pork

Buy British (there's lots of
continental pork around and the animals
may not have enjoyed the welfare
standards you would expect)

Look for outdoor-reared or free-range pork

Meat should be deep pink in colour
and should have a close and fine texture

Look out for marbling; it will be
more evident in rare breeds

Rare Breeds of Pork

TAMWORTH

GLOUCESTER OLD SPOT

SADDLEBACK

MIDDLE WHITE

BRITISH LOP

PLUM PUDDING

Five Ways
to Cook Chicken

•••

Rolled Chicken Thighs
with Spinach and Berkswell

Preheat the oven to 180°C/350°F/gas mark 4. Bone and flatten 6
chicken thighs under some cling film with a rolling pin. Cook 2 chopped
shallots in a little oil without colour, add 2 minced garlic cloves and 150 g
of washed spinach and allow to wilt. Remove from the heat, season and
stir in 50 g of nutty Berkswell cheese and 75 g of fresh breadcrumbs
(see page 29) followed by a beaten egg and a good grating of nutmeg
(don't be shy here). Stuff the thighs with this and close each with a
toothpick. Colour them in a little oil in a hot ovenproof frying pan and
finish in the oven for 20 minutes, or until cooked through. Serves 6 as
a starter.

Bonfire Sauce Chicken Wings

In a bowl, mix 3 tbsp of runny honey, 75 ml of soy sauce, 75 g of tomato
ketchup, 3 tbsp of white wine vinegar, 50 ml of sunflower oil, 2 splashes
of Worcestershire sauce and 2 tbsp of white wine. Add 1 tsp of smoked
paprika, a pinch of chilli flakes, 1 tsp of sea salt and a grinding of black
pepper and stir. Put 1 kg of chicken wings in a plastic food bag and add
the marinade. Seal and put in the fridge overnight. Next day, return to
room temperature and preheat the oven to 180°C/350°F/gas mark 4.
Cook the chicken for 35 minutes until charring on the edges. Serves 6.

Whole Roast Thyme and
Quince Chicken

A British quince in season will effortlessly perfume a roast chicken with its delicate flavour. Wash and chop a quince or two, skin on and core in, and stuff into the cavity of a well-seasoned chicken. Push thyme butter (should be made in the same manner as page 250) under the breast skin and roast in your usual way. Serves 4–6.

Lemon and Buttermilk
Chicken Goujons

Cut 2 chicken breasts into finger-width strips. Mix them in a bowl with 150 ml of buttermilk. Cover and place in the fridge for 2 hours. Remove from the buttermilk and follow the method for breadcrumbing food (see page 29), zesting 1 unwaxed lemon into the beaten egg before coating. Bring a shallow pan of sunflower oil up to temperature over a moderate heat, so it is shimmering and sizzles if you drop in some crumbs. Cook the goujons in small batches, turning, until golden and cooked through. Drain on kitchen paper before serving. Serves 6 as a nibble.

Pot-roast Chicken Legs

Preheat the oven to 180°C/350°F/gas mark 4. In a casserole, season and colour 4 chicken legs in hot oil. Gently sweat 2 sliced onions, 2 chopped carrots, 2 chopped celery sticks, some baby turnips and 100 g of bacon lardons. Add plenty of garlic, thyme and bay. Once the vegetables are softened but not coloured, place the chicken legs on top and cover with 500 ml of chicken stock and add 300 ml of white wine. Bring to the boil very slowly, then cover and place in the oven. Cook for one hour. Remove from the oven and lift out the chicken. Keep it warm while you boil down the juices. Serve the chicken with its juices and the vegetables. Serves 4.

PHEASANT

A small bird will serve 2

A large bird will serve 4

Young pheasants are best roasted
and served slightly pink

Older pheasants are best
pot roasted

Snipe

Very small so allow
2 snipe per person

Innards are left in during
cooking to add flavour

Innards can then
be scraped out and
served on toast

It only takes between
5 and 15 minutes to cook

Venison

Haunch and saddle are best for roasting
and taste a bit like beef

GROUSE

Red grouse is unique to the UK.
It has lean, dark brown meat,
bursting with flavour

Woodpigeon

Try the delicate breasts fried
They taste good because they're
fussy eaters themselves

HARE

Has a stronger taste than rabbit
Needs to hang longer than rabbit
Feeds up to 6 people

Partridge

Subtle flavour

Best roasted or pan fried

1 bird serves 1 person

Shooting Seasons

Pheasant
1st October – 1st February

Partridge
1st September – 1st February

Grouse
12th August – 10th December

Woodcock
1st October – 31st January

Woodpigeon
No closed season at present

Snipe
12th August – 31st January

Venison
Varies

Wild Rabbit
No closed season at present

Hare
Varies

Wild Rabbit

Is best at
3 to 4 months old

It's very low in fat and very
good when casseroled

Be careful not
to overcook

WOODCOCK

Pot roast slowly
Innards are left in during
cooking to add flavour

Storing Fresh Meat

All fresh meat should be stored in the fridge. It's a good idea to remove it from any packaging, placing it on a plate and covering with greaseproof paper, rather than let it sit in plastic.

When storing meat in the fridge, ensure that no juices can drip on to other foods, paying particular attention to keeping raw and cooked meats – and other ready-to-eat foods – well apart. For these reasons, it is safest to store fresh meat on the bottom shelf.

A fresh piece of red meat will keep in a fridge for up to five days for a large joint, though the smaller it is the less time it will keep. Chicken is safest when cooked within two or three days. Of course, in all cases, you can refer to the use-by date.

• •

Smoked Poultry

Curing and smoking poultry is a good way to extend the life of the bird as with any meat, although a milder smoke is needed to maintain the balance of flavours. Often hardwoods, such as oak, are used to smoke chicken to really enhance the flavour.

Duck has a more pronounced flavour than chicken and so stands up to different smokes well. The smoking process also renders some of the fat, making the meat even more intense and tasty.

Smoked duck is common in Chinese cuisine. The classic Sichuan dish of tea-smoked duck is one of the most famous. It is prepared by hot-smoking over tea leaves, after marinating in Sichuan pepper, ginger and garlic.

Brining Meat

Soaking meat in brine will help it retain moisture while roasting and gives a good, deep, all-over seasoning. Brining helps to break down proteins, giving a softer eating quality. A basic brine is a solution of 6 per cent salt to water. Depending on the meat you can add sugar or aromatics such as bay leaf, crushed garlic, juniper berries or peppercorns. Boil the salt and water to dissolve – with the aromatics if using – then cool. Now submerge the meat in the brine overnight (but for no longer than 12 hours) with a plate and a heavy weight on top. Dry with kitchen paper and bring to room temperature before roasting. It won't require further salt.

Preserving Pork

There was a time when, once your livestock had been slaughtered, you needed to find a way to make sure the animal you'd fed for the past six months would now feed you for the next six. All manner of meats can be preserved, but the one animal that has been paid most attention is the pig. Pork seems to lend itself to preserving more than other meat; just look at the number of different ways it's preserved around the world – ham, bacon, terrines, pâtés, sausages, salami – to see how successful it is.

There's an increasing interest in the revival of rural food practices and a new and energetic generation of pork butchers and curers are honing their skills and selling their wares at markets and specialist food shops. They're adhering to the time-honoured traditions while experimenting with new flavours and ingredients. The French, Italians, Germans and Spanish produce delicacies that are world renowned. We in the UK have some experience too... and it seems we are now catching up.

British Ham

•••

Ham is a generic term for meat from the upper hind leg of a pig that has been cured using salt or smoke, then matured or air-dried. It's the nuances of the preservation which define different hams around the world.

In the UK we're used to cooking our hams once they're brined, whereas our continental cousins are more well-versed in air-drying. That's all due to climate and the dampness that we have here in the UK. However, there are artisan companies now successfully making air-dried hams here, too.

Here are some hams we've been producing over the past few centuries:

Bradenham Has a delicate, sweet flavour. The recipe is said to have originated from Bradenham Manor in Buckinghamshire in 1781. When the butler fell out with his master, he left to set up his own ham business using the household's method and the Bradenham Ham Company was born. The ham is dry-cured in salt, then soaked for a month in a mixture of molasses and spices, including coriander and juniper berries, before being left to mature over six months. Then it is smoked. The process leaves the ham with a distinctive shiny black skin, which is why it is sometimes known as 'black' ham.

Shropshire Black Ham Is made to a similar recipe, but only matured over three months.

Wiltshire Ham A mild, unsmoked meat named after a curing method that originated in the 1840s from the Harris family in Calne, Wiltshire. They discovered that they needed less salt to cure the meat and it stayed fresher if they kept the pork at lower temperatures, so they chilled their curing rooms with ice. They dry-cured the hams, salting the meat for 10 – 14 days, but clearly there was an element of moisture (from the ice) which made the process unique. It wasn't until after the First World War that Wiltshire cured ham was truly a wet cure, with the meat now soaked in brine for five days.

However, reader beware: what is sometimes labelled as 'Wiltshire cured ham' and sold in packets in the larger retailers may not be the real thing. They've appropriated the name by the fact that it has been through a quick process of wet curing, rather than the artisan process above.

Suffolk Ham Said to grace the Royal table every Christmas, this is not widely available these days. The pork is brined, then pickled for at least three weeks in a mixture of stout, ale or cider and sugar from a rich source (such as molasses or dark brown sugar), plus a unique blend of spices. Then the meat is smoked for four or five days over oak and aged for at least a month. Depending on the alcohol used, this ham has a golden or deep brown skin and a sweet meaty flavour. The best-known producer who still makes this traditional recipe is Emmett's of Peasenhall, one of the first to make the Suffolk ham in 1840, using local free-range pigs.

Cumberland Ham A traditional English ham from Cumberland pigs but, since that breed is sadly extinct, it is now made from Middle White pigs. It is dry-cured for a month in salt, saltpetre and brown sugar or treacle, then washed and air-dried for a further two months. It is usually unsmoked, but can occasionally be found smoked over juniper wood.

York Ham A dry-salted ham cooked on the bone and matured for at least two months. The pork should be from Yorkshire and allowed to grow for longer than usual to enhance the flavour and size, which is also bigger because the leg is cut over four rather than three muscles. The large, pear-shaped ham is the impressive cut sitting on the best British deli counters. It is pale with a dry, firm texture and deep, salty flavour.

Marmalade Glazed Ham

•••

There's nothing like slicing a ham to share at a summer buffet or a festive spread. The secret – as with all boiled meats – is to cook it very slowly. The water should just shudder as it cooks.

Makes about 25 slices

Ingredients

For the ham

1 unsmoked gammon joint
   (about 2 kg)
1 onion, halved
1 carrot, halved
6 cloves
3 bay leaves
1 tsp white peppercorns
1 tsp fennel seeds
3 strips of orange zest

For the glaze

100 g marmalade, warmed and
   strained, to remove peel
100 g dark muscovado sugar
½ tsp ground cloves
1 tsp mustard powder
1 tsp sea salt

Equipment

saucepans
sieve
sharp knife
roasting dish

Preparation

Rinse the gammon under cold, running water.

Heat the marmalade in a small pan, then pass it through a sieve to remove the peel.

Method

Place the gammon in your largest saucepan and cover with cold water. Add all the other ingredients. Bring to the boil and cook, uncovered, over the lowest heat.

Cook for 30 minutes for every 450 g of original weight, then remove and allow to cool a little.

Before the ham has cooled completely, peel off the outer skin, leaving a layer of fat. Do this slowly, coaxing away the skin with a sharp knife if needs be. Discard the skin and score the fat with the sharp knife in neat criss-crosses about 2 cm apart. Don't cut too deep.

Place the ham in a roasting dish lined with foil and preheat the oven to 200°C/400°F/gas mark 6.

Heat all the ingredients for the glaze in a saucepan and pour over the ham.

Pop into the oven until you have a deep glaze on the ham with the edges slightly scorching and the fat deep golden. This should take no longer than 15 minutes.

Remove and cool.

Hams from Further Afield

•••

Italy

Italian hams are all 'prosciutto' and are *cotto* (cooked) or *crudo* (raw).

Prosciutto di Parma An air-dried ham produced in the hills around Parma. The pigs are fed on a diet of grains and the whey from Parmesan production. The hams are cured with sea salt before being left to hang. They are aged for at least 12 months and, once approved, fire-branded with the Dual Crown. The end result is a sweet, moist ham.

Prosciutto di San Daniele Made along very similar lines, except that maturation is for a minimum of 13 months, the trotter is kept intact and each ham is mechanically pressed, which results in a squashed or flattened ham. The result is a creamy texture and sweet flavour.

Speck A lightly smoked ham from the northernmost part of Italy, bordering the Alps. After curing, the hams are gently smoked using low-resin alpine wood. The crisp air results in a delicate, smoky but sweet ham.

France

Jambon de Bayonne Another air-dried ham. A paste of flour and lard is applied during maturation to moderate the rate of moisture loss. It has a sweet flavour, but can be chewier than Italian hams.

Spain

Jamón Ibérico de Bellota Comes from the Pata Negra ('black foot') pigs found in south western Spain. They are famously fed on a diet of acorns *(bellota)* which are said to give the ham a unique flavour. It is made in a similar way to other air-dried hams. It has a hefty price tag and is definitely not one to have with egg and chips. A glass of fino sherry will do.

Sausages, Salamis and Saucissons

...

British Sausages

The practice of making sausages is almost as ancient as civilisation itself. There are many people more qualified than us to relate histories of Ancient Greek, Roman and Chinese versions of sausages. In essence, it was always going to fall to any savvy butcher to find an outlet for the odd pieces of meat to make most effective use of an animal, using intestines to encase the mix. In time, spices and herbs were introduced, so recipes and processes were refined. Before refrigeration it was necessary to preserve sausages using salting and smoking, which is where all the cured and fermented recipes originate. But the humble sausage that we know as an integral part of the breakfast fry-up is something wholly different.

There are hundreds of types of sausage, often named after the city in which they were made, or the region they come from. We have picked a few of our favourites to highlight different recipes and flavours:

Cumberland A full-flavoured coarse sausage that stands out from the crowd as it is coiled into a continuous spiral. The seasoning is spicy and warm, including pepper and mace or nutmeg. It is said that these spices were added to the traditional recipe when the spice trade first came through the Cumbrian port of Whitehaven in the 18th century. In 2011, the traditional Cumberland sausage became the 44th UK food and drink product to have its name protected with the status-giving Protected Geographic Indication (PGI).

Lincolnshire A herby, meaty pork sausage made with the sage that thrives in Lincolnshire soil. Sage is a good preservative, used that way since Roman times, so is ideal for sausage making. Sometimes other herbs such as thyme or parsley are added. The meat is coarsely ground, so this is a meaty sausage that is best cooked slowly in the oven.

Black Pudding Less popular than the traditional British banger, black pudding is a sausage traditionally made from oatmeal soaked and cooked in pig's blood, flecked with pork fat and onions, then wrapped in a natural casing. It's often served as part of a 'full English' breakfast in the morning, sliced and fried, although it has been gentrified these days and can often be found on restaurant menus, to the extent that it is now something of a cliché served with pea purée and seared scallops. But, as with most things, there is a middle way: you can use black pudding to add to stews, crumble it into salads and soups and even add it to a risotto. The new charcutiers are now experimenting with black pudding recipes, carefully sourcing their raw ingredients and playing with novel spice blends. And if black pudding is not for you, you can always show your feelings by participating in the World Black Pudding Throwing Championships, held each year in Ramsbottom near Manchester.

Sausages from Further Afield

Merguez A spicy North African sausage made from lamb or mutton (sometimes beef) and a bold flavouring of warm spices. The distinctive red colour comes from paprika, chilli and harissa and these are balanced with even more bold flavours such as cumin, coriander, fennel, garlic and sumac. They are traditionally served with couscous, though make a great spicy sandwich served in pitta bread with yogurt dressing.

Toulouse Originates from the south west of France and was originally made with no crumb added, so was purely pork, salt and pepper which, over time, has evolved to include stronger flavours such as red wine, garlic, bacon and herbs. The meaty filling benefits from slow cooking such as braising. The sausages are the primary ingredient of the regional hearty French dish: cassoulet.

Salami The collective noun for a range of cured, fermented, air-dried sausages which are made across Europe. Salami is the plural of the Italian *salame*, or 'salted meats' and can therefore refer to a variety of products. They are made from all sorts of meats, flavoured with different herbs and spices and can be salted, smoked or air-dried. The salted and spiced meat is ground and extruded into an edible outer casing (generally animal intestine), then fermented over a period before being air-dried. They vary in shape, size and recipe and there are traditional versions all over Europe.

Chorizo A pork sausage which originated in Spain and Latin America and comes in many different guises. Made from minced pork flavoured with paprika, the sausage is then fermented, cured and smoked. It has a relatively coarse texture, sometimes with large chunks of fat embedded in the meat. The different sausages can be either raw or cooked, smoked or unsmoked, sweet or spicy, so read the packaging carefully. The most well known to the UK market is the hot *(picante)* cooked version with a chilli kick which is eaten as is, or added last-minute to a recipe for an injection of flavour. The sweet *(dulce)* is much milder. Cooking chorizo (which is raw) is mildly cured so it is soft, ideal to fry and serve as hot tapas.

Mortadella This is Italy's most popular sausage. Traditionally from Bologna, it is made from finely minced pork, ham and pork fat seasoned with white pepper and garlic and is sometimes studded with pale green pistachio nuts. The original preparation is said to date back to the Roman era, when a sausage called *farcimen mirtatum* was a firm favourite, using myrtle berries as the flavouring. This recipe has evolved and the modern version now has PGI status, ensuring that it can only come from a particular region of Italy. It has a smooth texture and a pale pink colour flecked with white fat, is sold ready cooked and usually eaten cold.

Saucisson This is a French dry-cured sausage with recipes that date back to Roman times. Typically made from pork, although other meats are sometimes mixed in, it is a combination of lean and fatty meat which is combined with salt, sugar, spices and sometimes other flavourings such as garlic, alcohol, nuts, dried fruit and even cheese.

• •

Terrines and Pâtés

Making a terrine or pâté dates back to ancient times in the same way as sausage making or curing, primarily because it was yet another way of preserving all elements of the animal. History tells us of Egyptians and Romans enjoying the delights of goose liver pâté. But it was Catherine de Medici who really established the fashion for more refined terrines as well as pâtés, featuring them prominently on her state banquet tables.

It is the layer of fat on a pâté – or the jelly in a terrine – that seals in the freshness and preserves the meat. However, what separates them from other cured meats is just how impressive a turned-out terrine can look. These are luxurious speciality dishes that are just right for celebratory meals and that's the reason why, even today, we turn to them at special occasions such as Christmas.

Other Parts of the Pig

•••

Bacon This is pork cured in the same way as a raw ham (gammon) but it is taken from a different cut of meat, usually the back and sides. It may be unsmoked (green) or cold-smoked. Back bacon is cut, as the name suggests, from the back of the loin of pork, giving it that eye of meat and single side of fat. Streaky bacon is made from boned belly of pork and is streaked with a combination of fat and flesh.

Coppa This is an Italian-cured meat. It is known in Italy as *capocollo*. It is made from the muscle of pig that sits directly behind the back of the head, at the top of the shoulder. The meat is initially lightly seasoned, often with wine, garlic and a mixture of herbs and spices that vary between regions. It is then salted and put into a natural casing, then dry-cured for up to six months. Additional flavours are created by rubbing the casing with paprika or smoking over different woods. In Italy, it is regarded as a premium product and is always an impressive addition to an antipasti platter.

Gammon A raw ham, needing cooking. It can come either smoked or unsmoked (green).

Ham Hock The cut of pork that sits above the trotter. You can buy hocks cured and smoked and they benefit from slow cooking to make a really tasty, great-value meal. Any leftover hocks are wonderful in a terrine with pear and parsley (see page 282).

Pancetta The Italian version of streaky bacon, taken from the same cut – *pancia* – or belly of pig. It, too, is a raw product, cured in salt and spices such as nutmeg, juniper and fennel to give it that unique flavour before it is dried. Its main difference from bacon is that it is never smoked. It is a milder, sweeter alternative in any recipe.

Preserved Beef

...

Biltong A speciality of South Africa, this is cured beef or game. It was developed by Dutch settlers in the late 1600s as a way to preserve meat in that hot climate. It is cut into chunks, then rubbed with vinegar, salt and spices including pepper, coriander and cloves. It is then hung up on hooks and cool air-dried for three to seven days, which results in a hard, chewy, intense product to be sliced or eaten in pieces as a snack.

Corned Beef This is finely minced, salted beef compressed with gelatine, packed in cans. The name comes from the large kernels of rock salt ('corns') in which the meat is processed. Corned beef was popular during both world wars, when fresh meat was rationed. Please note: in the USA corned beef is what we British call salt beef (see below).

Jerked Beef The American equivalent of biltong, the word is from the Inca Quechua word *ch'arki* (dried meat). Some say it was first made by an ancient Inca tribe, others that it was Native Americans who first made it from buffalo thousands of years ago. It is air-dried with salt, spices and sugar and is only dried for a few hours, so is less tough than biltong.

Pastrami Made from beef brisket and cured in brine. It starts out as salt beef (see below), but it is then partially dried, coated in herbs and spices such as garlic, coriander, black pepper, cloves and allspice, then smoked. Finally, the meat is steamed, resulting in succulent spicy beef that is a favourite in Jewish delis when served in a rye bread sandwich.

Salt Beef Meat that has been cured or preserved in salt by brining (see page 267). Made with beef brisket, the brined meat is then boiled with seasoning and spices to turn a well-worked cut into delicious soft meat. Salt beef is commonly associated with Jewish cuisine, served simply with pickled cucumbers to get the classic salty-sour combination.

Five
Classic Sauces
for Meat

•••

Bread Sauce

Stud a peeled onion with 4 cloves and cover with
500 ml of milk. Add a blade of mace, 3 bay leaves,
2 crushed garlic cloves and 6 peppercorns and
simmer gently for 15 minutes until the milk is infused.
Pass through a sieve, discarding the flavourings, and
add 200 g of fresh, fine white breadcrumbs. Season
and cook until starting to thicken, then stir in 25 g of
unsalted butter and serve. Very good with poultry,
particularly chicken, while for some it's obligatory
with the Christmas turkey.

Apple Sauce

Peel and core a large Bramley apple (about 350 g).
Slice and toss with the juice of ½ lemon. Melt 25 g
of unsalted butter in a pan and cook the apple, with
2 tbsp of water and 2 tbsp of granulated sugar. Add
2 star anise and cook until the apple breaks down into
a smooth sauce. Cool, remove the star anise and serve.

M

Horseradish Sauce

Peel and grate 6 tbsp of fresh horseradish. Squeeze over 1 tsp of lemon juice to stop discoloration. Stir in 200 ml of crème fraîche and ½ tsp of English mustard powder. Season well with salt and pepper and serve with roast sirloin of beef.

Mint Sauce

Pick and wash the leaves from 6 large sprigs of mint, roughly chop, then crush in a mortar and pestle with 2 tbsp of golden granulated sugar to form a paste. Add 6 tbsp of white wine vinegar and season to taste. Allow to stand for one hour before serving with roast lamb.

Cumberland Sauce

Zest 1 orange and 1 unwaxed lemon and add to 200 ml of port in your smallest saucepan. Bring to a gentle simmer. Add 1 tsp of ground allspice and 1 tsp of English mustard and cook until reduced by half. Stir in 220 g of redcurrant jelly and cook until dissolved. Pass through a fine sieve and add a little sea salt and freshly ground black pepper. Cool slightly before serving with ham or game.

M

Sausage Rolls

•••

The balance of flavoursome fat to meat is important for a good sausage roll. Some use pork belly, but we use streaky bacon to bring extra flavour. Breadcrumbs help retain the moisture and give a soft eating quality.

Makes 6

Ingredients

1 onion
6 sprigs of oregano
4 rashers of streaky bacon (rind cut off)
250 g ready-made puff pastry sheet
½ tbsp flavourless vegetable oil
½ tsp sea salt
300 g minced shoulder of pork
50 g dried breadcrumbs (see page 29)
½ tsp freshly ground white pepper
1 egg, lightly beaten
fennel and onion seeds (optional)

Equipment

sharp knife and chopping board
rolling pin
frying pan
mixing bowl
piping bag and 5 cm nozzle (optional)
pastry brush
baking sheet

Preparation

Peel and finely chop the onion.

Wash and pick the oregano and chop the leaves.

Mince the bacon.

Roll out the pastry into a rough 50 x 20 cm rectangle and chill in the fridge.

Preheat the oven to 190°C/375°F/gas mark 5.

Method

Sweat the chopped onion and oregano in the oil in a frying pan, seasoning with the salt, until all is soft and translucent, but without colour. Set aside to cool.

Mix the pork and bacon together in a bowl and add the onions, breadcrumbs and white pepper. Stuff into a piping bag fitted with a 5 cm nozzle, if you like.

Pipe the meat down the length of the pastry. Or form it into a sausage shape and place it there.

Brush one side of the pastry with the egg. Flip the other side of the pastry over to cover the meat. Seal the pastry with a fork and cut into six neat rolls. Place on a baking sheet.

Glaze with more egg and, if you like, sprinkle with the seeds. Bake for 25 minutes until golden brown and cooked through. Best served warm.

Chicken Stock

•••

We make dark and light chicken stocks depending on the recipe. Dark stocks are added to recipes for red meat, such as cottage pie, while the lighter stocks are called for in a delicate chicken noodle soup. To make a dark stock, roast the bones in a moderate oven until well coloured but not scorched, as this will impart a bitter flavour to the stock.

Makes 1.5 litres

Ingredients

4 onions
1 carrot
1 fennel bulb, or trimmings
2 celery sticks
1 small leek
herbs for 1 bouquet garni
  (see page 236)
1 kg chicken bones, wings
  or carcass
6 white peppercorns
1 tsp fennel seeds
1 glass of white wine (optional)

Equipment

sharp knife and chopping board
kitchen string
large saucepan or stockpot
slotted spoon
fine sieve

Preparation

Peel and slice the onions (though leave the skins on if you want a dark stock).

Wash and slice the carrot, fennel and celery.

Slice the green part of the leek and wash under running water to remove any dirt. Slice the white part of the leek finely.

Tie up the bouquet garni with string.

Method

Place the bones in a large saucepan or stockpot. Cover with the chopped vegetables, tuck in the bouquet garni, tip in the peppercorns and fennel seeds and cover with 2.5 litres of cold water, making sure everything is submerged. Add the wine (if using) and bring slowly to the boil.

Leave to cook on a low heat, uncovered, for two hours, removing any scum that floats to the surface with a slotted spoon. Cool and pass through a sieve. Freeze for up to three months or keep in the fridge for five days in an airtight container.

Note: If you want a more intense flavour in the stock, return it to the heat after passing it through a sieve, boil hard for 15 minutes, then taste. Continue to reduce until you are happy with the flavour.

RECIPE
281

Ham Hock, Pear and Parsley Terrine

•••

Great as part of a buffet or to take on a picnic. We suggest setting it in one dish or terrine, but feel free to set it in three smaller containers. It's most successful when the hock is cooked long and slow, to break down the meat and release the flavour.

Makes 750 g

Ingredients

1 unsmoked ham hock
  (about 1 kg)
1 carrot
1 onion
6 garlic cloves
500 ml dry cider
1 pig's trotter, cut in half lengthways (get your butcher to
  do this)
6 cloves
4 star anise
1 dried chilli
1 tbsp white peppercorns
1 tbsp fennel seeds
3 bay leaves
1 Conference pear
1 tbsp chopped parsley leaves

Equipment

sharp knife and chopping board
large saucepan
sieve
box grater
lined terrine

Preparation

Rinse the hock and soak it in clean water overnight.

Peel and roughly chop the carrot and onion.

Crush the garlic cloves.

Method

Remove the hock from the soaking water and rinse it under fresh water.

In a large saucepan, cover the hock with the cider and fresh water and bring slowly to the boil, then add the trotter, carrot, onion, garlic, spices and bay.

Bring to the boil and simmer for four hours until the meat falls away from the bone. Remove from the heat and allow to cool in the poaching liquor.

Discard the trotter (it will have released its gelatine into the poaching liquid). Strain the liquid through a sieve, then heat and boil to reduce by one-third.

Shred the ham hock meat, discarding all the fat.

Peel and grate the pear and mix with the shredded meat and the parsley.

Place the meat into a lined terrine, cover with the reduced poaching liquid and allow to chill and set in the fridge overnight.

This will keep for five days in the fridge. Serve with Pear piccalilli (see page 451).

12

NUTS AND SEEDS

An Introduction to Nuts and Seeds

These days, it's not just the health crowd who are turning to nuts and seeds. As meat and fish become more of a luxury, it makes sense to get proteins from a wider variety of sources. Rich with flavourful oils, omega fatty acids, fibre and nutrients, nuts and seeds make an excellent addition to the diet. They are an essential storecupboard ingredient, equally dazzling in savoury and sweet dishes, and they keep well if stored correctly.

We always keep nuts and seeds close at hand in the kitchen. Large jars of our favourites are at arm's reach to be thrown into bread doughs and cake batters, home-made granola, a quick nut brittle, used to add crunch to a salad or to whip up a quick pesto.

But nuts are not inexpensive. Long prized for their oils and nutrient-filled calorie content, it is no surprise that they have featured historically in feast-time food, where they could be justifiably splurged on. Luckily, we find you don't need many to add a sense of luxury to your cooking. What we love about nuts and seeds is their ability quickly to transform dishes and make them feel special. Leftover couscous becomes an impromptu warm 'salad' with sautéed greens, herbs and just a few hastily sliced pistachios – elegant and satisfying – and most importantly ready in just minutes. And a sneaky late-night bowl of ice cream is transformed into something lip-smacking with the simple addition of a handful of toasted hazelnuts and grated dark chocolate.

We like to make nuts and seeds work harder for us by turning them into nut butters, milks and creams, or grinding them for use in our kitchen. These products variously add texture, flavour or brilliantly replace dairy in many dishes. We strongly urge you to try them, too.

Whole Nuts vs Pre-prepared

Nuts are sold in various states: whole, raw, roasted, sliced, slivered, blanched and ground, to name but a few. However, we think it's nearly always worth buying them in their whole raw state and preparing them yourself. Firstly, because if you use a lot of nuts then pre-prepared can be pricey, especially if you want the best... which you do. Secondly, because anything other than whole raw nuts will not store as well, so you have to use them up more quickly before they go off. Keeping nuts whole until you need them means you are in control.

The only exception to this is if a recipe calls for finely sliced or slivered nuts, where that sort of precision cutting would be difficult or impossible to replicate at home.

Storecupboard Stars

Whole Skin-on Raw **ALMONDS**	Raw **WALNUT** Halves	Whole Roasted **HAZELNUTS**
For the ultimate home-made nut milk and butter	For toasting and tossing through salads, or making spinach pestos	For quick ice cream sundaes and adding to cake batters

Nuts

•••

The Best Varieties and Their Uses

	Raw Nut Butter	Toasted Nut Butter	Nut Milk	Ground Nuts
Almonds Heart-shaped Spanish marcona are widely regarded as the best you can lay your hands on	●	●	●	●
Brazil Brazils cannot be farmed and so must be ethically harvested from natural rain forests	○		○	○
Cashews Processing cashews is a labour-intensive job, so Fair Trade protects Indian workers	●	●	●	●
Chestnuts Pick your own wild in the British countryside each autumn, or buy pre-cooked and vacuum-packed				○
Cobnuts Buy fresh Kentish cobnuts each autumn, the milky nuts are still in their papery green skins	●	●	●	●
Coconut Fresh whole coconuts feel heavy; shake and you should hear the water sloshing	○		○	

	Raw Nut Butter	Toasted Nut Butter	Nut Milk	Ground Nuts
Hazelnuts	●	●	●	●
Macadamias	○		○	
Peanuts		●		
Pecans	○	○	○	
Pistachios	●	●	●	●
Walnuts	○	○	○	○

Hazelnuts

Turkish 'Giresun' hazelnuts are regarded as the best in the world

Macadamias

Artisan-grown Australian nuts and extra virgin oils

Peanuts

Buy raw monkey nuts and toast them whole in the oven (see page 292), to make a ridiculously moreish nibble to go with drinks

Pecans

Shell-on Texan pecans, particularly the Old Mississippi 'Forkert' variety

Pistachios

Shell-on Iranian pistachios

Walnuts

Fresh 'wet' walnuts from Verona each September

Seeds

•••

The Best Varieties and Their Uses

	Raw Seed Butter	Toasted Seed Butter	Seed Milk	Ground Seeds
Chia Buy only certified 100 per cent pure seeds			●	
Flax (Linseeds) nuttier brown or milder gold, whole or milled seeds	●		○	○
Hemp Whole for baking and raw hulled for seed milk and butter (see page 298)	●		●	
Pine Nuts Resinous Siberian nuts (actually seeds)	○	○	○	
Poppy Sweeter black or milder white			●	
Pumpkin Styrian pumpkin seeds from Austria	○	○	○	○
Sesame Black seeds are nuttier, white seeds are mild	●	●	●	
Sunflower Toast hulled seeds for the best flavour (see page 292)	○	○	○	

Sourcing and Spotting Quality

As with spices, it's worth making a trip to an ethnic grocers to buy nuts and seeds. In supermarkets, both can be terribly overpriced and sold in tiny little packets. Specialist online nut and seed merchants are also worth looking up.

Wherever possible, look out for the source; good suppliers should be able to tell you about the product, its provenance and what sets it apart.

Look out for whole, undamaged nuts and seeds, with little extraneous debris or dust. Look out for packing, sell-by and best-before dates and keep in mind how long you intend to store them when buying in bulk.

Storecupboard Stars

Raw

PUMPKIN SEEDS

For toasting and stirring through grains and herbs

Raw

SUNFLOWER SEEDS

For topping muesli and granola

White

SESAME SEEDS

For home-made flapjacks and sesame brittle

Nuts Go Well With

...

Almonds
apricot, cauliflower, cherry, chicken, fig, honey, mackerel, plum, raisin, sherry

Brazil Nuts
apricot (dried), banana, caramel, chocolate (dark), cinnamon, orange, plum

Cashews
broccoli, chickpea, duck, fish (white), honey, lime, mandarin, prawn, rice

Chestnuts
apple, bacon, Brussels sprout, caramel, meringue, pear, turkey, vanilla

Cobnuts
beetroot, game birds, nectarine, pear, watercress, wild rice

Coconut
beef, chilli, coriander, crab, ginger, lemon grass, lime, mango, passion fruit

Hazelnuts
berries, celeriac, chicory, chocolate (milk), langoustine, peach, scallop, toffee

Macadamias
butterscotch, cranberry, ginger, orange, rose veal, wild mushroom

Peanuts
banana, chicken, chocolate, lime, rice noodle, strawberry jam

Pecans
carrot, cinnamon, French bean, maple syrup, parsnip, pumpkin, toffee

Pistachios
lamb, nectarine, orange, pomegranate, rice, rose water, saffron, strawberry

Walnuts
beetroot, cinnamon, coffee, goat's cheese, lentils, Parmesan, rum

Skinning Nuts

•••

Some nuts, most notably hazelnuts, but also almonds, pistachios, walnuts and peanuts, have a thin, protective skin that can taste a little bitter. This skin tends also to be quite dark, which could taint your cooking. So, for both reasons, some recipes call for the skin to be removed. Blanching or toasting, depending on the type of nut, will loosen the skin and allow it to be removed. Be warned, however: skinning nuts is a bit of a labour of love, so first ask yourself if you really need to skin them, or whether a more rustic finish would suffice...

The Toasting Method

Best for hazelnuts, peanuts and walnuts

1

Toast the nuts in a dry pan, or roast in the oven (see page 292) until the skins are starting to split and come away from the nuts.

2

Cool the nuts slightly so they can be handled.

3

While still warm, gather them in an old tea towel and rub them vigorously until the skins come away. A coarse-textured fabric works best; the tea towel may never be quite the same again so use one you don't care about and keep it for this job. It takes some rubbing and not all the skins will be removed; this is normal and a little skin won't affect the recipe.

4

Cool the nuts completely before storing.

The Blanching Method

Best for almonds, pistachios and hazelnuts

For both almonds and pistachios, place the shelled nuts in a large pan of boiling water and boil for one minute. (For hazelnuts, add 1 tbsp of baking soda per 150 ml water and boil for three minutes.) Take the pan off the heat. Remove a nut and, pinching the end, check to see if the skin slips off easily. If not, return the pan to the heat and boil for another 30 seconds or so.

Drain the nuts in a colander, then rinse them in cold water. Pinch each nut to slip off its skin.

Dry the skinned nuts in a single layer on a baking sheet at 110°C/225°F/gas mark ¼ for around one hour before storing. It's important to dry nuts thoroughly before making ground nuts or nut butters, as any water will affect the final product (if you are making nut milk, you don't need to dry the nuts).

Oven Roasting and Pan Toasting

•••

Raw nuts have a fresh milkiness that is very appealing. Toasting or roasting nuts takes them to another level, bringing out their true 'nuttiness' and richness, making them rather difficult to resist.

Both toasting and roasting nuts and seeds involves heating them to release their essential oils and begin to caramelise their natural sugars, enhancing the flavour at the same time.

Oven roasting tends to give a more even, thorough browning as well as a slightly crunchier nut, whereas pan toasting gives you a bit more control and tends to be a slightly faster process, producing very delicious nuts. So both have their place.

Pan Toasting

1

Set your largest frying or sauté pan over a low heat.

2

Add the nuts and dry-toast them in a single layer, moving them about every few seconds until you see them changing colour to the correct shade of toasty brown; this could take five to 10 minutes.

3

Remove from the pan and allow to cool.

4

Toast seeds in the same way, paying particular attention to them as they toast even faster than nuts.

5

If you are toasting a selection of nuts and seeds, it's prudent to do so in batches, ideally one variety at a time, or at least in batches of similar-sized nuts and seeds, so they can all cook evenly.

Oven Roasting

1

Preheat the oven to 160°C/325°F/gas mark 3. Lay the nuts in a single layer on a large baking sheet. Roast in the middle of the oven for 10–15 minutes.

2

Exact timings are not useful here; watch carefully and judge when to remove the nuts (this isn't the time to leave the room and make a phone call: you need to watch them like a hawk so they don't burn).

3

Stir every couple of minutes to ensure an even colour and make sure nothing catches; they should turn a couple of shades darker and look and smell appealingly toasty.

4

Allow to cool slightly.

5

Seeds can be roasted in the same way, they just take less time and so will require an even sharper eye on their progress in the oven.

Grinding Nuts

···

Ground almonds can be easily bought and are essential in many cakes and desserts. To make them yourself, you only need a food processor, and you can custom-grind to get any texture from coarse 'meal' to fine powder.

Any nut or seed can be ground. We use ground hazelnuts to make light little biscuits scented with orange flower water, or ground almonds to make a stunningly rich, moist chocolate torte. Ground macadamias are great in chocolate truffles, while coarsely ground pistachios and pumpkin seeds with spices make a bright green, nubbly coating for roast salmon.

There are two ways to grind nuts: the first is to blitz in a food processor; the second is to use the byproduct of home-made nut milk (see page 296).

Blitzed Nuts Method

1

Choose your nuts or combination of nuts and seeds to be blitzed. Make sure they are completely dry.

2

If using almonds or hazelnuts, decide if you want a fine pale grind or a more textured grind containing the nut skins (to remove the skins, see page 291).

3

Decide if you need raw ground nuts to use in baking, or toasted, perhaps for a coating or spice blend (to toast nuts, see page 293).

4

Add your nuts and / or seeds to the food processor bowl – in batches if need be – and pulse until you get the texture you desire. Do this slowly until you become familiar with how the nuts behave: you want the ground nuts to be free-flowing and not clumped together.

5

If you blitz for too long, you will create nut butter, where the oils are released and the flour becomes a paste. It's very nice indeed, but not what you are looking to create here (see page 298).

If possible, store nuts in their shells; if not, ensure shelled nuts are completely dry, as moisture speeds up spoiling

Nuts and seeds can take on flavours, so store them well away from onions, garlic and other pungent items

Nuts and seeds have a high oil content which means they can turn rancid relatively quickly if not stored properly. The higher the oil content, the more quickly they will go off. Keep them in airtight containers. Label each with the expiry date, so you can easily track their freshness.

Storing Ground Nuts and Seeds

Home-made ground nuts can turn rancid quite quickly, so it's important to keep them in an airtight container in the fridge if you're not planning to freeze them. They will last around a week in the fridge and up to two months in the freezer. Seeds can be a little more volatile – particularly flax seeds – so these should be used up immediately or frozen straight away

If stored properly, shelled nuts will keep at room temperature for on average three months, in the fridge for around six months, or in the freezer for up to a year

Making Nut (and Seed) Milk

•••

Much more flavoursome than anything you can buy, nut milks are so easy to make you almost think you must be missing something. Of course you can flavour or sweeten nut milk if you like, but it's useful to have the unadulterated version in your fridge for using hot in porridge, cold over granola or muesli, to make nutty hot chocolate and anywhere else you would otherwise use cow's milk; try it in a custard or ice cream. Use raw, whole organic nuts and seeds if possible and work in small quantities, as they won't last more than a couple of days in the fridge.

Plain seed milks, on the whole, have a little less charm. Those worth trying solo are pumpkin, with a pleasing pale green complexion and light nutty taste, and pine nut, which is deliciously milky, if a little extravagant given their price. The best way we find to use them is as an addition to nut milks to create complexity and to lend their nutrients without overpowering.

1

Soak the nuts in just enough water to cover overnight, or for up to two days: the longer you soak them, the creamier the milk.

2

Drain the nuts and add to a blender or food processor with fresh water in a ratio of 1:2 nuts:water. Grind until you have a creamy, smooth mixture.

3

Pour into a large piece of muslin placed in a sieve over a bowl. Pull the muslin around the mixture and squeeze the milk out.

4

Flavour and sweeten your nut milk if you wish (see right) and keep it covered in the fridge for up to two days.

5

Spread the nut mash out on a baking tray and gently toast it (see page 293) to make ground nuts, or use straight away in baking or to add texture and flavour to porridge.

6

Dried and frozen, nut mash lasts for a few months in the freezer. (Seed mash can't be used in this way and should be discarded.)

Nuts for Milking	Sweeten the Milk	Flavour the Milk
Almonds	Blitzed Dried Dates	Almond Extract
Brazil Nuts	Date Syrup	Cacao (raw)
Cashews	Honey	Cardamom
Hazelnuts	Maple Syrup	Chocolate
Macadamias	Pomegranate Molasses	Cinnamon
Pecans	Raw Cane Sugar	Ground Ginger
Pistachios		Vanilla Extract
Walnuts		

Nut Cream

To make nut cream, follow the steps for nut milk (see left), but pass the nut mixture through the sieve without the muslin to give a thicker, heavier and much more creamy texture. Nut creams are useful for when you need something richer with a more pronounced nutty flavour.

Making Nut Butter

...

Nut butters are another dangerously easy thing to make yourself. Even easier than nut milk – if that were possible – and much more satisfying and delicious than most versions you can buy. On the whole we prefer to toast nuts and seeds first before grinding, as it adds a richness and depth of flavour, but there is a purity to raw nut butters that is very satisfying, particularly if you are using very good-quality blanched almonds (see opposite for a guide to which nut is considered better in a raw butter and which is best toasted).

1

Toast whole raw nuts or seeds in batches in a pan or in an oven (see page 292). Allow to cool slightly.

2

While still warm, place the toasted nuts or seeds in a food processor and blitz.

3

The nuts will go from coarse grains to powder before they start to clump and look oily, then become a solid mass and finally break down into a paste: around five minutes.

4

Scrape the sides of your food processor bowl every 30 seconds or so, to make sure all the nuts are being incorporated.

5

Once you have the consistency you like, a little raw coconut oil is a good way to loosen it up if its a bit stiff, season with salt if you want and add any flavourings. Nut butters tend to have enough of their own sweetness not to need anything other than a light sprinkling of sea salt.

Seed Butters

These can be slightly bitter, so a little sweetness from honey or maple syrup is usually a good idea. As with seed milks, the best way we find to use seeds is alongside nuts or as seed blends, where you can get the benefit of their nutrients without one flavour being the star of the show.

Nuts for Butters

Almonds
Brazil Nuts
Cashews
Cobnuts
Hazelnuts
Macadamias
Peanuts
Pecans
Pistachios
Walnuts

Seeds for Butters

Flax
Hemp
Pine Nuts
Pumpkin
Sesame
Sunflower

Nut and Seed Butter Combinations, and Flavoured Butters

Cashew AND **Almond**

Almond AND **Vanilla**

Pecan AND **Macadamia**

Peanut AND **Chocolate**

Hazelnut AND **Orange Zest**

Pistachio AND **Pumpkin Seed**

Pumpkin Seed AND **Sunflower Seed** AND **Maple Syrup**

Pine Nut AND **Honey**

299

Breads

Cakes, Tarts and Tray Bakes

Chocolate-covered Chocolate Truffles

Crumble Toppings

Dukkah

Granola

Honey

Meringues

Muesli

Nougat

On a Cheese Board

Porridge

Praline

Raw with a
Glass of Wine

Sweet and
Savoury Biscuits

Tahini

To Dust

Toasted and Salted
with a Glass of Beer

Toasted, for Salads

Za'atar

High in antioxidant vitamin E, which combats harmful free-radicals, and B-vitamins, which help in energy metabolism

Mineral-rich: they contain manganese, magnesium and copper which help maintain bone health and keep blood sugar at healthy levels

Their good fats – omega-3 and omega-6 fatty acids – are excellent for heart health

Fuller for longer; nuts and seeds help keep you feeling satisfied for longer after eating

Tiny parcels of protein, nuts and seeds are the perfect portable way to ensure you are getting your daily dose

Spiced Nuts and Seeds

•••

This recipe will make a large amount. They keep well, but they won't last long once shared at a party. Feel free to use different nuts if the selection here is not to your liking, just make sure the total weight remains the same.

Makes just over 500 g

Ingredients

1 medium-hot red chilli
2 sprigs of rosemary
½ tsp each cumin and
   fennel seeds
100 g Brazil nuts
100 g hazelnuts
100 g pecan halves
100 g cashew nuts
50 g pumpkin seeds
50 g sunflower seeds
50 g light muscovado sugar
1 egg white, lightly beaten
2 garlic cloves, very
   finely chopped
¼ tsp cayenne pepper
1 tsp sea salt

Equipment

sharp knife and chopping board
baking tray
mortar and pestle
baking parchment
large mixing bowl

Preparation

Preheat the oven to 130°C/265°F/gas mark ¾.

Deseed and chop the chilli very finely. Pick the leaves from the rosemary and chop.

Toast the cumin and fennel seeds on a baking tray in the oven for 10 minutes. Crush in a mortar and pestle.

Line a baking tray with baking parchment.

Method

Mix everything together in a large mixing bowl, spread out on the prepared baking tray and roast in the centre of the oven for one hour. Make sure you stir them every 20 minutes or so, to avoid scorching.

Remove when the nuts are deep golden brown. While they cool, stir them from time to time so they don't stick together. Once cooled, feel free to bash them to break them up. Store in a large airtight jar.

Nut Wellington

•••

We add spinach and pears to the spiced nut stuffing to give this dish a lovely fresh quality. Serve with Tomato and oregano sauce (see page 254).

Makes 1 x 1 kg loaf / Serves 4–6

Ingredients

350 g shortcrust or puff pastry
plain flour, to dust
1 large onion
2 garlic cloves
2 Conference pears
juice of 1 lemon
100 g each pecans, hazelnuts
 and almonds
½ tsp cumin seeds
½ tsp coriander seeds
200 g spinach
drizzle of olive oil
25 g unsalted butter
pinch of cayenne pepper
1 egg, lightly beaten, plus 1 egg
 to glaze
50 g fresh breadcrumbs
50 ml milk
sea salt and ground black pepper

Equipment

rolling pin
1 kg loaf tin
sharp knife and chopping board
vegetable peeler
frying pan
mortar and pestle
colander

Preparation

Roll out two-thirds of the pastry on a floured work surface and use it to line a 1 kg loaf tin. Chill.

Peel the onion and chop it finely. Peel and very finely chop the garlic. Peel, core and chop the pears and toss with the lemon juice.

Toast the nuts in a dry frying pan for 10 minutes (see page 293), then roughly chop. Crush the cumin and coriander with a mortar and pestle.

Method

Wilt the spinach in a hot pan in a drizzle of oil and drain in a colander. Sweat the onion and garlic in the butter, then add the spices and pear and cook until everything is softened.

Make the stuffing by mixing the nuts with the egg, breadcrumbs and onion mixture. Add the milk if the stuffing is too stiff, then season to taste. Layer half the mixture in the prepared tin.

Squeeze out excess water from the spinach and lay on top. Cover with the remaining stuffing.

Roll out the remaining pastry and neatly crimp on the loaf. Decorate with pastry leaves, using the trimmings.

Cover and chill for a few hours, or overnight.

Preheat the oven to 180°C / 350°F / gas mark 4. Glaze the loaf with the egg. Bake for 40 minutes, until golden. Allow to stand for five minutes before carefully turning out of the tin and slicing.

Peanut Butter Biscuits

•••

These are dangerously moreish to have to hand. As ever when baking, use vanilla extract, not anything labelled 'essence', please.

Makes 20

Ingredients

250 g plain flour
½ tsp fine sea salt
½ tsp bicarbonate of soda
115 g unsalted butter,
  at room temperature
120 g light muscovado sugar
100 g caster sugar
1 egg, lightly beaten
200 g peanut butter
1 tsp vanilla extract
20 peanuts, to decorate

Equipment

sieve
baking sheet
baking parchment
electric mixer

Preparation

Sift together the flour, salt and bicarbonate of soda.

Line a baking sheet with baking parchment.

Preheat the oven to 180°C/350°F/gas mark 4.

Method

Put the butter and both the sugars in an electric mixer and beat until smooth.

Add the egg, peanut butter and vanilla and beat again. Stir in the flour mixture. Roll into 20 balls, flatten them slightly and push a peanut into the centre of each.

Place on the prepared baking sheet 2 cm apart and bake for 15 minutes, rotating the tray halfway for an even bake. Cool and serve with a cup of tea.

Fruit and Nut Bar

•••

You really can't call this a flapjack, as I once said to a customer. It's in another league. The bars will keep for two weeks in an airtight container and are ideal for lunch boxes. Best of all, they are both wheat-free and utterly delicious.

Makes about 14

Ingredients

70 g dried apricots
70 g dates
60 g pecans
180 g unsalted butter
120 g golden syrup
60 g honey
200 g demerara sugar
225 g rolled oats
70 g raisins
60 g hazelnuts
35 g pumpkin seeds
35 g sunflower seeds

Equipment

30 x 20 cm baking tray
baking parchment
sharp knife and chopping board
saucepan

Preparation

Preheat the oven to 180°C/350°F/gas mark 4.

Line a 30 x 20 cm baking tray with baking parchment.

Chop up the apricots, dates and pecans.

Method

Bring the butter, golden syrup, honey and sugar slowly to the boil and cook until the sugar has dissolved.

Remove from the heat. Mix in all the other ingredients, then fill the prepared tray with the mixture.

Bake for 20–25 minutes, until golden brown and bubbling.

While still warm, score into 4 cm wide bars in two rows of seven, to make it easier to divide them when cool.

Pan-toasted Granola

Very good with cold milk or thick yogurt, with or without compote, for breakfast. Or sprinkled over vanilla ice cream with dark chocolate sauce, or added to a crumble mix for orchard fruits.

Over very low heat, toast a couple of handfuls (75 g) of chopped almonds, hazelnuts, cashews, coconut flakes or any other nuts in a dry frying pan until toasty smelling. Set aside. Toast a handful (50 g) of whole pumpkin and sunflower seeds in the same pan, until the pumpkin seeds pop and puff up a little. Set aside.

Now toast 4 good handfuls (125 g) of jumbo rolled oats in the pan until starting to smell nutty. Reduce the heat to low and add 1 heaped tbsp of coconut oil and the same of honey or maple syrup and stir to coat. Once combined, add 1 tsp of good vanilla extract and ½ tsp of ground cinnamon. Return the nuts and seeds to the pan and stir until starting to clump together.

If it's not looking wet enough, add a little coconut oil and honey or maple syrup until it is a little sticky but still relatively loose.

Pour out the granola on to a flat dish or large plate to cool, then store in an airtight jar. Makes 4 servings.

M

Pistachio Frangipane

A colourful alternative to almond. It keeps for at least a week in the fridge, or can be frozen once in tart shells. Blitz whole roasted pistachios in a food processer until finely ground. Combine 225 g of unsalted butter with 225 g of golden caster sugar in an electric mixer (don't incorporate too much air), add 225 g ground pistachios, then gradually add 4 lightly beaten eggs. Finally, fold in 115 g of plain flour. This looks great made in a blind-baked tart with pink rhubarb, blueberries or figs. Bake in a preheated oven at 180°C / 350°F / gas mark 4 for 30 minutes.

Coconut Macaroons

Whisk 3 egg whites in a clean metal bowl placed over simmering water with 200 g of caster sugar. Once the mixture reaches 45°C / 113°F, pour into a food mixer and beat on a medium speed until cooled, glossy and stiff. Fold in 200 g of desiccated coconut and a few drops of vanilla extract. Using 2 dessertspoons, make 20 mini scallop-shaped macaroons on a baking sheet lined with baking parchment. Allow to dry for 1 ½ hours before baking at 220°C / 425°F / gas mark 7 for 10 minutes, until slightly scorching on the edges. Cool and serve.

M

13

An Introduction to Oils

Even the most meagrely stocked kitchen cupboard will have a bottle of cooking oil stashed away somewhere; in fact, except for boiling an egg, it's hard to imagine cooking without it. It is essential. So it's pretty difficult to understand why it's so often treated as an afterthought rather than a carefully considered ingredient. (Unless you are talking olive oil, of course, which has benefited from some very good PR since the love affair with Provençal and Tuscan cuisine that gripped Britain in the 1990s.)

When we were young, olive oil was something you bought in the chemist in little pale bottles, purchased to ease skin complaints. For us there was a heavy emphasis on animal fats in the kitchen: butter (of course) and the lard that was requisite in pastry making. Sunflower oil was seen as the 'healthy option' (though that view is now changing) and soon established its place in the storecupboard at home. Rather pale and uninteresting, it was quickly eclipsed by a passion for olive oil.

The use of cooking oil has been a part of cultures around the world for millennia. The Eastern Mediterranean's first bubbling of civilisation was accompanied by that of olive oil; stone mortars and oil presses have been found dating back to 5,000 BC. The ancient Egyptians used olive oil in religious ceremonies and as a skin ointment, while Homer's *Odyssey* and *The Iliad* both mention the olive tree.

Of course, olive is not the only fruit. At a similar time, it seems that we in northern Europe were using flax seed, poppy seed and camelina oils in cooking. Coconuts and soy provided the source for China and South East Asia's cooking oils, while many other cultures made good use of other seeds, nuts and fruits to extract the oils they needed for fuel, to improve their skin and for cooking. But it's only since the middle of the 20th century that we have started to think differently about the role of oil in our diets.

Oil is – of course – a fat. Fats of all kinds were the scourge of the calorie-counting 1970s and 1980s, but in recent years they have seen a bit of a renaissance with the health crowd. In fact, 'good fats' have been embraced wholeheartedly into our diets and many lesser-known but beneficial oils have been added to our kitchens, bringing health-giving minerals, nutrients and vitamins and exciting new flavours.

Methods of Producing Oils

Extra Virgin This indicates the first extraction from a fruit or nut's pressing, which is also the one that releases the majority of the nutrients, flavours and aromas. In fact there are many health-giving compounds that are only present in extra virgin oils and not in subsequent pressings. Olive oil is undoubtedly the best-known extra virgin oil; it must have no more than 0.8 per cent acidity and is considered to have a superior taste.

Expeller-pressed The extraction method used for thousands of years to produce oil from nuts, fruits and seeds. They are ground and pressed with granite millstones or – these days – modern stainless-steel presses.

Cold-pressed Cold-pressed oils also use expeller-pressing, but under much stricter temperature control. Unfiltered, these oils often contain sediment and particles, which carry a lot of the nutrients and give an oil its character. To be regarded as cold-pressed, the temperature of an oil must not exceed 49°C. (With extra virgin olive oils, it must not exceed 25°C; any warmer and the oils' qualities, flavours and aromas are diminished.)

Unrefined These retain the integrity of the fruit, nut or seed that they come from, and tend to receive little or no filtering before being bottled. They have a good flavour, aroma, colour and nutritional value. Some may be cloudy or have sediment, but don't be put off; that's a sign of quality.

They have a relatively low smoke point and shouldn't be used at high temperatures. They are prone to oxidation and spoiling, so keep in a cool, dark place and use for dressings, marinades and light cooking.

Refined If the oil you buy is pale, odourless and clear, it's probably refined. Refining involves either a natural process of extensive filtering or – more commonly – chemical extraction, which by default also refines the raw oil to remove pulp and foreign matter. This leaves a pure, stable oil. The more refined the oil the longer the shelf life and, typically, the higher the smoke point. Most useful for high-temperature cooking and frying.

Chemically Extracted Much of the refined oil in supermarkets has been extracted using hexane. The oil goes through processes to remove that chemical before bottling, but it's still not something you'd want in your diet. There is no law requiring manufacturers to specify their method of extraction so, if the label doesn't state 'cold-pressed', 'expeller-extracted' or 'expeller-pressed', expect chemicals to have been used.

Single Estate Much like grapes for wine, an olive, nut or seed's 'terroir' or specific geography, as well as its treatment while being grown and processed, can greatly influence the quality and flavour of the oil. A rise in interest in provenance and the search for specialist flavours and characters in our food has fuelled an interest in single estate oils.

Organic Organic farming techniques often go hand in hand with the desire to retain old practices that enhance the final product. Farmers need to go through strict regulatory procedures, which can take years, in order to become certified as organic and the more labour-intensive farming methods mean these oils often carry a higher price tag. They will always be cold- or expeller-pressed with no chemicals used.

Olive Oils

···

Prized across the Mediterranean since time immemorial and widely recognised as one of the most health-giving oils available, olive oil has become so specialist these days that specific harvests from single estates are given vintages. High in monounsaturates, olive oil's reputed health benefits extend to lowering cholesterol and even preventing rheumatoid arthritis, while the antioxidant components in extra virgin olive oil stave off the cell damage which can lead to heart disease and cancer.

Light Olive Comprising a blend of oils from extra virgin through to low-grade refined olive oil from the last pressings. The lighter in colour and flavour, the more refined oil it contains.

Virgin Olive From the first pressing, this oil has an acidity level between 1 and 2 per cent (too high to be labelled 'extra virgin'). Less intense in flavour and colour than extra virgin, it has a medium smoke point.

Beyond Extra Virgin Extra virgin olive oil has been trumped by some specialist oil producers, who offer *flor de aceite*, the small amount of oil collected before the first cold pressing of the olives has even begun. This naturally secreted oil is said to be so special that each harvest is batch numbered: you can track each bottle's specific origin. This oil must be used on its own to enjoy its full character.

Olive Investors

Hardcore olive oil fans can even guarantee a supply of their own extra virgin, with some small-scale olive growers starting to offer investments in the form of rows of olive trees. This allows farmers to expand their farms and investors to receive a year-round supply of specialist olive oil.

Olive-picking Season

•••

As with all fruiting trees, olives have a season. In the Northern hemisphere, the least-ripe green olives are harvested from the end of September to the middle of October, followed by 'blond' olives (turning from green to black) picked from mid-October to the end of November, and the most ripe black olives from mid-November into early February. Oils deteriorate over time – a one-year-old oil will be less fragrant than a fresh oil – so look out for 'new season' olive oils during the winter months.

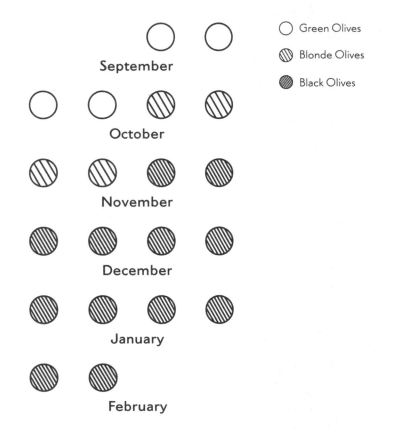

Other Oils

...

Corn

A hugely popular cooking oil with a high smoke point, making it ideal for frying. The hard kernel of the corn means it is most commonly chemically extracted, but some naturally expeller-pressed versions are on the market, often labelled 'corn germ oil'.

Citrus

If you've ever pressed a thumbnail into a citrus fruit and experienced the aromatic puff that immediately fills your nose with a pungent aroma, then you've discovered its oil. Cold-pressing the zests of citrus fruits gives a pure oil that can be used in cooking, baking and dressings. Beware: these are very pungent and should be used as flavourings, not as cooking oils.

Lemon Very good with fish and meat, it also adds amazing intensity to cakes, biscuits and meringues.

Lime Works alongside other fruits to add a zesty dimension when you want to combat cloying sweetness. Very good in jellies, too.

Orange Inherently sweet, orange oil is best used in puddings, desserts and ice creams and can introduce a strong orange flavour to chocolate.

Coconut

One of the few highly saturated vegetable fats, in its raw form it is highly nutritious. Used across the tropical world, it's fast becoming popular with the health food community in the West for its many nutrients and ability to mimic butter in baking. It comes in jars as it has such a low solidifying point. When warmed, the nutty, sweet white solid turns to a clear oil. Unrefined but stable at high temperatures, it's great for roasting and frying.

Palm

Controversial due to its links to the deforestation of Indonesian orang-utan habitats. A rare saturated vegetable fat, in its raw red form it carries many health-giving nutrients. But, if you can't find genuinely CPSO (Certified Sustainable Palm Oil) or GreenPalm certified, it's best to give it a miss.

Nuts

These oils have many nutrients and often a high smoke point, making them ideal for cooking. But it's the unique nut flavours that make them so sought after. Some of our favourites are:

Hazelnut Virgin cold-pressed, rich and intensely flavoured, this versatile oil can be used in desserts and baking, as well as forming the basis of a classic salad dressing with cider vinegar, shallot, honey and a little garlic.

Peanut Good varieties are made from pressed steam-cooked peanuts. It has little flavour and a high smoke point, so is pretty versatile.

Walnut Strong flavoured and aromatic, this makes a great dip for bread and cheese. Considered by chefs to be the supreme salad oil, it has a distinct sweet nuttiness. It is high in monounsaturates, omega-3 and powerful antioxidants and minerals.

Seeds

Like nuts, seeds are high in oil and offer excellent flavour as well as high nutritional value. Look out for:

Argan Made from the seeds of a Moroccan tree, this has a rich nutty flavour and light golden colour. It has high nutritional benefits and was developed through a women's co-operative formed in the 1990s. This oil is ideal for finishing dishes and dressing salads. It should be used cold for the benefits of its powerful antioxidants and high levels of vitamin E.

Hemp Another oil that's started replacing olive on restaurant tables due to its pleasant nutty, sometimes grassy, flavour. Highly nutritious, 1 tbsp provides your daily requirement of omega-3 fatty acids.

Pumpkin Made from either raw or low-temperature-toasted pumpkin seeds, this oil is highly flavourful (particularly when toasted) and filled with vitamin E, omega-3, zinc and magnesium. It is very good in marinades, salad dressings or just drizzled over grilled vegetables and meats, where its nuttiness can be fully enjoyed.

Rapeseed Fashionable in recent years, British cold-pressed rapeseed oil is bright yellow, rich in omega-3 and vitamin E and contains half the saturated fat of olive oil. It has a high smoke point, making it ideal for high-temperature cooking, roasting and frying.

Sesame Cold-pressed for a light cooking oil or hot-pressed to make the darker, nuttier toasted sesame oil. It is prized in Asian cooking and rich in the antioxidants reputed to lower blood pressure. When toasted, it has a distinctive nuttiness, making it good for use in robust dressings and marinades, or just as a dip for crusty bread.

Sunflower One of the most common culinary oils; polyunsaturated, neutral in flavour, high in vitamin E and low in saturated fat. You can now find first cold-pressed, unrefined versions which are light golden and with a gentle nutty flavour, but neutral enough to be used in a variety of dishes, making it the ideal oil for mayonnaise and emulsions.

Flavoured Oils

Also known as macerated or infused oils, these are standard oils (often light olive), which have had flavour-giving herbs, spices, flowers or fruits added. They provide a shortcut, adding flavour to cooking. Flavoured oils can be a lot less stable than other oils, so are worth keeping in the fridge. Among the most useful are:

Chilli Great as a standby for adding a quick hit of heat to dishes and for drizzling over pasta and pizza. It also makes a great speedy marinade for chicken and pork.

Garlic A very useful shortcut when your cupboard is bare. Look for a good-quality oil that has had the garlic crushed with the olives, imbuing a soft fragrance. Keep it in the fridge; always check the use-by date and discard anything that's gone over.

Lemon Again look for an oil that has been made by cold-pressing the lemons with olives to create an oil with a citrus pepperiness, that is ideal for drizzling over fish, risottos, chicken or salads.

Truffle Usually made with extra virgin olive oil infused with white or black truffle. A little of this pungent oil goes a long way, which is a good thing as it carries a high price. A great larder standby, it is best employed in simple mushroom or egg dishes: sautéed mushrooms or scrambled eggs, for example, suddenly become luxurious with a heady hint of truffle and can be whipped up in seconds. Beware of anything containing 'truffle essence': this is not the real thing and will taste like the imposter it is.

Heat, light and oxygen are the enemies of oil, particularly polyunsaturated oils that deteriorate more quickly

Some oils become cloudy or solidify in the fridge (or in cold weather). Don't worry, the oil is not affected and will return to liquid at room temperature

Keep oils in a cool, dark place, far enough from the oven not to absorb too much heat

Old or rancid oil takes on a characteristic bad smell and taste, so check your use-by dates and throw anything past those dates in the bin

Very expensive, specialist oils are best kept in the fridge

Getting the Best
Out of Your Oils

•••

Using Oils Cold

Use top-quality, cold-pressed, extra virgin, unrefined oils so the character of the oil can shine through. Save your very best oils for using cold, to show off their unique flavours and take advantage of their nutrients.

Dipping Extra virgin cold-pressed olive oil is the obvious choice, a classic served with crusty bread and just a little salt. The restaurant classic, albeit a bit 1980s, is to combine good-quality balsamic vinegar with olive oil for another flavour dimension.

Other classics are olive oil and Middle Eastern spice mixes such as dukkah and za'atar; just dip bread into pungent olive oil before dunking it into the spices. The Portuguese like to float aromatic thyme and pink peppercorns in bowls of olive oil to serve with crusty bread.

A strong-flavoured oil such as walnut or pumpkin seed would work well with walnut bread and goat's cheese, while the unusual grassy quality of rapeseed and hemp oils make them good for dipping, too.

Dressing This is another case for top-quality oil, but as you are adding other flavours – such as vinegar or citrus juice – you can afford to be a bit more playful. The classic combination of olive oil, white wine vinegar, French mustard and garlic can be adapted to make a British version from golden rapeseed oil, lemon juice, English mustard and honey (British, of course) to make a lively, bright dressing for lentils and bitter leaves to accompany traditional British cold meats. Nutty, fruity dressings work well with goat's cheese and pickled fruits, and a dressing made from hemp oil and pomegranate molasses flatters a salad to accompany grilled lamb.

Drizzling One of the most delicious things you can do with a good piece of meat is to simply chargrill it then, once rested, drizzle it with some very good olive oil and a spritz of lemon juice. Save your best oils for this and experiment with whole fish and seasonal vegetables as well.

Argan oil makes an excellent and highly nutritious addition drizzled over hot porridge for breakfast. The nuttiness complements the oats and also works very well with honey, toasted nuts and dried fruits should you want to add them, too.

Toasted pumpkin seed oil is very nice drizzled on roasted vegetable soups such as butternut squash; a drizzle of the oil with some croutons, shaved Parmesan or even fried sage leaves also works surprisingly well.

Cooking with Oils

There is no point in spending lots of money on a lovely cold-extracted extra virgin oil and then cooking with it. All the interesting vitamins and minerals will be immediately ruined, taking with them a lot of the special flavours and aromas.

As a rule, you only want to heat and cook with oils that are designed for the job; that usually means naturally refined oils. They have had volatile organic particles – that will burn and cause the oil to break down – filtered out. As a rule, the more refined and lighter in colour the oil, the higher the temperature, or 'smoke point', to which you can take it (see overleaf).

Get to Know the Smoke Point

Different oils and fats react differently to heat. Heating oil to the point where it begins to smoke produces toxic fumes and harmful free-radicals. Using an appropriate oil greatly reduces the chances of this.

It is worth noting that the longer you heat an oil, the lower its smoke point becomes. When deep-frying, any pieces of food left in the oil can also lower the oil's smoke point. You can also raise the smoke point of an oil by combining it with another oil with a higher smoke point.

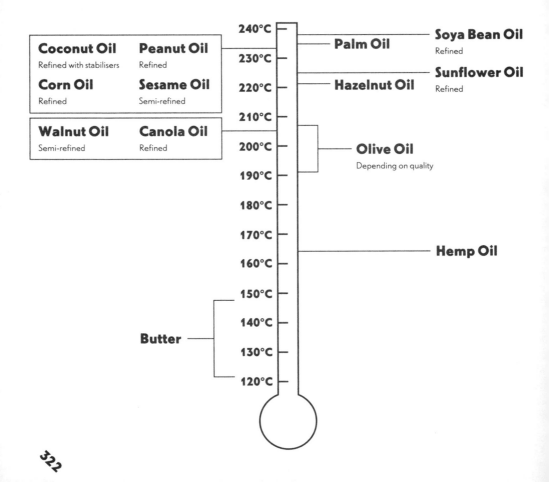

Coconut Oil
Refined with stabilisers

Peanut Oil
Refined

Corn Oil
Refined

Sesame Oil
Semi-refined

Walnut Oil
Semi-refined

Canola Oil
Refined

240°C
230°C
220°C
210°C
200°C
190°C
180°C
170°C
160°C
150°C
140°C
130°C
120°C

Palm Oil

Soya Bean Oil
Refined

Sunflower Oil
Refined

Hazelnut Oil

Olive Oil
Depending on quality

Hemp Oil

Butter

Make Your Own Flavoured Oils

•••

Dried

The simplest way to add flavour to oil and a good entry point to explore infusions. Oils flavoured with dried spices or herbs can last up to a year in a cool dark place, though very good oils should always be kept in the fridge.

Cold Infusions If you have a very good-quality oil you want to flavour, cold-infusion is for you. (Heat would remove some of its nutrients and flavours.) Best suited to dried flavouring ingredients that pose no risk of bacterial growth.

First add a couple of tablespoons of dried spices or herbs to a sterilised bottle (see page 408) with a stopper or cap, then cover with the oil. Let it infuse for a few weeks somewhere dark and cool, then strain off the flavouring and decant into the same bottle.

Warm Infusions A quicker process, using less good-quality oil you are happy to heat. Pour the oil into a saucepan over a medium heat, add dried flavourings and simmer for a few minutes. Cool, then strain into a sterilised bottle.

Fresh

Fresh ingredients contain water that can lead to bacterial growth which can permeate your flavoured oil, even in a sealed bottle, so follow a few rules:

Small Batch, Quick Cold Infusions Place the fresh flavouring ingredients and oil into a sealed, sterilised bottle or container, refrigerate and use within a week. Ideal for using up leftover chillies or a small glut of soft herbs such as tarragon, chervil or basil.

323

Quick Hot Infusions Heat oil over a medium heat and simmer the fresh ingredients for a few minutes, being careful that they caramelise but don't burn. This will cook the flavourings, so choose things that can stand up to heat, such as whole heads of garlic, pieces of root ginger, robust herbs such as rosemary, or citrus zests. The slightly caramelised flavour works well as a drizzling oil or a dip for crusty bread. Refrigerate and use within a few weeks.

Preserved Infusions Preserving fresh ingredients in vinegar before adding them to oil is another way to combat bacterial growth while adding a new flavour. Pickled garlic adds an unusual piquancy. Refrigerate and use within a few months.

Dehydrated Infusions The more adventurous might consider a food dehydrator, or just leave fresh ingredients in the sun to dry fully before adding them to oil. Whole sprigs of herbs, chillies or citrus zests all work. If thoroughly dried, the strained oil should last for a year, but keep it refrigerated.

Hazelnut Oil

Wonderful nutty aroma for classic dressings, dipping and for use in baking

Virgin Olive Oil

Light-tasting, for flavoured oils, mayonnaises and everyday cooking; a medium smoke point makes it good for sautéing

Coconut Oil

For dairy-free baking and to fry spice pastes when cooking coconut milk-based curries

Peanut Oil

Unobtrusive flavour and a high smoke point; a versatile oil for frying, roasting and high-temperature baking

Extra Virgin Olive Oil

Top-quality; grassy, pungent or spicy, take your pick, used for drizzling, dipping and dressing

Truffle Oil

For adding an instant sense of luxury to the simplest storecupboard ingredients

Aubergine Caviar

•••

We use virgin olive oil in this summer dish. The charred aubergine skins impart a delicious smoky flavour. Use a fork to break up the flesh for the best texture. Serve as a starter with crispbreads or with barbecued lamb.

Serves 4

Ingredients

2 large aubergines
½ lemon
1 tbsp chopped coriander leaves
1 tbsp chopped mint leaves
2 garlic cloves
virgin olive oil
2 tbsp crème fraîche
pinch of ground cumin
sea salt and freshly ground
   black pepper

Equipment

juicer
sharp knife and chopping board
baking tray
mixing bowl

Preparation

Wash the aubergines.

Juice the lemon.

Wash, pick and chop the herb leaves.

Preheat the oven to 190°C/375°F/gas mark 5.

Method

Place the aubergines on a baking tray and roast in the oven for 45 minutes until charred and slightly collapsed. Fifteen minutes before the end of cooking, rub the garlic cloves with olive oil and place next to the aubergines to roast and soften. Remove the garlic and aubergines and allow to cool.

Once cool, scrape out the flesh of the aubergines into a bowl, discarding the skins. Break up the flesh with two forks.

Squeeze in the soft interior of the garlic cloves, add the crème fraîche, measure in the lemon juice, cumin and herbs. Give the dish a good season. Finish the dish with a generous slug or two of your best peppery virgin olive oil. Give a final stir before serving.

Montgomery Cheddar and Tomato Muffins

...

We use sunflower oil to keep these light and moreish. Montgomery Cheddar, with its full flavours, works well, but use other well-made mature Cheddars if you prefer. These are excellent to take on a picnic.

Makes 6 large or 12 mini muffins

Ingredients

120 g mature Cheddar cheese, plus more for the tops
unsalted butter, for the tray
300 g cherry tomatoes
fine sea salt and freshly ground black pepper
drizzle of olive oil
20 g chives
300 g self-raising flour
2 tsp baking powder
150 g polenta
3 large eggs, lightly beaten
240 g live yogurt
150 ml sunflower oil
2 tsp whole grain mustard
1 tbsp pumpkin seeds, for the tops

Equipment

box grater
sharp knife and chopping board
sieve
mixing bowl
muffin tray and 6 large or 12 mini muffin cases

Preparation

Grate the cheese.

Preheat the oven to 140°C/275°F/gas mark 1.

Wash the tomatoes, cut in half, season with salt and drizzle with olive oil. Slow roast for one hour, then cool. Finely chop the chives.

Increase the oven temperature to 180°C/350°F/gas mark 4.

Method

Sift the flour and baking powder together into a mixing bowl and stir in the polenta.

Make a well in the flour mixture and add the cheese, eggs, yogurt, sunflower oil, tomatoes, chives and mustard and season with ½ tsp fine sea salt and ¼ tsp freshly ground black pepper. Bring the mixture together quickly.

Divide between six large or 12 mini muffin cases placed in a muffin tray. Cover with seeds and a grating more Cheddar.

Bake for 25 minutes until cooked through and well risen; a skewer inserted should emerge clean.

Salad Cream

•••

A British classic. Once you have discovered home-made salad cream you will find it difficult to return to the shop-bought factory-made variety. Serve this with almost anything when it comes to summer salad plates, though its perfect partner is a ham and egg salad with butterhead lettuce and thinly sliced cucumber.

Makes 175 ml

Ingredients

1 egg
1 tbsp Dijon mustard
1 tsp honey
20 ml white wine vinegar
80 ml double cream
sea salt and freshly ground
  black pepper
80 ml olive oil

Equipment

small saucepan
food processor

Preparation

Boil the egg for 10 minutes until hard, then cool and remove the yolk (discard the white, or eat it).

Method

Place all the ingredients apart from the oil into a food processor and blitz until smooth.

Pour the olive oil in very slowly so as to emulsify.

Check and adjust the seasoning.

Covered, this will keep in the fridge for a week.

Dairy-free Pastry

Substituting butter with oil can leave pastry heavy and brittle, so we use self-raising flour to add lift and a light flour – spelt – to help the texture. Sift together 210g of self-raising flour and 60g of spelt flour in a bowl. Mix in 1 tsp of sea salt and make a well in the middle. Pour in 100ml of light olive oil and 125ml of water and bring together into a soft dough. Give it a gentle knead, then roll it out on a floured surface and use to line tart shells. The shells will need blind-baking (see page 253) for 30 minutes in an oven preheated to 180°C/350°F/gas mark 4.

Fried Beetroot Crisps
with Sea Salt

If you can, use a selection of colourful beetroots from ruby to golden; the stripy Chioggia will look great here. Peel the beetroots and slice wafer-thin on a mandoline. Dry on kitchen paper. Pour one litre of sunflower or rapeseed oil into a wok and bring slowly up to 180°C (350°F). Fry the vegetables a spoonful at a time for up to three minutes. Once golden brown, scoop them out and drain on more kitchen paper. If needs be, keep warm and crisp in a very low oven while you cook the rest. Season with salt and pepper and serve warm with drinks.

M

Olive Oil-mashed Potato

Good mash is made from floury potatoes. Yukon Gold are an excellent choice, or Maris Piper. Boil 1 kg of peeled and chopped potatoes in plenty of salted water until soft. Drain and keep back half a ladle of the cooking liquid. Mash the potato, using a ricer or a potato masher. Add the reserved cooking liquid and beat until smooth. Stir in 50 ml of extra virgin olive oil. Add plenty of fresh ground black pepper, adjust the seasoning and serve.

Oven-dried Tomatoes in Oil

Preheat the oven to 110°C/225°F/gas mark ¼. Wash and halve a punnet or two of cherry tomatoes and lay them on a baking parchment-lined baking sheet, cut-side up. Season each with sea salt and one or two leaves of thyme and drizzle with light olive oil. Cook for about 2 hours, depending on size. Try one: they should have shrunk to half the size and taste intense. Place into sterilised jars (see page 408) and cover with sunflower oil (see page 317). Keep in the fridge and eat within one month.

14

PASTA AND NOODLES

An Introduction to Pasta and Noodles

Pasta and noodles seem to be equally matched when the vexed question arises: what shall we have for supper tonight? Supermarket aisles are packed with seemingly endless varieties of both.

In their make-up there is not much difference between pasta and noodles. Both are unleavened doughs made from flour and water. Yet we think of them in culinary terms as poles apart; the noodle is generally thought of in an East Asian context, whereas pasta is synonymous with Italian food.

The noodle has probably been part of the diet in the East for thousands of years, whereas pasta is a little younger (probably by two or three thousand years) and only really became a staple of the Italian diet in the latter part of the 19th century. To help understand what to use, in the pages that follow we need to dip a toe into the history and politics, geography and home climate of noodles and pasta.

Storecupboard Stars

SOBA

Made from buckwheat, that gives a strong nutty flavour

UDON

Chewy, soft and thick, these are great in a soup

RICE VERMICELLI

Use in stir-fry, or cold in a salad

Noodles

•••

Made from a variety of flours and salt mixed with water, though some have egg added. The paste is stretched by man or machine into strands, or rolled into sheets and folded to make stuffed parcels. They are boiled in water and added to broths or soups, or fried and served with a sauce. Most that we buy today are dried, so they can easily be reconstituted in boiling water or a broth. Fresh noodles are becoming more widely available, too.

Noodles are a relative newcomer to our grocery shelves, but now are often our default healthy dish, cooked with lots of vegetables and without much oil. They are also so easy to put together with a bit of this and that... inauthentic, but a great user-upper.

Cooking

Most dried noodles have been pre-cooked and therefore take only a few minutes to prepare. As a general note, they already contain salt, so you don't need to salt the cooking water. Bring about 1 litre of water for every 100 g of dried noodles to a rapid boil and place the noodles in a few at a time until all have been added, stirring to stop them sticking. When you think they are ready, taste them. Correctly cooked, they will be soft, plump, slightly chewy and the same colour throughout. Drain and run under cold water to prevent them sticking together. The noodles can then either be added to a broth or stir-fry or served chilled as part of a salad.

Storing

Dried Once you've opened a packet, store in an airtight container. They will probably last for at least 12 months if stored correctly.

Fresh Large supermarkets and speciality Oriental shops sell these. Most can be kept, chilled, for three days, but follow the packet instructions.

Japan

Most Japanese noodles are wheat based. The Japanese rarely use noodles made from rice, preferring to keep their rice in its original form. When eating them, slurping is requisite; it's also thought bad form to bite through a noodle.

Ramen

Thin wheat noodles with an added alkaline water called kansui. The dough is allowed to rise before being rolled and the noodles can be of varying shapes, widths and lengths. Usually served in a meat-based broth flavoured with soy sauce or miso.

Soba

Made from buckwheat, these are a good gluten-free alternative (although read the packet as many sold in shops these days contain wheat flour, too). Served cold or in a hot broth, they are a particular favourite in Tokyo. When moving house, the Japanese give them to new neighbours as a greeting.

Somen

Thin wheat noodles that have been stretched with a coating of vegetable oil, then dried. These are usually served cold with a light dipping sauce, but can also be used in a salad.

Udon

Generally thick, white wheat noodles served in a soy sauce-based broth, often with meat or fish as well as vegetables. They can be served chilled with a dipping sauce.

China and South East Asia

Alongside rice, noodles are a staple. Rice noodles are generally eaten in the south and wheat noodles in north China, due to the cereals grown in each region. In China, dishes with long noodles are served at birthdays to represent hope for a long life.

Cellophane Noodles

So-called due to their translucence once cooked, these thin noodles are made from mung bean flour. They are used in all sorts of dishes, from soups and stir-fries to salads.

Egg Noodles

Wheat noodles containing egg that gives them a yellow appearance. They can be thick or thin and tend to retain their egg flavour even when added to a potent sauce.

Rice Noodles

Rice flour and water is spread into sheets, steamed and cut into strips. In Canton they are simmered in a broth, while Thai people fry them. Very thin rice noodles (rice vermicelli) can be served in soups, stir-fries or salads. They are our first choice for a stir-fry, or with a broth.

Rice Wrappers

Paper-thin sheets of rice batter that have been steamed until translucent. Most renowned as the Vietnamese spring roll or as dim sum in China, when sheets are stuffed with meat, seafood or vegetables and often served with a dipping sauce.

Wheat Noodles

Wheat and water made into a dough and stretched into long strands. Referred to as mein, as in chao mein, a dish of stir-fried noodles and vegetables.

Wonton Noodles

Wheat noodles containing egg, these are filled most commonly with pork – but could have any number of different fillings – and added to soup.

Three Noodle Sauces

•••

Here are three sauces to keep in your fridge and use when serving noodles. The teriyaki is also perfect to liven up a piece of salmon or chicken: simply spread the sauce over the salmon or chicken before roasting, then serve with a simple bowl of noodles in a vegetable broth, or fried in a wok. The peanut sauce is great on a noodle salad. The simple dipping sauce is for a bowl of plain noodles. It is versatile, though, and perfect with spring or summer rolls, or works well as a dressing for an Asian-style salad.

Enough to coat 2 servings of fish or meat

Teriyaki Sauce

3 tbsp dark soy sauce

3 tbsp mirin

2 tbsp sake (or dry white wine)

1 tbsp caster sugar

1 garlic clove,
crushed or finely grated

1 cm root ginger,
peeled and finely grated

juice of ½ lime

Boil the soy, mirin, sake and sugar with the garlic and ginger in a pan until reduced and thickened. Pass through a sieve, then add the lime juice.

Makes about 200 ml

Peanut Sauce

4 tbsp peanut butter

2 tbsp soy sauce

4 tsp honey

2 tbsp sesame oil

pinch of chilli flakes

juice of 1 lime

2 tbsp rice vinegar

Whisk all the ingredients together
to form a smooth sauce.

Makes about 200 ml

Dipping Sauce

3 tbsp fish sauce

juice of 1 lime

2 tbsp caster sugar

1 garlic clove, crushed
or finely grated

¼ tsp chilli flakes

Whisk all the ingredients together
with 2 tbsp of hot water
until the sugar has dissolved.

Pasta

•••

Even though kneaded doughs have been part of Italy's food heritage for a number of centuries, it was only after the Second World War that the word 'pasta' was used to refer to all the forms of foods that now fall under that banner. It's said that there are 310 specific types of pasta, known by some 1,300 different names that vary from Italian village to village and even street to street. The name often gives a clue to the pasta's shape; think of cappellini d'angelo (angel's hair), or orecchiette (little ears).

We didn't have such variety in our youth – that was back in the Pre-Pesto Era – though we do remember those very long, blue packets of spaghetti in our mothers' kitchens. We ate spag bol at home, but that was it. These days, pasta is a staple. Of course, pasta dishes can be very complex, or come with a sauce that has taken hours to make. But, mostly, dried pasta is the sustaining, comforting and quick meal when our brains can't think about anything more taxing, or if you're just cooking for yourself. If you buy dried pasta and a tub of sauce, you can even kid yourself you are doing 'proper cooking'... Have a quick rummage in the fridge and find something to add to your bought sauce: spinach? Goat's cheese? Purple-sprouting broccoli? Dinner, without the need to peel anything.

Dried vs Fresh

Dried pasta is made with hard durum wheat. If you're making fresh pasta at home, an Italian 00 flour works well (the 00 reflects the grade of milled flour, 0 being coarse and 000 being the very finest).

Hard strong flours contain lots of gluten, so nothing other than water is needed to make pasta. Softer flour contains less gluten, so eggs are needed to bind the pasta together. If making fresh pasta at home, as a general rule, the more '0s' your flour contains, the more eggs you will need to use!

Originally, dried pastas were favoured by southern Italians, as the hot sun helped the production of durum wheat and made the air-drying of pasta easy. In the centre and north of the country, softer flours and a wetter climate meant that pasta was more often used fresh. Today it's widely accepted that different types of pasta suit different types of dishes.

When buying dried pasta, look for those made only from durum wheat. Generally, the smaller the producer, or more artisan they are, the better the quality. The best dried pasta is made by extruding the dough through bronze dies, with each die producing a different shape or size. The dies create small imperfections on the surface of each piece, making them rough rather than silky smooth. This roughness plays a part in helping the sauce to coat the pasta rather than just sliding off. A good test of quality is to run your finger along dried pasta and see how rough it is.

With fresh pasta, it's preferable to make your own unless you have access to an old-school Italian deli that makes it in-house, or to one of the new artisan pasta makers springing up in larger towns and cities. Supermarket fresh pasta is a poor substitute. Fresh pasta generally works well with a fresh filling. In addition, if you make your own pasta you can flavour it with spinach, herbs, pepper, squid ink, even chocolate. The flavour should of course complement the sauce with which you intend to serve it.

Storing

Dried Once you've opened a packet it's always best to store it in an air-tight container. Most dried pastas will store easily for at least 12 months if not longer if kept correctly.

Fresh This has a much shorter shelf life. If making your own, it's always best to make and serve it on the same day.

SPAGHETTI

The one we all know and love; quick and versatile. Dress it up with a complex sauce, or take it easy and add some garlic, chilli, lemon and olive oil

LASAGNE

Makes a great sharing or family dish

ORZO

If you're bored with risotto try this rice-sized pasta, which is also great added to soups and stews

PENNE

A perfect partner for meat and thicker-style sauces

COUSCOUS

'No cook', simply pour over stock, fluff up, then serve with meat and vegetables, or as a great salad base

Which Pasta Shape Goes with Which Sauce?

Much has been written about pasta sauces and which is the right sauce to serve with which pasta. (Incidentally, Italians lightly coat pasta in sauce, rather than drowning it.) Some simple rules can be followed:

For light sauces and dressings, use long pasta such as spaghetti, linguine and tagliatelle

For thicker sauces and light ragus, use pasta shapes: farfalle, conchiglie

For heavy, rich sauces, use tubular pasta: rigatoni, penne, macaroni

Other Types of Pasta

Couscous Couscous is made by combining granules of durum wheat, otherwise known as semolina, with water. The dried granules, when steamed over water, become soft and moist. It has its origins in north west Africa and is traditionally used to mop up stews and sauces. It has little or no flavour by itself but works well with African-style tagines and other sauces and can be used as the base for a salad.

Giant couscous is also called mougrabieh, Israeli couscous or Lebanese couscous. These little pearls can be up to 6mm in diameter. Just like its smaller brother, it can be steamed before serving, or toasted in a pan with butter until soft and tender. Or, more simply, cook it like most pastas in a large pan of boiling water.

Gnocchi Best made and eaten fresh, these little 'knots' of flour and water, some with added potato or egg, are cooked and served in a similar way to pasta. Often served simply with a coating of sage butter or pesto.

Gnudi Similar to gnocchi, with less flour: think ravioli filling without the casing. A paste of flour, egg, ricotta and/or Parmesan, fried in butter.

Cooking Pasta

Pasta should always be boiled in a large pan of water, say 1 litre for every 100 g of pasta. The pan should be low and wide to ensure an even heat distribution. Always use plenty of sea salt, allowing 1 tsp per litre of water, but only add it once the water is boiling, as salted water takes longer to boil. Don't be tempted to add oil to the water. (The one exception is that a few drops can help pieces of filled pasta – such as ravioli and tortellini – from sticking to each other.)

Only put the pasta in the water once it has been salted and has reached a rolling boil. Then balance the lid on two-thirds of the pot to help return it to the boil quickly. Once it's reached a rolling boil again, the lid can be removed and the heat reduced a little, always maintaining the rolling boil. A quick stir will help prevent the pasta from sticking.

Dried pasta should always be served *al dente* or 'to the tooth'. Follow the recommendations on the packet, but always taste the pasta a minute or so before the packet suggests, to ensure it is *al dente*. (Most dried pasta takes between seven and 10 minutes to cook.) Keep tasting until it has reached the desired texture.

Once cooked to your taste, remove the pan from the heat and drain, but don't let it stand or start to dry out; it should appear and remain slippery. (Never run your pasta under cold water.) Add the drained pasta to the sauce, either in a warmed bowl or directly to the pan the sauce has been cooked in, then serve straight away. The sauce or dressing should coat your pasta, rather than sitting in a lump on top!

For fresh pasta, follow the same method as above but reduce the cooking time to between two and five minutes. Again, taste as you go to see when it's cooked.

Which Pasta Shape Goes with Which Cooking Technique?

Once you've decided between fresh or dried pasta, the style of cooking helps you make your next choice.

Boiled

Pasta Asciutta

Spaghetti

Penne

Fettuccine

Orecchiette

Cappellini

Rigatoni

In soups or stews

Pasta al Borda

Macaroni

Quadrucci

Orzo

Farfalle

Baked in the oven

Pasta al Forno

Lasagne

Cannelloni

Four Seasonal Pasta Ideas

Spring • Wild Garlic

Steam stems of purple-sprouting broccoli and toss with a
drained jar of artichokes, then with cooked, drained penne.
Lubricate with basil oil and finish with torn wild garlic leaves
and shaved Berkswell cheese.

Summer • Goat's Curd and Broad Beans

Melt goat's curd over cooked, drained orzo. Add blanched
broad beans and peas. Stir in finely grated unwaxed lemon zest
and chopped mint leaves and finish with pea shoots.

Autumn • Wild Mushrooms and Cavolo Nero

Sauté wild mushrooms. Stir in crème fraîche and Dijon mustard,
adding black pepper. Discard the ribs from cavolo nero and
tear the leaves. Wilt in a separate pan, then squeeze out excess
water. Toss through cooked, drained fettuccine with the
mushrooms. Finish with sourdough crumbs fried in sage butter.

Winter • Oregano and Nut Crumb

Make a nut crumb by blitzing equal amounts of pine nuts,
almonds and pistachios in a food processor. Fry dried oregano
with finely chopped shallots until soft and season well. Add the
nuts and serve over cooked, drained spaghetti. Sprinkle with
a peppery extra virgin olive oil and grated Parmesan cheese.

PULSES

An Introduction to Pulses

If you have pulses in your storecupboard, you have dinner. We believe that, in future, pulses will make up more and more of the protein in our diets. It's no hardship; pulses are delicious. They are a highly nutritious protein and vegetable all wrapped up together in one neat package, and they are almost fat-free.

As good-quality meat becomes more of a luxury, if we don't know how to cook pulses already – and many of us don't – we've got to teach ourselves to embrace them. In Japan they have already learned this; they use bean curds and pastes (such as tofu, made from soy beans) in everything – even sweets – and have done so for centuries (and, as a nation, they have always been impressively healthy).

When we opened our first shop a decade ago, we couldn't sell pulses. People were simply not interested. But in the last five years there has been a definite shift back to those bags of dried seeds, as appetites, awareness and shoppers' budgets have changed.

You can eat pulses in so many different forms that we couldn't be without them. All home cooks need some pulses in their storecupboard, whether they're in a can, jar, dried, or fresh from the garden or greengrocer. They form a great low-GI alternative to potatoes and other starchy side dishes and come in a wide variety of styles, shapes, sizes and colours, all best suited to different treatments. So why are they often cruelly left on the grocer's shelf?

We think it's down to bad PR. While highly prized for their versatility and health-giving properties since the time of the ancient Greeks, pulses have at the same time often been disregarded as poor man's food. In addition, they still bear the 'knitted-lentils' legacy left over from the mania for (largely poor) vegetarian food during the 1960s.

However, fond childhood memories of the baked bean mean that, for many of us, pulses have always held a place in our hearts. Far less likely to be consigned just to that famous blue tin, these days clever cooks know that pulses are a brilliant substitute for grains in the rising fondness for gluten-free diets. They have also been given a lift by chefs who champion *la cucina povera*, that elevates humble ingredients.

• •

Larder Credentials

Infinitely versatile, pulses can be used
in a mind-boggling range of dishes.

Low-cost – particularly if dried –
and widely available.

No-cook if bought ready-prepared in cans
or jars (but stick to good-quality examples).

A portion (3 heaped tbsp)
is one of your five-a-day.

Pulses are 20–25 per cent protein
content by weight, double that of wheat
and three times that of rice.

Canned or Jarred vs Dried

We stock pulses according to their quality, not their ease of use, but we understand that not everyone has hours to spare simmering beans. Most aficionados prefer the dried variety, but canned and bottled pulses are widely available and all have earned their place in the larder. The latter are hugely convenient, as you cut out all of the soaking and simmering required for dried beans. When using canned or jarred beans, though, always rinse them after draining and before adding to a dish.

Pre-cooked, canned or jarred beans can be eaten cold or added to cooked dishes. They do, however, tend to be saltier and less flavourful, with an inferior texture, than dried beans cooked from scratch. Pulses in glass jars usually command a higher price than canned, as they tend to be of a much better quality. Also, the shopper can see the quality of the pulse – and its preserving liquor – through the glass.

Dried pulses are very cheap. When buying dried beans and pulses, look for those that are brightly coloured and uniform in size with a smooth appearance. Even very good-quality dried pulses can carry impurities, so it's sensible to sift through and remove any unwanted grit and stones, or wrinkled-looking beans or pulses, before cooking.

LOW IN FAT AND SATURATED FAT

FREE FROM CHOLESTEROL

A good source of plant-based protein

High in potassium, magnesium and calcium, which counter the effects of sodium and normalise blood pressure

High in iron, zinc and phosphorus as well as folate and other B-vitamins, but low in sodium

High in fibre

Very low risk of allergy

349

Lentils

...

If you think you have nothing to eat in the house, go into your cupboard and haul out your lentils. You can make something really quite special in minutes (see page 361).

Lentils are eaten around the world, due to their relatively high protein and calorie content. They have huge importance in Asian subcontinental diets, where 'dal', their generic name, is an inexpensive bulker that can be transformed into a myriad of delicious recipes. Lentils are also traditionally eaten in Italy on New Year's Eve, to symbolise hope for a prosperous year to come, probably because of their round, coin-like shape.

Soaking isn't necessary for whole lentils, but one or two hours may make them more digestible and reduce their cooking time. Split lentils don't need soaking at all.

Lentils vary in shape and colour and come both with and without their skins. The name is derived from Latin meaning 'lens', due to their shape. There are hundreds of varieties, but here are some of the best known:

Beluga

Whichever marketing genius came up with the name, these are almost glamorous. Whoever thought that was possible for a lentil? Where other lentils can be dull-looking when cooked, the tiny beluga retains its gloss and so looks great in a salad and has a deep earthy flavour.

Brown

By far the most common variety, these are great for adding to soups, casseroles and bakes, as well as to salads. Our favourites include the Spanish pardina lentil which has an earthy, herbal flavour.

Puy Lentils
(Sometimes Known as 'French Green')

Small, round and green-grey, these have blue marbling across robust seed coats that allow the lentils to retain their shape during cooking. So called because they are cultivated in the Le Puy-en-Velay region of France, they are considered by many to be the best lentil. A relative newcomer to our storecupboard, these are responsible for giving lentils their more exotic makeover of recent times. They have a peppery taste and are a great accompaniment to meat or fish when cooked in stock. They are also particularly good in salads, as they don't turn mushy. A classic dish of cooked, drained Puy lentils dressed with vinaigrette while still warm (see page 361) is a great fridge stand-by. We love to eat a dish of lentil vinaigrette with grilled lamb chops, or roasted cod.

Red

The home-cooked soups of our childhoods were bulked up with this popular pulse, which is widely used in Indian cooking and as an ingredient in dal. Coloured red to orange to yellow, these lentils have had their seed coats removed, so they become soft and tend to break up in the cooking process. It must be admitted that these are great in curries or for thickening soups and arguably have the sweetest, nuttiest flavour of all lentils. But... we are in the business of editing the choice for our customers. What we sell is what we like and what we believe in. We don't stock red lentils; we dislike the mushy texture.

Beans

•••

The Second World War left a strange legacy surrounding dried beans and other pulses in the British kitchen. Rationing had forced home cooks to use a lot of dried foods. As a result, we kicked against the habit, so we don't remember many dried foods in our mothers' kitchen cupboard. There were only really the token canned red kidney beans in the British take on chilli... Instead, fresh pulses were what we were accustomed to: peas, green beans and runner beans from the garden.

These days, as the decades have erased the link between dried beans and austerity, clever cooks always have a supply in their kitchen cupboard. There's something indulgent about cooking them at the weekend, when you have the time. Braise beans simply, in bulk (see page 364) and keep them in a jar in the fridge in their own stock. We always do this these days, scooping out what we need as the basis of soups, side dishes, starters or salads. They go amazingly well with meat or fish.

Safety and the Bean

If not soaked and cooked properly,
bean toxins can cause food poisoning.

Following soaking, always cook
beans thoroughly until they
are totally soft all the way through.

Whole or split lentils, chickpeas,
mung beans and aduki beans are safe
to sprout, but avoid other beans.

Dried beans offer great variety to suit cooking styles from around the globe. Here are some of the better known:

Adzuki / Aduki Native to the Himalayas and East Asia, these are small, round and a fairly uniform russet colour. Strong, nutty and sweet in flavour, they work well in curries and zesty salads and, in Asian cuisine, are mixed with coconut milk and made into sweets.

Black Eyed The small 'eye' marks the point (the hilum) where each bean was joined to its pod. Essential to southern US Creole and Caribbean cooking, some say they are easier on the stomach than other pulses. Use them in Jamaican 'rice and peas' and Mexican refried beans and chilli.

Borlotti A variety of kidney bean, championed in Italy, these are pale beige with crimson- or rose-coloured marbled veins. They are sweet and soft in texture and work well in classic Italian dishes, often alongside meat. The fresh beans are also great; we recommend you grow them if you have an allotment or garden. They have an amazing texture and flavour and beautiful mottled red and cream pods. Braise the fresh beans slowly for up to 40 minutes, depending on size and age, with bay leaves and olive oil. If you grow your own and have a glut at the end of summer and are not able to freeze them, you can dry them. It's thought best to dry them on the plant, but watch out for wet or frosty autumn days as you may lose them.

Broad or Fava Most often used dried in North Africa and the Middle East, these are often eaten fried as salty snacks, or in the famous Egyptian dish of ful medames, cooked over coals with oil and eaten for breakfast.

Butter Beans Butter beans were our mothers' go-to pulse, though they are in fact far more exotic than that, being Andean and Mesoamerican in origin (unlike us). Large and creamy-white in colour with a lovely mealy texture and an almost meaty depth, they absorb flavours beautifully. They are the most popular bean in our shops. They form the basis of many stews or roast veg salads, and we blitz them up as an alternative to houmous. Our very favourite variety are the huge gigantes, dried and (unusually and very successfully) vac-packed. (Look out for the latter; when cooked, they come up even bigger than the jarred kind.) Serve butterbeans dressed in olive oil as a vegetable side dish with grilled pork chops.

Cannellini A bean similar to haricot, these kidney-shaped pale beans are a staple in Italian cookery and work very well with tomato, garlic, sausage and olive oil. The Italians love them with slow-cooked lamb, and they also make a tasty white bean and oregano whip.

Flageolet These small pastel-green beans are soft and creamy. They are actually young haricot beans taken from the pod before they are fully ripe, which accounts for their great, tender-yet-firm texture. The French like to eat them with duck confit. Often used in stews or mixed bean salads, they also work well simply tossed in butter or olive oil to serve with meats.

Haricot The bean we know better than any other in the famous blue can. Small, pale and creamy, they are incredibly versatile, though marry well with fatty meats. Classically paired with slow-cooked meats in dishes such as French cassoulet and soups, they also make the original Boston baked beans. They are cheap and a good bulker and, although they have little taste in themselves, they readily absorb the other flavours in a dish.

Kidney The biggest group of beans, this term covers any bean that has a kidney-like shape without being flat. The type we most commonly think of as 'kidney' in Britain is the dark red bean used in our islands' bastardised but wonderful version of the Texan chilli con carne. Highly toxic until cooked, you must never use the bean soaking water for cooking.

Mung Olive green and very small, these are one of the most commonly used for making bean sprouts but, when cooked, the beans themselves are soft and sweet. They make a very good pancake when soaked and blitzed with stock and herbs.

Soy One of the most nutritious foods you can eat, these sadly lack much flavour and need substantial coaxing with herbs and spices to make them enjoyable. They are famously used to make both Chinese and Japanese bean curd, soy sauce and a very popular alternative to dairy milk. Young soy beans are familiar to us these days as the salty snack edamame, cooked in their pods and ubiquitous in sushi bars and sandwich shops.

Dried Beans

Will keep for up to a year, but toughen over time and take longer to cook. Ideally you should use your beans within six or nine months of their harvest to get the best out of them.

In order to get the freshest beans, buy them in small quantities from shops you expect to have a regular turnover of stock

Beans should be kept away from direct contact with air in a cool, dark, dry place. The best way is in a glass or plastic container with a tight-fitting lid.

Preparing Dried Beans: the Soak

As a general rule, the larger and older the bean, the longer the soaking and cooking time. Soaking dried beans will partially rehydrate them, reducing cooking time, softening the skins – which prevents splitting during cooking – and, most importantly, removing the toxins and some of the complex carbohydrates that can make them, for many of us, indigestible. Also, changing the soaking water once or twice will aid this process.

1

Before soaking, remove shrivelled or broken beans or any foreign matter such as grit or pebbles, then place the beans in a sieve and rinse under cold running water.

2

Measure the beans in a measuring jug and use 750 ml of water for every 250 ml of beans.

Quick

Bring the beans and water to the boil together from cold. Boil them rapidly for two minutes, remove from the heat, cover and let stand for one hour.

or

Long

Cover the beans generously with cold water in a very large bowl. Let stand for 12 hours, or overnight, in the fridge.

or

Extended

Cover generously with cold water in a very large bowl. Let stand for two or three days in the fridge. Change the water twice daily until the beans are starting to sprout. This is ideal for those who really struggle to digest beans.

No matter which method you favour, at the end of soaking always discard the water and cook the beans with fresh cold water, according to the recipe.

Cooking Dried Beans

After soaking, put your beans in a large saucepan with plenty of cold water and bring gently to the boil. At this stage you can add flavourings such as onion, garlic and fresh herbs, but be careful not to add any salt or anything acidic such as lemon or vinegar, as these will toughen the skins.

As a general rule, you need to cook the beans for between 45 minutes and two hours, depending on their size and age. Once they're cooked, season well to taste. Beans can take a fair bit of seasoning. If you are to eat them cold they may need even more than usual, so always check and re-season if necessary.

Beans form part of one of the first recorded instances of 'companion planting': native Americans planted corn, beans and squash together in a formation known as the 'three sisters': corn to provide a structure for the beans to climb, squash to cover the ground to prevent weeds and shield the earth from the piercing sun, and beans to provide essential nitrogen to the soil and fertilise all three crops.

Peas

•••

With far fewer varieties on sale than either lentils or beans, the humble pea still stands its ground and packs a punch with its flavour... arguably more so than its legume cousins. Peas were important in the Middle Ages and even staved off famine. They may become, for future generations, a main source of protein once again.

We remember dried marrowfat peas gathering dust at the back of our mothers' kitchen cupboards. We think it was one of those larder staples that was bought but never used... and that's probably the right decision!

Chickpeas

These days, chickpeas can claim to be a staple of the British diet. Nutty in flavour and hazelnutty in shape, they are used widely in North African and Middle Eastern cooking, such as in the classic chickpea dip, houmous, and in falafel. It is of course an exaggeration to say that every Brit eats houmous every day, but it often seems to be getting that way... Chickpeas are also ground to create gram flour, used in Indian and Mediterranean cuisines to make protein-rich flatbreads such as chapatis and socca. We put chickpeas into almost all the curries we make at home, with roasted cauliflower and parsnip.

However, you have to work at a chickpea to make it tasty. Making a good houmous is quite difficult. You have to achieve the balance of acidity and spice, then there's the question of whether to add herbs. The version we make contains chilli and coriander. Many popular varieties on the market have roasted red peppers or even black olives in the mix. You must decide on your own favourite.

Split Peas

If we were forced to decide between a green split pea and a marrowfat pea, the split pea would win every time. Grey-green and mealy when cooked, marrowfats are used to make the 'mushy peas' traditionally eaten with fish and chips. Whereas split peas, as the name suggests, have had their skins removed, allowing the pea to split into its two halves. The classic British split pea and ham hock soup is one of our most comforting winter dishes. They can also be used in a variety of winter stews and soups to bulk and thicken the pot.

Pulses and Digestion

To aid digestion, many cultures cook pulses with natural stomach-soothing spices such as aniseed, coriander seed and cumin, or asafoetida, a natural (and very stinky) resin that reduces indigenous microflora in the gut (see page 372). Simply adding a small amount of any of these to the cooking water of pulses can greatly help the digestive process.

Soaking in frequently changed water prior to cooking can help to rid beans of their more indigestible, less welcome complex sugars. Cooking pulses thoroughly, until they can be easily mashed with a fork, is another way to reduce their indigestibility. Though, let's face it, who wants mushy bean salad or exploded lentils in a casserole?

Fermented beans produce fewer of these problems than unfermented beans, since the yeast produced in fermentation consumes the offending sugars, thus making Japanese miso and other eastern fermented bean preparations less hazardous for the delicate belly.

Storecupboard Stars

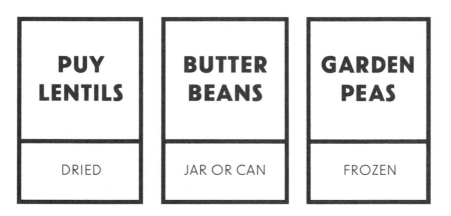

PUY LENTILS	BUTTER BEANS	GARDEN PEAS
DRIED	JAR OR CAN	FROZEN

Spiced Chickpea Salad
with Aubergines
and Roast Peppers

•••

A satisfying salad that can be eaten cold or warm and keeps well in the fridge. Excellent with barbecue food, or serve as a starter with peppered yogurt. Good-quality canned or jarred chickpeas speed up the process.

Serves 6

Ingredients

400 g canned chickpeas,
  or 200 g dried chickpeas
2 red peppers
2 yellow peppers
2 aubergines
½ tsp fennel seeds
½ tsp cumin seeds
½ tsp coriander seeds
20 g flat-leaf parsley leaves
2 tbsp light olive oil
fine sea salt
150 g Tomato and oregano
  sauce (see page 254)

Equipment

can opener
sharp knife and chopping board
frying pan
mortar and pestle
mixing bowl
oven tray

Preparation

Drain and rinse canned chickpeas, or soak and boil dried chickpeas (see page 356).

Wash all the peppers and cut into bite-sized pieces, removing seeds and stalks. Wash the aubergines and cut into bite-sized cubes, removing the stalks.

Dry-fry all the whole spices over a low heat until they start to colour.

Crush the spices in a mortar and pestle.

Wash and chop the parsley.

Preheat the oven to 200°C/400°F/gas mark 6.

Method

Place the vegetables in a mixing bowl, toss with the oil and season well with salt. Spread on an oven tray in a single layer. Roast for 15 minutes until coloured and still holding their shape.

Meanwhile, warm the tomato sauce and add the ground spices from the mortar. Cook gently for five minutes, allowing the flavours to meld.

Dress the chickpeas in the tomato sauce, then gently stir in the roasted vegetables.

Scatter with parsley and serve.

RECIPE
360

Lentil Vinaigrette

•••

A classic salad that goes well with highly seasoned sausages, or roast fish. We have added kohlrabi for a refreshing crunch, but replace it with fennel if kohlrabi is unavailable. This salad looks delightful if you take care in chopping the vegetables as finely as possible.

Serves 4

Ingredients
For the salad

200 g Puy lentils
1 carrot
1 kohlrabi
1 banana shallot
1 onion
6 sprigs of tarragon
6 sprigs of flat-leaf parsley
2 bay leaves

For the dressing

60 ml virgin olive oil
20 ml sherry vinegar
spot of Dijon mustard
sea salt and freshly ground
   black pepper

Equipment

colander
vegetable peeler
sharp knife and chopping board
saucepan

Preparation

Rinse the lentils under cold running water in a colander, then leave to drain.

Peel the carrot, kohlrabi and shallot and chop them all finely. Peel the onion, leaving the root intact, then cut into quarters.

Wash, pick the leaves and chop the tarragon and parsley.

Whisk all the dressing ingredients together, then taste and season.

Method

Cook the lentils in plenty of cold water, adding the onion and bay, for 20 minutes, until tender. Do not add any salt.

Drain the lentils and remove the herbs. While warm, dress in the vinaigrette and then add the chopped vegetables and herbs. Serve.

Summer Minestrone Soup

•••

We serve this all year, making a winter version with cavolo nero and this classic 'summerstrone'. Parmesan rind adds depth and flavour. Use a good-quality canned bean if you don't have time to soak dried beans.

Serves 4–6

Ingredients

1 carrot
1 onion
1 celery stalk
3 large garlic cloves
4 tomatoes, on the vine
1 Baby Gem lettuce
100 g dried cannellini beans, soaked overnight (see page 356), or 200 g canned beans (drained weight)
3 tbsp olive oil
1 litre Vegetable stock (see page 163)
1 leftover Parmesan rind
50 g peas, shelled weight
50 g broad beans, shelled weight
Pesto, to serve

Equipment

vegetable peeler
sharp knife and chopping board
large bowl
large saucepan

Preparation

Peel the carrot and onion, wash the celery, and chop them all finely. Peel and finely chop the garlic cloves.

Plunge the tomatoes into a bowl of boiling water for one minute, remove, slip off the skins and finely chop them, retaining the juice.

Wash the Baby Gem lettuce and separate the leaves.

Method

Drain and rinse the soaked beans, tip them into the large saucepan and cover with cold water. Cook the beans (see page 357).

Sweat the onion, carrot and celery in the oil until soft but not coloured. Add the garlic and continue to sweat for a few minutes. Stir in the tomatoes and season with salt. Add the beans, cover with the stock and add the Parmesan rind. Bring everything to the boil, then reduce the heat and cook gently for 20 minutes. Remove the Parmesan rind, then check the seasoning.

Tip in the peas and broad beans for the last few minutes of cooking so they still have bite and a good green colour. Finally add the Baby Gem lettuce.

Serve in a warmed bowl with a spoon of pesto that you should encourage diners to stir into the soup.

White Bean Salad

Dress 4 tbsp of softly cooked white beans with 1 tbsp of Sherry vinegar and shallot dressing (see page 455). Add 2 tbsp of Oven-dried tomatoes in oil (see page 330) and a handful of finely chopped parsley. Season and add a glug of olive oil if you want. Serve with grilled mackerel, or spread on hot buttered toast. Serves 4.

Butter Bean Whip

Drain and rinse a 400 g can of good-quality butter beans. Whip them in a food processor with the juice of ½ lemon, 4 tbsp of olive oil and ½ tsp of smoked paprika. Add 1 tbsp of finely chopped chives and season well. Serve with charred sourdough toast, grilled chorizo, or good-quality roast peppers from a jar.

Potted Peas

Perfect on toasts as a finger food, or with fishcakes or scallops. Place 200 g of frozen peas in a pan, pour in vegetable stock to cover and bring to the boil. Boil for five minutes, until almost all the stock has gone. Drain, then cool. Pulse-blend in a food processor with the stock, 100 g of cream cheese, a handful of mint leaves and 2 finely chopped spring onions. Season and pot into a jar. This keeps in the fridge for five days.

M

Curried Chickpea Pops

Preheat the oven to 190°C / 375°F / gas mark 5. Pat dry 400 g of cooked chickpeas. Mix 3 tbsp of olive oil, 3 minced garlic cloves, ½ tsp of curry powder, ½ tsp of chilli flakes and ½ tsp of fine sea salt and stir with the chickpeas. Spread them over a baking tray lined with baking parchment. Bake in the hot oven for 20 minutes until deep golden brown and the skins have slightly popped, stirring from time to time. Cool and serve on the same day with cocktails or cold beer.

Braised Beans

Dried beans vary in quality, so use the best you can find. Always try and soak overnight but, failing that, use the quick method (see page 356). Use plenty of water and add aromatics such as thyme, rosemary and bay. A sliced carrot can add sweetness; a celery stalk and onion gives depth. Skim any scum that floats to the surface. When they are ready, a bean should give way but hold its shape. Avoid overcooking, as they will be soggy and lose flavour. Never add salt until the beans are cooling. Cool them in the seasoned cooking liquor, adding a spoon of olive oil. Store in an airtight container in the fridge for up to a week. Serve as a side dish, or use to bulk up salads, soups or curries.

M

16

SPICES

An Introduction to Spices

Curry may well be the nation's favourite dish, but a lot of people seem to be terrified of using spices in their home cooking. You may be forgiven for thinking that spicing plays little part in traditional British cooking... and if you look towards fish and chips, the classic 'meat and two veg' and our more austere post-war culinary offerings, you could argue that was the case. Apart from in traditional Christmas sweet foods, British cooking seems to shy away from using spices to any great degree of complexity. But don't be fooled into thinking that spices don't figure at all; subtle spicing and the coaxing of flavours with carefully chosen spices is very much part of our food heritage.

We have a long history of importing spices; the 15th- to 17th-century Spice Wars' quest to conquer the world's supply of spices, among other things, defined much of the Age of Discovery. Battles were fought, fortunes won and lost and many a man risked his life to secure the trade of these most precious seeds, fruits, barks, roots and other strange dried plants. How anyone first discovered that these odd vegetal specimens actually tasted good is anyone's guess.

Spices were hugely expensive and sought-after both for their culinary and medicinal properties. They were kept for the great celebrations of the very rich; the only occasions that could justify the use of these precious, rare and expensive ingredients.

So it's not that surprising that some of our most traditional and best-loved feast foods – think Christmas cake and pudding, mince pies, mulled wine and hot cross buns for starters – all rely on a heady mix of spices. What is possibly more surprising is that a lot of the spices you find in sweet Christmas cakes and pastries are the same spices that make Jamaican jerk chicken (bar the copious scotch bonnet chillies, of course), or form the backbone of many of our much-loved curries, as well as classic savoury dishes from Africa, Asia and Central and South America.

It's no accident that every dinner table in the land is equipped with a salt and pepper pot, but what about the quintessentially British gin and tonic? London dry gin is in fact made with coriander seed, cassia bark, cinnamon, liquorice root and – of course – the main flavouring, juniper berries. What about the good old British picnic? Well, what would pickled onions be without pickling spices, or pork pies and scotch eggs without a grinding of mace? Even jellied eels have a pinch of cayenne pepper and one of our most famous condiments, Worcestershire Sauce, contains cloves.

Spices are arguably the ultimate storecupboard ingredients. They pack a serious amount of flavour but take up little space; if bought whole they have a relatively long shelf life; and most importantly you can take your cooking on a trip around the world in a couple of twists of a lid and a few grinds in a mortar and pestle.

Buyer's Guide

Spices used to be one of the most precious and expensive commodities on earth. Some, such as saffron and vanilla, still carry a fairly hefty price tag, but these days we are very lucky to be able to pick up spices at relatively low cost from anywhere from speciality food retailers, to supermarkets and even from the corner shop.

However, opting for the cheapest and most readily available isn't always the best idea. High-quality spices will carry a slightly higher price tag, but understanding their origin, and the date and method of harvest in some cases, will make a difference not only in flavour, but also in how long they can survive in your storecupboard.

Spices that have been properly treated when growing, picking and packing will last longer and have a far superior flavour. So seeking out and spending a bit more to get good-quality spices is worth every penny if you are serious about using them in your cooking repertoire.

Whole Whole spices retain more flavour and potency than ground. As with coffee beans, the seeds and pods of many spices often have a hard protective coating that conceals the essential, flavour-giving oils inside. It is only grinding that releases these oils and allows the full flavour of the spice to emerge. With a whole spice you are also more sure of what you are buying: seeing its shape, size and colour will reveal much about its quality and freshness, as will its aroma. Also, whole spices cannot be added to or adulterated in the same way as ground spices sometimes can be.

Ground Ready-ground spices have their uses, but be careful to steer clear of cheap, mass-produced ground spices, or those whose origins are unclear, as you can't be sure of their purity. Lots of ground spices contain other ingredients such as salt, flour or rice which act as anti-caking agents, but that might not be immediately obvious when buying. If you do buy ground, make sure you check the 'Spotting quality' section (see right).

Sourcing

Don't automatically head to the supermarkets with their little jars of mass-produced and rather overpriced (when you consider the quality) spices. Instead head to an ethnic grocers or market, where you will find a much wider selection of whole spices at a better price. If ethnic grocers are thin on the ground in your area, look out for specialist spice merchants, either on the high street or those trading online. Specialist food shops will often carry very good-quality spices, some organically grown.

Spotting Quality

Whether buying from an ethnic grocers, market, supermarket, spice merchant or specialist food shop, chat to the staff, ask their advice and also request to smell the spices on offer. Fresh spices give off a strong, often pungent aroma. If smelling the spices is not an option – not everyone will be happy to offer this – then be sure to check the turnover of the seller's stock and the sell-by date and, if possible, the packing date of the spices you intend to buy. Good-quality whole spices will be intact and free from dust and other debris.

Most spices are not in fact 'spicy' in the hot, fiery sense. Many people avoid spices because they fear they will burn, but true heat only really comes from peppers and chillies. Spices are better described as pungent, rather than mouth burning.

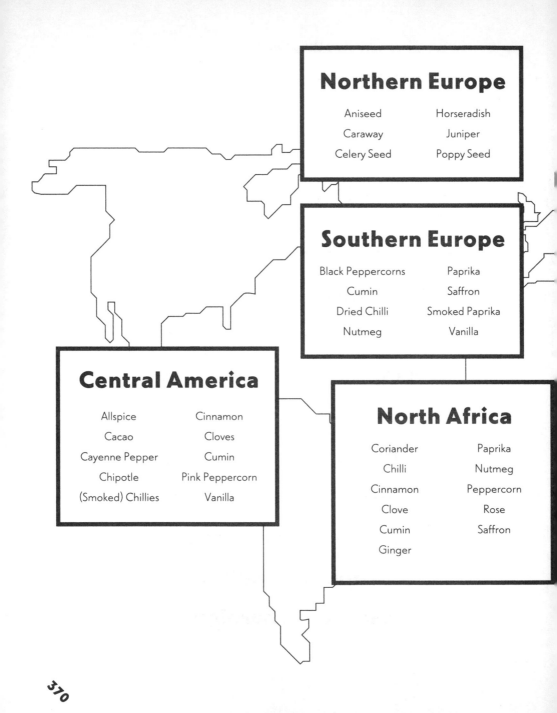

Northern Europe

Aniseed   Horseradish
Caraway   Juniper
Celery Seed   Poppy Seed

Southern Europe

Black Peppercorns   Paprika
Cumin   Saffron
Dried Chilli   Smoked Paprika
Nutmeg   Vanilla

Central America

Allspice   Cinnamon
Cacao   Cloves
Cayenne Pepper   Cumin
Chipotle   Pink Peppercorn
(Smoked) Chillies   Vanilla

North Africa

Coriander   Paprika
Chilli   Nutmeg
Cinnamon   Peppercorn
Clove   Rose
Cumin   Saffron
Ginger

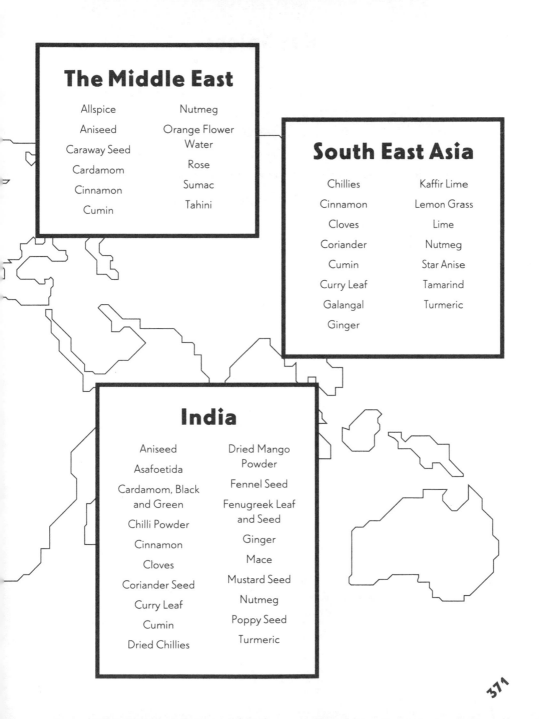

The Middle East

Allspice

Aniseed

Caraway Seed

Cardamom

Cinnamon

Cumin

Nutmeg

Orange Flower Water

Rose

Sumac

Tahini

South East Asia

Chillies

Cinnamon

Cloves

Coriander

Cumin

Curry Leaf

Galangal

Ginger

Kaffir Lime

Lemon Grass

Lime

Nutmeg

Star Anise

Tamarind

Turmeric

India

Aniseed

Asafoetida

Cardamom, Black and Green

Chilli Powder

Cinnamon

Cloves

Coriander Seed

Curry Leaf

Cumin

Dried Chillies

Dried Mango Powder

Fennel Seed

Fenugreek Leaf and Seed

Ginger

Mace

Mustard Seed

Nutmeg

Poppy Seed

Turmeric

Key Spices

•••

Botanically speaking, spices can be categorised as the dried seeds, fruits and flower buds, roots, bulbs, barks and resins of aromatic plants. Health-giving, highly flavoursome and essential to many cuisines, when used correctly spices are the cook's equivalent of the artist's paint palette, adding depth, colour and unique dimensions to food.

Allspice Also known as pimento. Used in both savoury and sweet cooking and with an aroma reminiscent of cloves, cinnamon and nutmeg, it is in fact a small berry that, when dried, looks like a smooth large black peppercorn. Often confused with mixed spice, or mistakenly thought to be a blend of 'all' spices. Its pungent fragrance makes it a favourite in Caribbean cooking.

Aniseed Liquorice-like in flavour, this tiny seed is used both in sweet foods, such as European cakes and breads, and in savoury cooking, such as Middle Eastern soups and stews. It is also thought to aid the digestion.

Asafoetida A very pungent spice used in Indian and Middle Eastern food. Made from the resin of a root from a plant in the fennel family and an acquired taste, used wisely it can give a garlicky aroma. It is often found with pulses, as it aids digestion.

Caraway Widely used by Scandinavians and middle Europeans in rye breads and as a seasoning for sauerkraut, sausages and cheese. This is also the 'seed' that is baked into old-fashioned English seed cake. Also considered a digestive aid.

Cardamom, Black Gnarly and black-brown. Not to be confused with more fragrant green cardamom, it lends an earthy, smoky fragrance to curries. It is not so well-suited for use in sweet dishes.

Cardamom, Green Bright green and fragrant, a little of this goes a long way. Most famously used in Indian curry blends and sweets, it is also widely used in Scandinavian breads and sweet pastries.

Celery Seed Tiny seeds with a strong, savoury celery flavour. Famously used to make celery salt, traditionally included in a Bloody Mary or used as a dip for boiled quail's eggs, it is also used in pickling spices.

Cinnamon Sweet, woody and versatile. In both ground and stick forms, this spice is widely used in baking, in sweet and savoury dishes and as a key component in a lot of preserving. A close relative is the bark from the cassia tree, which can be used in place of true cinnamon in cooking.

Cloves Pungent and sweet tasting, these dried unopened flower buds are essential to festive baking, and are key components in mulled wine, mincemeat and baked ham. Use sparingly to get the best from their fragrance without overpowering other ingredients. Cloves have a curious numbing effect and were used in dentistry to numb pain before anaesthetics were available.

Coriander Seed The small round or oval seeds of the coriander herb. They impart a citrussy, warm note and, when dry-toasted, give off a nutty fragrance. A key component in Indian cuisine where it is often paired with cumin seeds, it is also used widely across Africa, Central Europe and Russia and features as an aromatic in some Belgian beers. Oval-shaped Indian coriander is thought to be superior to the rounder Moroccan variety.

Cumin Seed Earthy and woody in flavour, the small brown seeds are a key part of Indian garam masala, as well as widely used in Mexican cooking. It partners very well with coriander seeds. Toasting brings out its character and warmth as a spice.

Fennel Seed Pale green seeds with a soft anise-like flavour, fennel goes well with fish and is a classic in Italian sausage and pork dishes. Like its anise-flavoured cousin aniseed, fennel can aid digestion.

Fenugreek Yellow-amber seeds used widely in food across the whole Indian subcontinent. Pungent, bitter-sweet and very savoury in character, they should be used in moderation to get the best from their distinctly 'curry-like' flavour.

Ground Ginger When powdered and dried, ginger takes on a new characteristic: still strong and pungent but with a curious sweetness not found in the fresh root.

Juniper Berries The classic flavour of gin, these bitter-sweet dried black berries marry very well with rich meat and game; they are classically paired with venison and rabbit.

Long Pepper Sometimes known as pipali, this flowering vine fruit is related to black, white and green peppercorns but is stronger and hotter in flavour and in shape resembles dry, dark brown catkins. A key component in many Indian, Indonesian and North African spice mixtures.

Mace The outer casing of nutmeg, this is most commonly found ground but the whole 'blades' can also be bought; they resemble pale strands of shoe leather. Similar in flavour to nutmeg, but with a more delicate fragrance.

Mustard Seed Strong and spicy, these make mustards: the peppery English, several French incarnations and the yellow American variety. The whole seeds are used in Indian cooking and in pickling spices.

Nutmeg This hard oval nut comes from the same tree that produces mace. Sweeter and more aromatic than mace, it is mostly used for baking cakes and puddings and is a key component in English custard tarts, though it has savoury uses in classic white sauces and bread sauce, too.

Peppercorns The most universally used spice, true pepper has nothing to do with the chilli or capsicum family, but is the berry of the *Piper nigrum* shrub. Bought as black peppercorns, the ripening and spiciest berries; white peppercorns, ripened on the vine and soaked to remove their outer black casing; or green peppercorns, unripe berries often found preserved or used fresh in vibrant South East Asian dishes.

Pink Peppercorns No relation to black, white or green peppercorns, these bright pink berries are the dried fruit of the Peruvian pepper tree. Peppery and fruity, they add an interesting pungency to both savoury and sweet cooking.

Saffron The world's most expensive spice; pricier by weight than gold. Saffron is the stigma of *Crocus sativus*, painstakingly harvested and dried by hand. The bright orange strands impart a spicy, woody fragrance to Middle Eastern cooking and are also widespread in Europe; famously used in bouillabaisse and paella.

Sichuan Peppercorns No relation to the black pepper family, pink peppercorns or chillies, these small dried seed husks are used whole in Asian cooking and ground as part of Chinese five spice, imparting a hot, pungent, mouth-numbing quality when used in even small quantities.

Star Anise Brown star-shaped seed pods with a strong anise-like flavour. Used predominantly in Asian cuisine, it is a chef's secret ingredient: when used as a marinade or as part of a slow-cooking liquor, it adds an undetectable richness to any meat.

Sumac Dark purple-red in colour, this is the dried ground berries of the sumac tree. Used predominantly in Middle Eastern cooking to add a zingy, lemony flavour to vegetable and meat dishes, it is also a key component of the spice blend za'atar.

Tamarind The dried fruit of the tamarind tree, used for its fruity souring effect. Used extensively across Asia as a souring agent in place of, or alongside, lime to create balance in curries.

Turmeric Most commonly bought in its ground form, this bright orange spice is a root related to ginger. Used for medicinal purposes in Ayurvedic cooking because of its natural antiseptic properties, it has a mildly aromatic flavour, but can turn bitter in anything other than small quantities. Strong orange in colour, it can also be bought as a fresh root for grating from Asian supermarkets, resembling smaller, thinner pieces of root ginger.

Vanilla The long, sticky dried seed pods of a tropical orchid, vanilla's sweet perfume is one of the most familiar and comforting to us and is used in cakes, custards, biscuits and ice cream. Buy the pods whole, or as a good-quality extract or paste containing the prized black seeds. Avoid anything called 'essence', which is not the real thing.

Curries are often blamed
for causing tummy aches, but many spices,
rather than being bad for digestion,
are in fact positively beneficial to it.
Fennel and aniseed are very good
digestive aids, ginger counteracts nausea,
turmeric is a natural antiseptic and
anti-inflammatory, cinnamon helps regulate
blood sugar levels, coriander seed eases
gastro-intestinal spasms, cumin is the
virtual 'cure all' with its digestive qualities,
antioxidant, stress-relieving and
cholesterol-fighting properties and
nigella seed has been said since
ancient times to 'cure all diseases except
death' (and modern medicine is increasingly
finding evidence of its worth).

BHUT JOLOKIA

Scoville Scale 1,000,000

HABANERO

100,000–200,000

CAYENNE

30,000–50,000

CHILE DE ARBOL

10,000–23,000

CHIPOTLE

3,500–10,000

PAPRIKA

100–900

Chillies

•••

There are hundreds of varieties of chillies, far too many to mention in this book. However, here are a few dried chillies that you might encounter and some that are worth looking out for:

Aleppo Sweet medium-heat chilli flakes from Turkey. Bright red in colour, with lots of flavour without burning heat.

Ancho A Mexican chilli, central to the country's traditional mole. Fruity and rounded, they have a mild heat.

Bhut Jolokia One of the hottest chillies in the world, these hail from Assam in northern India. They are surprisingly fresh and citrussy alongside the searing heat.

Bird's Eye Chilli Small and tapered, these are very hot indeed. Used most often in Thai cooking, where the seeds are left in and the chilli often left whole.

Cayenne Pepper A fiery powder made from dried cayenne chillies. It has little aroma but lots of heat. Anything 'devilled' has usually been spiced with cayenne.

Chile de Arbol Small, hot and earthy, these Mexican chillies are used to make oils or crumbled directly on to cooked meat.

Chilli Flakes Crushed dried chillies chosen for their heat, from various sources unless the jar specifies an origin or variety.

Chilli Powder A blend of different dried ground chilli peppers, so spiciness can vary.

Chipotle Mexican dried smoked peppers with a lovely smoky heat.

Habanero Caribbean bursts of heat, these smallish teardrop-shaped chillies are prized for their fruitiness and fire.

Kashmiri One of the most prized Indian chillies, for its warming rather than searing heat and also the wonderful red-orange colour it imparts. Essential to achieve the correct colour for tandoori chicken.

Long Thai Very hot and with a certain sharpness, these smallish thin, red chillies are used to make soups and curry pastes.

Paprika Associated with Spanish cooking, where it's known as pimenton, as well as in Hungarian food, where it's the key spice in goulash. It can be made from any number of dried powdered capsicums and can be anything from sweet to very hot.

Pequin Miniature fire bombs, these Mexican favourites are seriously hot, but the heat quickly dissipates on the palate to leave a nutty fruitiness.

Urfa Black-red in colour and mild and smoky in flavour, these Turkish chilli flakes can be sprinkled on to salads, houmous and dips as well as used in stews.

Classic Spice Blends

•••

Baharat A Turkish blend of paprika, cassia, black pepper, cumin, coriander, cloves and nutmeg. Earthy and warming, it makes a good rub for chicken, lamb or beef before grilling. It also pairs very well with aubergine: a pinch in a roasted aubergine dip with garlic would be excellent as part of a mezze.

Berbere A hot Ethiopian blend of cumin, coriander, black pepper, chilli, ginger, paprika, fenugreek, allspice, cloves, cardamom and cinnamon. Used like garam masala (see right).

Chaat Masala A salty, sour, spicy blend used in India to season vegetables, salads and fruit, typically containing amchur (dried mango powder), black pepper, cumin, coriander, ginger, mint, asofoetida and salt.

Chermoula This Moroccan blend is used predominantly with fish, but also with white meat and vegetables. It usually contains cumin, coriander, garlic, onion, parsley, coriander leaves, cayenne, black pepper and salt. This is a wet spice blend which needs to be made fresh each time.

Chinese Five Spice The name is often only symbolic and the blend can contain many more than five ingredients, including Sichuan pepper, cinnamon, star anise, nutmeg, cloves, fennel and ginger.

Curry Powder Much like the word 'curry', the idea of this is British rather than Indian and it is not authentic in the subcontinent. Typically containing turmeric, coriander, cumin, chilli and ginger, it comes in strengths from mild to very hot.

Dukkah An Egyptian blend of hazelnuts, sesame, coriander and cumin seeds, black pepper, paprika, cayenne and salt. Used as a snack where flatbread is dipped in olive oil and then dukkah, which sticks to the oily bread. It's very good sprinkled over thick yogurt with chilli and oil to accompany grilled fish, or used to coat chicken or halloumi before being fried and thrown into a salad.

Garam Masala The classic north Indian spice blend, typically of cumin, coriander, black cardamom, ginger, cinnamon, cloves, mace, bay and nutmeg. Used whole, the spices are fried in oil or ghee before onions are sweated to create a base for the curry. Then it is sprinkled over a finished dish in its powdered form to give a fresh hit of spice.

Harissa A fiery North African blend often using rose petals to add fragrance and complexity, it is chiefly comprised of paprika, chilli, caraway, coriander, cumin, garlic, mint and salt. A wet spice paste which serves as a very good marinade for meat and fish, or just as a hot condiment. Blended with yogurt, it is mellowed and together they act as a very good tenderiser.

Jerk Seasoning Very hot and highly aromatic, this Jamaican blend typically contains cinnamon, coriander seeds and leaves, black pepper, nutmeg, allspice berries, thyme, garlic, ginger, scotch bonnet peppers and lime. It is particularly good with pork and chicken. The term 'jerk' reflects a style of cooking using both a dry rub and a wet marinade with spices.

Mixed Spice A British sweet spice blend mostly used in baking and traditional puddings, this typically contains cinnamon, nutmeg, allspice, ginger, cloves and sometimes cassia and cardamom.

Mulling Spices The sweet mixture, usually containing cloves, cinnamon and nutmeg, used to create mulled wine, cider and wassail, drunk at Christmas.

Panch Phoran Often referred to as Bengali five spice, this blends cumin, fennel, nigella seeds, mustard seeds and fenugreek. The seeds are left whole rather than being ground and are used at the start of a curry, or to coat pieces of meat, fish or paneer before roasting or grilling.

Pickling Spices The basis of pickled onions, beetroots and eggs. It most often contains a mixture of cinnamon, chilli, yellow and black mustard seeds, allspice, coriander seed, peppercorns, dill seed, fennel seed, celery seed, cloves, mace and bay leaves, but could include any spices that you would like to flavour your pickles.

Ras El Hanout This is a hot, sweet blend of paprika, cumin, ginger, coriander, turmeric, black pepper, fennel, allspice, cassia, cardamom, galangal, nutmeg, long pepper, bay, caraway, cayenne, cloves, mace, black cardamom and sometimes rose petals, lavender and saffron. Its literal translation – 'top of the shop' – reflects the quality of the ingredients used.

Quatre Épices A staple of French kitchens, usually containing a mixture of peppercorns, nutmeg, cloves and ginger. Often found in charcuterie and sausages, it is also used in soups, vegetable dishes and sweet cakes.

Shichimi Togarashi A spicy Japanese blend dating back to the 17th century, with black and white sesame seeds, dried orange zest, chilli powder, ginger, dried nori and Japanese sancho pepper.

Za'atar Used across the Middle East and North Africa, this usually contains thyme, toasted sesame seeds, sumac and salt, but can also contain marjoram, oregano and savory. Used to flavour breads, to top houmous and labneh, and as a seasoning for vegetable and meat dishes.

Whole spices should last a year if kept in the right conditions, but spices such as nutmeg and allspice all have a protective outer shell which helps to prevent exposure to oxygen, thereby keeping them fresher for longer

Airtight glass jars, plastic containers or tins are best for preserving spices' essential oils and therefore flavours and aromas

Ground spices should be used immediately for best results, but can remain relatively fresh for a couple of months if kept airtight and cool

If you have a glut of oil-rich spices such as mustard seeds, then freeze them in well-sealed containers to prevent the oils from turning rancid

Spice Flavour Spectrum

Understandably, many people feel a certain lack of confidence about cooking with spices, because they feel a bit daunted by what to use where and which spice goes with what. Spices have a huge range of flavours, aromas and levels of pungency, both individually and even more so when employed in spice blends.

Broadly speaking, spices can fall into various flavour profiles; from woody to sweet, aromatic to floral, heating to bitter. Understanding these flavour profiles better can help the home cook know a bit more about how to employ spices to marry with and best bring out the flavour in their food.

There are of course some classic marriages of flavour, but there are no hard and fast rules. Spicing is a very individual thing and, once you start to get a bit of a handle on different spice flavours and characteristics, you can really start to find out what you like and become creative in the kitchen.

Storecupboard Stars

Good all-rounders in their own right, these spices are interchangeable in any combination: cumin and cinnamon give warmth, chilli and coriander give citrussy heat... Each works well with a wide variety of meat, fish, pulses, vegetables and dairy products. Cinnamon can be used in both savoury and sweet dishes, complementing anything from chocolate, orchard fruits and bread to pulses and game birds.

	EARTHY	WARM WOODY	WARM SWEET	HEATING FIERY	HEATING NUMBING
Cumin	●	●			
Black Cardamom	●	○			
Allspice	○	●	●		
Smoked Dried Chilli		●	○	●	
Smoked Paprika	○	●	○	●	
Cinnamon		●	●		
Dried Ginger	●	○	●		○
Mace			●		
Nutmeg	●		●		
Cloves		○	●		●
Cayenne Pepper				●	
Dried Chilli				●	
Paprika			●	●	
Black Peppercorn		●		●	
Green Peppercorn				●	
White Peppercorn	●			●	
Sichuan Peppercorn				○	●
Asafoetida					
Mustard Seed				○	
Aniseed			○		
Caraway Seed					
Fennel Seed			○		
Star Anise		○	●		
Green Cardamom			●		
Saffron		●			
Vanilla			●		
Juniper Berries	○				
Tamarind					
Coriander Seed		●			
Turmeric		●			

SPICES

● Dominant flavour   ● Secondary flavour   ○ Tertiary flavour

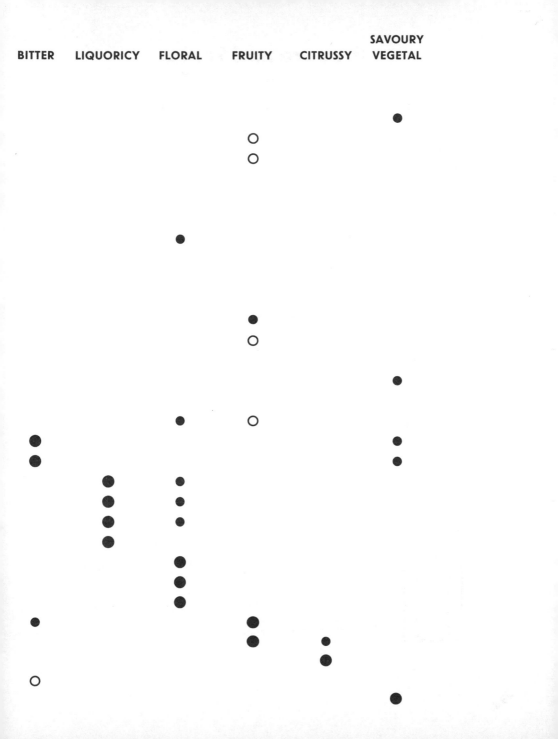

BITTER   LIQUORICY   FLORAL   FRUITY   CITRUSSY   SAVOURY
VEGETAL

Prepare and Serve

•••

Dry-frying Most whole spices benefit from gentle heating to release their essential oils, thus producing the greatest amount of flavour and aroma for your cooking. Apart from filling your kitchen with wonderful fragrances, the added benefit is that lightly toasted spices are easier to grind by hand.

To toast or dry-fry spices, heat a heavy-based frying pan over a medium heat, add the spices and keep them moving in the pan until they start to turn a shade or two darker and smell nutty and toasted. Whatever you do, don't take your eyes off the pan; it takes less than a minute to toast spices and they can turn from toasted to burned and acrid in seconds. (Adding whole spices to a pan of hot oil will also release their essential oils.)

Grinding There are several ways to grind spices. We keep a mortar and pestle, a Microplane and a small coffee grinder dedicated to spices near our spice drawer so we can turn to them at a moment's notice.

The time-honoured tradition of hand pulverising is thought by many to be the best way to grind spices. It's certainly great for small amounts of spices as it is instant, no faff and a mortar is easy to clean.

For larger amounts, or if you are grinding tough items such as cinnamon, cassia or nutmeg, an electric grinder is what you need. The important thing is to dedicate a grinder to your spices and not use it for anything else; who wants their morning cup of coffee tainted with last night's curry?

For grating small amounts of hard nutmeg, cassia and cinnamon, a Microplane comes in very handy. You don't want to get the electric grinder out for a couple of scrapes of nutmeg, for example. They are also invaluable for grating root ginger, garlic and chillies for making spice pastes, so are well worth the investment.

Store and Preserve

Nearly all of us are guilty of hanging on to spices for too long... who doesn't have a lonely, fusty old packet or two of half-opened something or other hidden up on the top shelf of a kitchen cupboard? The fact is that spices, especially ground spices, lose their pungency, aroma and colour fairly quickly and so need to be used up or discarded quite regularly.

If you really want to incorporate spices into your cooking, you need to have them ready at hand and easily accessible at all times. It's no wonder that that old packet of cinnamon is still sitting half-opened at the top of the cupboard five years past its use-by date if you can't see it.

If you have the space, dedicate a drawer to your spices near your cooker, but not so near that the heat from it has the chance to spoil the delicate essential oils contained in the precious spice. Use small clear plastic or glass pots with tight-fitting lids and store them upside down so you can clearly see which spice is which when you slide open the drawer.

If you don't have a drawer you can dedicate to spices, then keep the clear pots in a basket in a cupboard at eye level, so you can easily reach them and can't forget they are there.

Making Your Own Spice Mixes

•••

Spices are already the most brilliant storecupboard stars. Used individually they can transform your cooking, but when combined you have at your fingertips the makings of complex dishes with serious depth of flavour.

Dry Spice Blends

Having a few dry spice blends to hand in the kitchen is a brilliant shortcut to creating real spark in your cooking in seconds. Spice blends can be used as dry rubs and marinades, added to oil and citrus to create an instant wet marinade, used as a baste for barbecued meat and fish, added to dressings, sprinkled over salads, soups, dips... The list goes on. The beauty of making your own blends means that you can tweak them to your heart's content. Most importantly you know what's in them and how fresh they are, which is crucial if you want to get the most out of a spice's flavours and health benefits. Here are some favourites that we keep on hand at home:

Five Spice

In a dry frying pan over a low heat, toast 1 tsp of black peppercorns and 2 tsp of fennel seeds for a few minutes until their oils are released (you will smell their delicious fragrances).

In a mortar and pestle or a spice grinder, crush the pepper and fennel with 6 star anise and 4 cloves. Mix with 2 tsp of ground cinnamon. This makes 40 g and will keep in an airtight jar for a month.

Use to season pork, duck or chicken dishes.

A Spice Mix to Coat, Dip and Sprinkle

A mixture of ground coriander seed, cumin, chilli flakes and sea salt. Sprinkle over salad, add to houmous or yogurt dips, coat balls of labneh or slices of halloumi, or sprinkle over cooked meat, fish and vegetables.

Use this mix as a base and add to it: try crunchy toasted almonds, crushed pumpkin seeds and sesame seeds; pulverised herbs such as oregano, thyme or rosemary; or crushed garlic and lemon zest to give you different ways to spice up your supper.

Curry Standby, Garam Masala

•••

There are so many recipes for garam masala that it's impossible to give anything definitive. Balance is key, but like anything it is down to personal taste. This is the one we like to make, but use it as a base and have a play around with different flavours and levels of spicing. Garam masala is most often used alongside a myriad of other spices, but think of it as a sort of home-made (and far superior) curry powder upon which to base your curry making.

Ingredients

⅓ whole nutmeg
1 medium cinnamon stick
1 tbsp cumin seeds
1 tbsp coriander seeds
1 tbsp black peppercorns
1 tsp cloves
1 tsp black cardamom pods
1 tsp green cardamom pods

Equipment

rolling pin
frying pan
sharp knife and chopping board

Method

Wrap the nutmeg in a tea towel and crack it into small pieces with a rolling pin. Break the cinnamon into smallish pieces by hand.

Toast everything except the green cardamom pods in a dry frying pan, very gently, until they turn a couple of shades darker (see page 384). Remove from the heat and allow to cool.

Split the green cardamom pods with a small knife and prise out the seeds with your fingers, then mix them into the other toasted spices.

Seal in an airtight jar or pot, keep it on hand and grind fresh as you need it. Or grind a small quantity, just enough to fill a small pot with a tight-fitting lid, which you know you will use up in a month or two. If you keep it any longer, the flavour will start to diminish.

Successful curry making is about using whole and ground spices together, so keeping a jar of each to hand will mean you are always prepared and ready to go.

Curry-making Technique

•••

Curries are about creating layers of flavour: spices are used whole and ground and added at different times to achieve this. They are generally slow-cooked dishes, with melting, soft meat. If you want something in a hurry then opt for fish, which cooks in minutes, or vegetables or pulses. Rather than give a recipe, we have given suggestions for technique that will allow you to experiment confidently with curry making at home.

Gently fry a couple of teaspoons of whole garam masala spices in light-flavoured oil.

Make a paste with a medium onion in a blender, or just finely slice it, and spend time cooking it slowly in your hot spiced oil with a pinch of salt. The length of time you spend on this and the colour you decide to take your onions to greatly affects the flavour of the curry.

Make a ginger, garlic and fresh or dried chilli paste (the blender comes in handy for this) and fry 1 heaped tbsp or so gently in your softened caramelised spiced onions; it should smell fragrant and rounded. (You can also blitz a handful of herbs such as coriander or mint with the ginger paste if you want another flavour dimension.)

Add some ground garam masala, letting 1 tsp or so cook out in the fragrant paste,

creating a further layer of flavour. If you want a wet curry with a lot of gravy, add some water, stock or coconut milk, followed by the meat, fish or vegetables, which should gently poach in the sauce. If you want a dry coating curry, then simply add your meat, fish or vegetables straight to the paste. In both cases cook gently, covered, so it doesn't dry out, adding a little water from time to time if it needs it.

Towards the end of cooking, ask yourself: is there enough sweetness, saltiness, sourness, heat? You want a balance, so add sugar, salt, lime juice or tamarind, or chilli to taste.

To finish the curry, add 1 tsp of ground garam masala. Strew with herbs such as coriander or mint. Once you perfect this technique, you can introduce more spices into your curry making, either alongside garam masala or on their own.

Spice Pastes

•••

These are a combination of dried spices with fresh herbs and aromatics that are used as a base, most often for curries, but we like to use them as the foundation for deeply flavoured casseroles, as well as to marinate meat and fish before grilling or barbecuing. Highly flavoured and often spicy, these pastes are an incredible way to deliver flavour.

As they are a wet mix containing fresh and dried ingredients, they have a shorter shelf life than dry spice blends and should be kept chilled, covered with a film of oil, if they are not to be used immediately, though should ideally be made fresh each time. You can also freeze small pots of spice paste. The paste can go straight into the pot over the heat.

Making Fresh Spice Pastes

Really good spice pastes are perfectly merged together to create real complexity. This is a good argument for making your paste in a mortar and pestle instead of a food processor or blender. Pounding each ingredient by hand before adding the next means that each ingredient's essential oils can be released, allowing them to absorb the next flavour properly. It can also be an immensely satisfying and grounding way to cook.

Of course, this is fine if you are making supper for two and have time on your hands. When that's not the case, we don't think there is anything wrong with using a food processor to help, though the ingredients will only be finely chopped, leaving them rather more separate – and therefore the flavours less melded – than if you pound them by hand.

A quick short cut (if you don't mind a little extra washing up) would be to blitz your ingredients in the food processor, then transfer to a mortar and pestle for a quick bash to better meld the ingredients before using.

Aromatic Moroccan Spice Paste

1 tsp chilli flakes

1 tsp toasted cumin seeds
(see page 384)

1 tsp toasted coriander seeds
(see page 384)

½ tsp toasted caraway seeds
(see page 384)

3 cloves of garlic

1 tbsp chopped mint leaves

1 tbsp chopped parsley leaves

2 tsp thyme leaves

finely grated zest of ½ lemon

2 Oven-dried tomatoes
(see page 330)

3 tbsp olive oil

⅛ tsp salt

This is like a merging of harissa and chermoula, both classic Moroccan sauces. Use it as the base for a marinade for slow-roast lamb shoulder and add a spoon to some thick Greek yogurt to serve with flatbread alongside. Makes 2 good rounded tbsp of paste or enough to generously coat 4 pieces of salmon or 2 large pork chops, or to lightly coat a whole chicken.

M

All-round Rub

1 tsp cumin seed

1 tsp fennel seed

1 tsp coriander seed

1 tsp dried oregano

1 tsp black peppercorns

1 tsp paprika

4 star anise

50 g sea salt

50 g soft brown sugar

Toast the spices in a hot dry pan for a few minutes
to release their flavours, then cool and blitz in a spice
grinder. This will keep for a month in a sealed
container and is great with chicken, pork or duck.

M

Pickling Spice Bag

To pickle 1 litre of vinegar, use 25 g of spice. The spice
should be a mixture of coriander seed, fennel seed,
black peppercorns, allspice berries, cloves, bay leaves,
mace blades and cinnamon sticks. Tie in a muslin
cloth, secure with butcher's string and anchor around
the handle of the pickling pot.

M

Spiced Salts

•••

Flavouring salts with spices and aromatics is a great way to add extra flavour dimensions to your, now bursting, panoply of storecupboard reserves. Only a dusting of salt provides fantastic crunch, texture and bursts of flavour when sprinkled over cooked meat, fish and vegetables.

Of course there are many pre-made versions on the market these days, all promising to deliver unique and wonderful things. But they are often hugely expensive and most can easily be made at home with a few simple ingredients, a mortar and pestle and some small jars. Here are some pointers to ensure you get the best from flavouring salt at home:

Flaky sea salt is best used here as it retains its own texture and crunch. Experiment with toasting spices, to bring out their nuttiness, and with the coarseness of the grind to give different textures and flavours.

Salt is a natural abrasive. Simply grind a small amount with flavourings until you get a texture you like – something nubbly with mixed-sized pieces gives the most flavour and texture – then mix through more flaky salt.

Salt is a preservative, so you can happily use small amounts of fresh herbs and citrus zests along with your spices, as long as you don't mind the salt clumping. If you prefer it more free-flowing, simply dry fresh ingredients on the lowest setting of your oven for a few hours before grinding.

Flavoured salts will keep indefinitely but fade in flavour over time. Fresh ingredients have more volatile essential oils which can lose flavour more easily than dried, so keep your flavoured salts in a well-sealed jar.

Home-made Spiced Salts

Sweet and Warming

Cinnamon
Cumin
Nutmeg
Allspice

Good with lamb, chicken, rice and couscous.

Floral and Aromatic

Fennel Seed
Saffron
Lemon Zest

Good with white fish, shellfish and chicken.

Warming and Earthy

Cumin
Allspice
Smoked Chilli
Thyme

Good with barbecued and slow-cooked meats, root vegetables, pulses and beans.

Fruity and Citrussy

Coriander Seeds
Orange Zest
Pink Peppercorns

Good with chicken, milky cheeses such as mozzarella, yogurt marinades and dressings.

Zesty and Piquant

Dill Seed
Lime Zest
Pink Peppercorns

Good with oily fish,
such as a whole roasted side
of salmon or trout.

Sweet and Warming

Mixed Dried
and
Smoked Chillies
Chipotle
Serrano
Ancho

Good with lamb, chicken,
rice and couscous.

Layered Heat

Black,
White and
Sichuan
Peppercorns

Good with beef, pork
and mushrooms.

Brunch Essential

Celery Seeds

Good with
Bloody Marys
and eggs

Coronation Chicken

•••

When Queen Elizabeth came to the throne in 1953 she was given this dish at her banquet. It was created by Constance Spry and Rosemary Hume, both principals of the Cordon Bleu school at the time. We have used it in salads over crisp Baby Gem leaves and finely chopped peppers and also in sandwiches between two slices of nutty multigrain bread.

Serves 4

Ingredients

600 g free-range chicken, roasted
100 g raisins
175 ml apple juice
25 g coconut flakes
3 shallots
5 cm root ginger
1 tbsp vegetable oil
1 tbsp medium curry powder
150 g passata
150 g yogurt
150 g mayonnaise
juice of ½ lemon
coriander leaves, to serve

Equipment

sharp knife and chopping board
baking tray
grater
1 small non-stick saucepan
juicer

Preparation

Shred the chicken. Soak the raisins in the apple juice until plump, while you get on with the recipe. Preheat the oven to 160°C/325°F/gas mark 3, spread the coconut flakes on a baking tray and toast them for five minutes, or until they start to turn golden brown.

Finely chop the shallots and peel and grate the ginger.

Method

Make the sauce. Fry the shallots in the vegetable oil in a small non-stick saucepan for a few minutes until they soften. Add the curry powder, ginger and passata and cook gently for 15 minutes until the flavours have been released and the sauce has reduced to a paste. Set aside to cool.

Once cooled, stir in the yogurt, mayonnaise and lemon juice. Stir and adjust the seasoning. Coat the chicken with the sauce, then drain the raisins and stir them in.

Sprinkle with the coconut flakes and coriander leaves.

RECIPE
395

Preserved Lemons

•••

We use this aromatic ingredient in our lamb tagine to give an authentic burst of deep citrus. You can also use them very finely chopped over salads by removing the flesh and just using the intensely flavoured skin; we add a little to our winter version of tabbouleh.

Makes 1 x 1-litre jar

Ingredients

6 unwaxed lemons
rock salt (the amount you need depends on the size of the lemons, but you will need a generous amount)
1 tsp coriander seeds
4 bay leaves
1 tsp pink peppercorns
6 cloves

Equipment

1 x 1-litre wide jar with lid
sharp knife and chopping board
juicer

Preparation

Wash and sterilise 1 x 1-litre wide jar and its lid (see page 408).

Wash the lemons.

Method

Cut three of the lemons in half and juice them. Roll the other three lemons under your hand to help soften them and release juice.

Cut each of the three whole lemons into 12, slicing from top to bottom. Pack the sliced lemons into the jar in layers, with the rock salt, lemon juice and spices, until full.

Seal and leave in a cool place. Try them after one month: the skins should now be soft and fragrant. They will keep for up to 12 months but, once the jar has been opened, keep it refrigerated.

Cardamom and Pistachio Cake

•••

Once upon a time we employed a very talented Swedish pastry chef called Daniel who introduced cardamom as a key flavour to our sweet pastries. The customers' reaction was unanimous: they adored it. This wheat-free cake has remained a favourite.

Makes 1 x 20 cm cake

Ingredients
For the cake

180 g unsalted butter, plus more for the tin
1 unwaxed lemon
200 g golden caster sugar
3 eggs, lightly beaten
60 g pistachios, plus more to serve
150 g ground almonds
100 g polenta
3 g cardamom seeds
1 tsp baking powder

For the icing

1 tbsp lemon juice
100 g icing sugar

Equipment

20 cm round cake tin
baking parchment
zester and juicer
food processor
large bowl
wire rack

Preparation

Butter a 20 cm round cake tin and line the base and sides with baking parchment. Zest and juice the lemon. Preheat the oven to 180°C/350°F/gas mark 4.

Method

Blend the butter, lemon zest and sugar in a food processor until smooth, or cream them together with an electric mixer. Add the eggs a little at a time, whizzing or beating between additions, until incorporated.

Mix the pistachios, almonds, polenta, cardamom and baking powder in a bowl. Add to the food processor and pulse-blend to combine, or beat in with the electric mixer. Add the lemon juice.

Bake in the prepared tin for 35 minutes in the centre of the oven. Remove from the oven, leave to cool in the tin for a few minutes, then turn out on to a wire rack and leave to cool completely.

To make the icing, whisk the lemon juice and icing sugar together and use to drench the cake. Finish with a sprinkling of ground pistachios.

Chilli Jam

•••

This is a simple preserve to make; the only secret is not to overcook it. The condiment won't set like a jam as there is no pectin, so use your judgement and keep tasting as it cooks and reduces. It's a full-flavoured preserve so will go well with many dishes, from stir-fries and curries to mild soft young goat's cheeses.

Makes 5 x 200 ml jars

Ingredients

125 g garlic cloves
125 g root ginger
1.25 kg tomatoes
60 g medium-hot red chillies
825 g granulated sugar
30 ml red wine vinegar
½ tbsp sea salt
2 tbsp Worcestershire sauce

Equipment

vegetable peeler
sharp knife and chopping board
box grater
5 x 200 ml jam jars with lids
food processor
large saucepan

Preparation

Peel and mince the garlic.

Peel and grate the ginger.

Wash and sterilise 5 x 200 ml jam jars (see page 408).

Method

Blitz the tomatoes and chillies in a food processor until smooth. Scoop them into a saucepan with all the other ingredients and bring slowly to the boil, stirring to dissolve the sugar.

Cook for about one hour, stirring more frequently at the later stages, until the chilli jam has thickened and is a good colour.

Decant it into the sterilised jars, store in a cool dry spot and consume within six months.

Whole Grain
Honey Mustard

Mix 40 g black mustard seeds with 40 g yellow mustard seeds and pound them in a mortar and pestle. Cover with tarragon vinegar, 2 tbsp strong honey and a pinch of salt and leave to steep for a week in a covered bowl. Drain off the excess liquid, stir and pot into a sterilised jar (see page 408). Leave to mature for three months. The mustard will keep for a further six months in a cool spot.

M

Spice Grinder

Fill your pepper grinder with black, white, pink and green peppercorns and Sichuan pepper. Play with the ratios until you have the right balance. White pepper has a floral note while Sichuan is intensely zesty.

M

Five Spiced Butters

...

To 125 g of soft salted butter add 1 tsp each of
the following freshly ground spices.
Form into a roll, cut into about 12 portions and
store in the fridge or freezer.

1

Nutmeg, cinnamon and dried chilli, to finish
off roasted pumpkin dishes such as risotto

2

Ground fennel seeds, celery seeds
and lemon zest, to fry fish

3

Cardamom seed, turmeric and fenugreek
seed, as a base for spiced rice or curries

4

Green pepper, black pepper and white pepper,
to melt over meats such as sirloin of beef

5

Caraway seed, nigella seed and
orange zest, to glaze carrots

17

SUGAR AND SYRUPS

An Introduction to Sugar and Syrups

For many of us, there is a certain nostalgic romance that surrounds sugary things. Not simply because of childhood memories of the post-school sweet shop dash – pocket money in hand – and visions of rows of glass jars filled with delightfully coloured boiled sweets.

We are born with a sweet tooth, and youth, most often, does nothing to diminish that. Thankfully a passion for mouth-twisting sugar hits is (usually) replaced by something a little more sedate. Our advice is to seek out the very best-quality raw, unrefined sugars you can find and avoid anything over-processed. Not only does this make nutritional sense, it will reward you in the enjoyment of eating as well. Choose your sweetener wisely for the job in hand and learn a few tricks to use it subtly – to bring out the flavour in food and drink rather than to drown it – and you will be even more rewarded for your efforts.

Much has been written about the sugar we eat today. When researching the subject, you start to question why we became so addicted to sugar when it plays little – if any – part in our daily dietary needs. All sugar does is sweeten. White sugar has no flavour at all. So are those of us with a sweet tooth doomed?

As in all things, moderation is key. Sugar only starts to do harm when it is eaten in large quantities. A big dietary villain is the highly refined sugar hidden in processed foods. Any trip down a supermarket ready-meal aisle will soon reveal some surprising examples. Would you like some sugar with your spaghetti bolognese, sir...? How about in your plain cooked prawns? Stomach-churning it may be, but the undeniable truth is that sugar sells. Avoiding these processed foods is an important step for your health... and for your enjoyment of meals.

Cane Sugar

The most common form of sugar in use today. The tall, jointed stalks of sugar cane – actually a grass – can be found in warm temperate-to-tropical regions. It has a chequered history, predominantly due to the large-scale use of slave labour to cultivate and harvest the crop in the 18th and 19th centuries. Today it is an important world commodity that provides some countries with a large proportion of their revenue.

Once the crop has been harvested, a liquid is extracted from the cane before undergoing a series of refinement processes to give a variety of sugars. It's most commonly sold as white table sugar, but is also the starting point for muscovado, golden and molasses sugars.

Beet Sugar

Another plant that can be refined to produce white sugar. It tastes no different from white sugar produced from cane, as its make-up is exactly the same: pure fructrose. The main difference is that only white sugar can be naturally produced by beets. Beets don't produce a molasses-type substance, hence no muscovado, or treacle, but they still accounted for 20 per cent of the world's sugar in 2009.

We have Napoleon to thank for beet sugar. During the Napoleonic Wars and the blockade of all ships to European ports, Napoleon charged French chemists with the task of finding an alternative source of sugar. They did: *Beta vulgaris*, a relative of beetroot. The natural role of the white fleshy root is to store sugars. It is processed or refined to produce a syrup which is then crystallised to produce white sugar crystals.

White Sugars

•••

The whiteness of white sugar comes from a complex refining process; all impurities are removed to leave a perfectly white product.

Caster The perfect sugar for baking: fine crystals make it easier to mix into a smooth batter and allow the sugar to dissolve quickly in the oven.

Cube The preserve of silver sugar bowls and tongs. White sugar is moulded into cuboid shapes with the help of sugar syrup, which acts as a cement.

Granulated The sugar most of us grew up with, to be sprinkled on cereal, added to cakes or spooned into tea.

Icing A powder produced by grinding sugar crystals, with cornflour added to prevent it from caking. As the name suggests it's great for icing – buttercream, glacé, royal – or even just to dust on top of a Victoria sponge.

Jam Similar to preserving sugar (see below) but with added pectin – and sometimes citric acid as well – to aid the setting of jams and marmalades. If you're using a low-pectin fruit, such as plums, to make jam, it's worth using jam sugar to get a good set.

Preserving The sugar crystals are left larger to allow for slow dissolving and less stirring during the preserving process. These crystals are also less likely to fall straight to the bottom of your pan and burn, or produce quite so much froth.

Golden and Brown Sugars

...

This group is becoming more and more important in the kitchen, as they offer more flavour than white sugars. The flavours can vary in intensity depending on the process of refining a sugar has gone through.

Black Treacle/Molasses and Blackstrap Molasses This residue from the refining process is dark, rich and viscous. It contains minerals missing from refined sugars. Its darkness gives a hint of its slight bitterness. It may also remind some of medicine and has in fact been used as a base for cough mixture for years. A more pleasurable use is to add to parkin, Christmas puddings and cakes, or to a marinade for hams and other meats. Molasses can now also be bought in a moist crystallised sugar form.

Demerara When we were growing up, you were posh if you had this in your cupboard; it was brought out when coffee was served. It is named after its place of origin in Guyana next to the River Demerara. The crystals are larger than granulated sugar, light brown and shiny. Try it in a crumble, or sprinkled on top of fruit cake. It has a spiced, fruity flavour with a crunch.

Golden Granulated/Caster/Icing The same as the white counterparts, but with light caramel and honey flavours because they retain some of the molasses flavour and colour.

Golden Syrup A bit of a British institution. The famous tin holds a 'secret' recipe of liquid sugar; nothing else is added. It's used in baking, perhaps most notably in steamed treacle pudding. It's very sweet.

Muscovado, Light and Dark These moist, crystallised sugars are full of flavour due to the molasses left within them. Light muscovado has a warm honey colour and aromatic flavour, whereas dark is rich and fudgy. Use both in baking and the dark is also good in savoury dishes and marinades.

Things to Put in Jam, Jellies and Marmalades

Apple	Loganberry
Apricot	Passion Fruit
Blackberry	Peach
Blackcurrant	Plum
Blood Orange	Quince
Cherry	Raspberry
Chestnut	Redcurrant
Damson	Rhubarb
Fig	Rose Petal
Gooseberry	Seville Orange
Grapefruit	Sloe
Kumquat	Strawberry

Flavoured Sugars

Simply add these ingredients to a jar of
sugar and leave for a week or two.

Sprinkle on biscuits when baking.
Dredge French toast.
Caramelise desserts under the grill.
Scatter over fresh fruit salad.
Fold into buttercreams.

Cardamom and Mint

Some crushed pods and
bruised leaves

Clementine and Cinnamon

Cinnamon sticks and strips of clementine zest
in darker sugars, for winter puddings

Lemon Grass and Lime

Lemon grass stalk, split lengthways,
plus strips of lime zest, for coconut macaroons

Liquorice Root

The bashed root,
for autumn meringues

Vanilla

1 used, deseeded vanilla pod

Sterilising jars: boil jars, bottles and lids in a deep pan of water, then dry the glassware in an oven preheated to 110°C/225°F gas mark ¼ for 20 minutes

Always use the best-quality fruit. Don't be tempted to use fruit that is going over

Cook the fruit before adding the sugar

JAM

Get a good jam thermometer and use it; stop guessing

POT THE JAM WHILE IT IS HOT (ABOVE 85°C) TO GET A GOOD SEAL

Once on a rolling boil, stop stirring, or you will interrupt the set

Setting point for jam is 104.5°C

Sugar Alternatives

•••

As the effects of too much sugar on our bodies becomes more apparent, sugar substitutes are proliferating: agave nectar, rice syrup and stevia among them. We'll look at some of these here and figure out if they have a place in our kitchen cupboards. What we won't do is give you the latest medical and nutritional findings; we'll leave that to the scientists.

Agave Nectar The concentrated sap from the agave plant, commonly found in Mexico and also now grown commercially in South Africa. The long fleshy leaves and hidden pineapple-like core produce a sweet sap that's extracted and filtered down to a syrup, but still considered a raw food as the processing is so light. Different degrees of concentration result in varying flavours. The light nectar is mild, almost neutral and can be used in delicate dishes and drinks. The amber nectar produces caramel-like flavours and is more intense. Dark nectar has rich caramel notes and can add real flavour to the dish you're cooking. Agave is 1.5 times sweeter than sugar, so you can use less. It is considered low GI and so less likely to trigger fat storage in the body. There are other bottles on the market labelled 'agave' that have been refined, so check the label.

Coconut Sugar This looks a little like dull brown sugar and is sold in a granulated form. It's produced from the sap of the coconut palm flower, which is heated to leave a thick sweet syrup, then further reduced to a crystalline product. It's not as sweet as other sugar substitutes, but does have a slight caramel flavour with hints of the original coconut. It has a low GI and is high in vitamins and minerals.

Date Syrup/Molasses The new kid on the block here in the UK, though it is widely used in Middle Eastern cooking. It is made from date juice and lends itself, of course, to all things Middle Eastern in the kitchen, but also to drizzling over goat's cheese, making salad dressings, or adding to stews. You can of course experiment and use it as a sugar substitute, but it is very sweet so use it carefully.

Jaggery A traditional Indian and African sugar made from sugar cane juice, date palm sap and sometimes coconut palm sap. The juice or sap is boiled in large wide pans over a fire until it becomes a dark, rich and intensely flavoured thick syrup. It is then typically sold in relatively solid, hard blocks that need to be chipped away at, or grated, before adding to dishes. It is highly flavoured and, as it is untreated or refined, retains a lot of the original nutrients.

Maple Syrup This rich, dark syrup from North America is the sap of the maple tree. In the cold northerly climes, the trees store starch in their trunks and roots during the winter and then, as the warmer weather arrives each spring, the starch starts to rise through the trunk as sap and in the process turns to sugar. The sap is collected by boring holes into the trees' trunks and is then heated to form a syrup.

Always read the label and beware of syrups that purport to be maple, when in fact they have only had flavours and colours added to give the appearance of maple. The price will be an indicator, as the real thing is not cheap. If you're confused (not surprising), we suggest asking a Canadian to intervene and pick the one that suits your needs. Maple syrup can be poured over pancakes, waffles and French toast. It also goes well with bacon (and more pancakes). Others like to add it to their porridge in place of the more traditional British sweeteners.

Chemically, it is primarily sucrose and has a similar calorific content to sugar. In the kitchen today, more bakers are finding ways to include maple syrup in cakes and biscuits.

Rice Syrup This is made from sprouted whole grain brown rice and has a mild and pleasant caramel flavour. It is largely composed from complex carbohydrates that take longer to digest than the simple carbohydrates found in regular sugar, so is thought to circumvent the 'sugar rush' effect of simple sugars. Use in the same way as other sugar substitutes.

Stevia Is this the great white hope for sugar alternatives? Stevia is a herb that grows in the tropical and sub-tropical Americas and is known for its sweet leaves. It contains no glucose, fructose or sucrose, yet it is 250–300 times sweeter than cane sugar. Current thinking has led the big sugar manufacturers to start developing ways in which it can be introduced into their range. At present it can be bought as a processed sweetener, or a product that has been developed to mimic the look of sugar, that contains half the calories for the same sweetness. The downside is, to get it to the point where it acts anything like sugar, it has to undergo heavy processing. And as yet, due to its newness, there are very few in-depth studies that can show the long-term effect of processed stevia consumption on the human body. Still, we predict this is the one to watch.

Honey

•••

We've collected and used honey for 8,000 years, so it has a far older place in culinary history than the youthful sugar cane. It has religious significance in a number of cultures and is used across the globe to heal and protect (and is now known to contain antioxidants). Bees collect nectar from flowers, then return to their hive to turn it into honey and store it in wax honeycombs as food for their community. To make one jar, bees travel the equivalent of three times round the world.

A bee-keeping revival over recent years has led to high-quality, small batch, often local honey being sold at farmer's markets and independent shops. This is fairly unadulterated. Once the bee-keeper has collected his frames of honeycomb and removed the wax coating, he spins it in a drum so it flows out of the combs. This is 'raw' honey. (Commercial honey is often pasteurised.) The bee's nectar source, geographic, or flower specific, is now often used to distinguish different types of honey.

All honey, like cane sugar, is predominantly glucose and fructose, but is generally thought of as a 'healthier' option. It can be enjoyed on bread, in hot drinks (and cocktails), to sweeten dressings and marinades and in baking. Don't use expensive single floral variety honeys in cooking; their qualities will be lost.

> If your honey has crystallised you can return it to its runny state by warming gently in a very low oven.
>
> M

Honey Bees

...

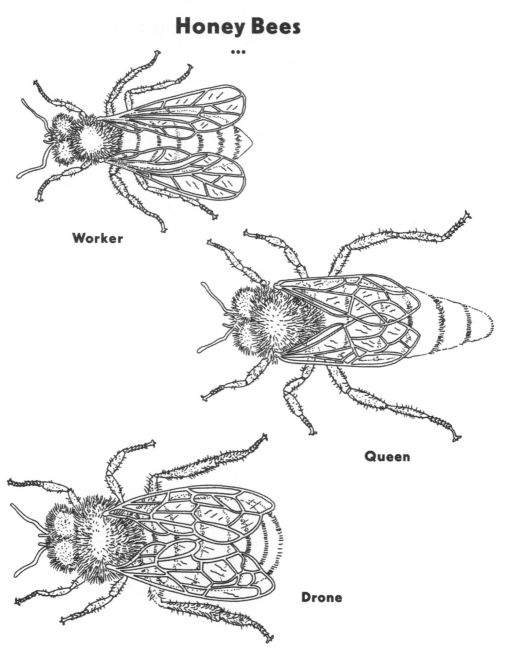

Worker

Queen

Drone

Muscovado Meringues

•••

The soft brown sugar will ensure a soft chewy centre. To make a dessert to welcome in the autumn, dip the bases in melted chocolate and fill with spiced poached plums (or blackberries) and whipped cinnamon cream. Blitzing the sugar gives the meringue a lighter texture and helps the sugar to dissolve. For a successful meringue, always use at least two parts sugar to one part egg white by weight.

Serves 6

Ingredients

200 g light muscovado sugar
4 egg whites (total weight 100 g)

Equipment

electric mixer
food processor
baking sheet
baking parchment

Preparation

Preheat the oven to 120°C / 250°F / gas mark ½.
Clean the bowl of an electric mixer thoroughly.

Method

Blitz the sugar in a food processor for three minutes. The structure will change, leaving the sugar with a sandy texture.

Whisk the egg whites in the electric mixer. Once they have doubled in volume, start to add the sugar, 1 tbsp at a time, leaving gaps between the spoonfuls to let the sugar dissolve. Continue until all the sugar has been added and the mixture is glossy and holds stiff peaks.

Using two tablespoons, spoon on to a baking sheet lined with baking parchment into apple-sized rounds, pushing a well into the middle with the back of a clean wet spoon to create a nest.

Bake for two hours, then turn off the oven and leave the meringues to cool inside, with the door closed. Remove gently from the baking parchment. Serve or store in an airtight container for one month.

Good Afternoon Jam

•••

If you don't have an abundance of fresh berries to hand, use mixed frozen berries instead; the bags often contain a good amount of varieties. Redcurrants and blackcurrants are high in pectin, which will help this jam set naturally. So make sure there is a good quantity of currants in the mix.

Makes 5 x 330 g jars

Ingredients

1 kg mixed berries (strawberries, raspberries, redcurrants, blackcurrants, tayberries, loganberries)
100 ml lemon juice, plus more if needed
1 kg golden granulated sugar

Equipment

juicer
5 x 330 ml jam jars and lids
plate
1 large saucepan
jam thermometer

Preparation

Pick over the fruit and give it a wash.

Juice the lemon.

Sterilise five 330 g jam jars (see page 408).

Place a plate in the freezer.

Method

Cook the fruit gently in a large saucepan in 300 ml of water and the lemon juice. The lemon juice will help extract pectin and also help the jam retain a good colour. Cook for about five minutes, to soften the skins.

Once the fruit has broken down, add the sugar and stir to dissolve.

Once the sugar has dissolved, increase the heat to reach a setting point of 104.5°C (220.1°F). Remove from the heat.

Spoon a small amount on to the chilled plate and see if it wrinkles when you push a finger through (though this should be a soft set jam). If not, return to the heat and boil again for 10 minutes with another dose of lemon juice, then test as above.

When the jam is set, pot and seal while still hot. The jam will keep for 12 months in a cool, dark place.

Maple and Chilli Sweet Potato Wedges

Preheat the oven to 200°C/400°F/gas mark 6. Wash and cut sweet potatoes lengthways into wedges. Toss in light olive oil and sea salt. Drizzle with maple syrup and chilli flakes. Lay out over an oven tray and roast for 30 minutes in the hot oven until soft inside and charred on the edges.

Honey and Sage Salad Dressing
for Winter Roots

Infuse 75 ml light olive oil by gently frying several sage leaves and a few slivers of garlic in it until they impart their flavour. Pass through a sieve and whisk in 25 ml of sherry vinegar, 2 tsp of good-flavoured honey and sea salt. Use over roast winter roots.

Sea-salted Chocolate Honeycomb

Sugar alchemy at its best and most fun, with dramatic results. You need a cook's thermometer. Sift 1 tsp of bicarbonate of soda on to a plate. Gently heat 110 g of golden granulated sugar and 60 g of golden syrup in a heavy-based saucepan until melted. Bring to the boil and heat until it reaches 150°C (300°F). Remove from the heat. Sprinkle the bicarb in and stir. Pour into a baking parchment-lined baking tin. It will start to set. Sprinkle flakes of sea salt on (or leave plain). Once cool, you could dip chunks into Tempered milk or dark chocolate (see page 71). Once set, keep in an airtight container.

M

18

An Introduction to Tea

Few could start the day without a cup of tea. There's a cup for nearly every occasion: that soothing morning mug; afternoon tea with cake and biscuits, or the 'tea break' signalling a moment of relaxation or the perfect way to calm a crisis. Few ingredients can be at the centre of so many social bonds. The simple act of making someone a cup of tea is nurturing, while the formal ritual of high tea is a vehicle for displaying social status and sophistication. In the UK, we have set ideas about tea and the role it plays in different situations, when to dive for the huge mug and when to bring out the best china and the jug for the milk.

At home, the cupboard is packed with boxes of the stuff: a golden snail China tea, an interesting-looking Earl Grey with blue flowers suspended in it, a solid block of gunpowder green, some emergency 'builder's' and box after dusty box of blended infusions, dried petals and strange-looking dried roots. All experiments and whims; some discarded, but plenty more we return to time and again.

The beauty of tea is you can afford to be fickle. There is a cup in hand at all times, but it will not be the same each time. Tea is infinitely adaptable; whatever your mood or need at a certain point, there is a tea to suit it.

First thing, we often reach for something strong from the black tea family, such as a punchy assam to awaken the senses. But it might equally be an earthy, malty oolong or a cleansing slice of lemon in a cup of boiled water. Mid-morning, it's several light infusions of green or white silver tip tea, or, if it's caffeine-free we are after, fresh lemon verbena will be on tap.

A simple slice of ginger in boiled water will sharpen the mind during a meeting or if some writing needs to be done. Afternoons are always for black tea: the 'afternoon blend' was made to accompany sweet treats that appear just in time to assuage the slump.

During the evening, cardamom pods or fennel seeds might be called for, just lightly bruised and flung into a cup of boiling water.

Despite tea being a quintessentially British tradition, tea drinking came from much further afield, in China. Tea containers have been found in Chinese tombs dating back to AD 206 and, by the 9th century (millennia before we had heard of it), tea had become the Chinese national drink.

Britain is certainly responsible for popularising tea drinking in the Western world. First seen in England in the mid-17th century, it was the tea-swilling Queen Catherine's marriage to Charles II that properly put tea on the map here, making it the fashionable drink at court.

The British East India Company began direct importation of tea from the Far East in 1689 and, by the mid-18th century, tea was widespread across the social classes. However, punitive taxes on the precious leaves meant tea smuggling was rife. To stop the huge loss of revenue, the government forced the East India Company to import enough without raising prices; finally making tea a democratic drink for all. However, tax relief was not extended to our colonies, who had also developed a keen tea habit. When a direct trade with Dutch importers was set up, the East India Company forced through a bill to ensure sole rights to import tea to the Americas. This resulted in the Boston Tea Party, civil war, the loss of America from the Empire and tea, to this day, relatively shunned on American soil.

Back at home, tea continued to influence society, first with its promotion during the 18th and 19th centuries as a healthy alternative to gin palaces, then as a morale-booster to the home front during the First World War, where its importation was secured at an affordable price by the government.

All in all, a lot of history is in that innocuous-looking morning cuppa.

A cup of tea has at least half the caffeine content of a cup of coffee

Ever wondered why Grandma was so keen to recommend a restorative cup of tea at times of need? Studies have shown that tea contains an amino acid called L-theanine, which is linked to a calm, relaxed mental state, similar to that attained through meditation

Heat, light, moisture and air all contribute to tea losing freshness

Black tea stored in a bag inside a sealed opaque container can keep for up to two years

Black tea has a longer shelf life than green tea; however, puerh tea can actually improve with age

Store tea in cool, dark, dry place in an airtight container

There are around 1,500 different varieties of the tea plant

Types of Tea Leaves

•••

Over 600 flavours and aromas have been identified in tea and the infinite varieties on offer mean there is a tea for every mood and time of day:

Black Black teas are complex and have an intensity of flavour. Like all tea categories, there is huge variation between those produced across the world, from fragrant darjeeling to malty assam and rare, sweet Chinese varieties. Beautifully hand-crafted black teas do not need milk or sugar.

Green Green tea has been steamed or roasted to prevent oxidisation and retain the fresh green flavours of the leaf. Green teas, like teas of all categories, can be purchased for just a few or as much as thousands of pounds per kilo, depending on quality. The best are bright, clean and refreshing. It is not caffeine-free; a common mistake.

Gunpowder The best-known green tea, gunpowder is rolled into small pellets with a characteristic metallic sheen. The smallest ('pinhead') of these plucked and rolled leaves are the best quality. Most is produced in China's Pingshui and Zheijian Provinces.

Orange Pekoe Every tea on the market is allocated a 'leaf grading', indicating the quality and condition of the tea leaves when picked. The highest and most prized grades are referred to as orange pekoe, and the lowest and least desirable (found in a lot of tea bags) as 'fannings' or 'dust'.

Seek out the abbreviation 'OP' on the packaging, which denotes whole leaf orange pekoe varieties of the highest quality. 'BOP' indicates broken orange pekoe, which is of a good, but not such excellent, quality.

White A sweet, soft, gentle flavour. The least processed of all tea types, they retain the most antioxidants. The best are made from the first leaves of spring; the most prized from new growing leaf buds: 'silver tips'.

Types of Tea

•••

Afternoon Tea Usually a blend of black teas devised to go well when drunk alongside cakes.

Assam A region of India producing typically robust, malty teas. Anything sold as assam will have these characteristics but may well be a blend. The best flavours come from single estates. An ideal tea to start your day.

Ceylon Famous for black tea, the term denotes tea from Sri Lanka. (It should be noted that 'Ceylon' is not the most politically correct term.)

Chai Or more correctly masala chai, meaning spiced tea. Its popularity in Britain soared along with the arrival of the 'chai latte' in coffee houses a decade or so ago. Originally hailing from South East Asia, it is typically a mix of black tea, green cardamom, cinnamon and ginger, sweetened heavily with sugar and drunk with reduced milk, although ingredients and brewing styles differ hugely throughout India.

Darjeeling One of the finest Indian teas, regarded as the 'champagne of teas' by many. Grown in the foothills of the Himalayas, darjeelings are light and delicate in flavour and perfect without milk or sugar.

Earl Grey Traditionally a black tea infused with the aromatic oils of the bergamot citrus. Thought to have been first blended in honour of the second Earl Grey. Now, a synthetic flavouring is commonly used in place of the essential oil. For the best flavours, look out for real bergamot.

English Breakfast Usually a blend of black teas from former British colonies. The Americans coined the term to categorise the style of tea enjoyed in the UK. It has come to be a catch-all term for black tea.

Irish Breakfast The tea you will tend to be offered on American soil, a blend of assam and several other black teas.

Lapsang Souchong One of the most famous China teas with a smoked flavour from drying the black tea leaves over pine wood fires. The best come from the hills in north Fujian province.

Matcha A finely powdered high-quality green tea used in Japanese tea ceremonies. The green colour and unique flavour are used to create ice creams and confectionery, as well as to colour soba noodles.

Russian Caravan A blend of keemun, oolong and often – but not always – lapsang souchong. The name originates from the camel caravans that undertook the transcontinental tea journeys from India, Ceylon and China, through Russia to Europe during the 18th century. A six-month journey under harsh, cold wet conditions is said to have enhanced the leaves, giving them an unique flavour.

Oolong Semi-oxidised or fermented teas from China's Fujian province and Taiwan, these are complex teas with their own categorisation process, from green-ish rolled oolongs, which make a light floral tea, to dark brown oolongs, which make a deeper, earthier brew.

Puerh Fermented 'large leaf' green tea from Yunnan province, but even specialists can't agree on its true definition. Aged for years, this tea is typically earthy and complex in aroma with a smooth, mature flavour.

Sencha A Japanese green tea and the most popular in Japan. *Sencha* means 'simmered tea', referring to the manner in which it is made by steeping actual tea leaves, rather than other powdered leaf versions.

Tea Geography

Tea is made from the small leaves of *Camellia sinensis*, native to China, and the larger-leafed *Camellia assamica*. Climate and geography are key to the quality of a tea. The plants favour tropical climates, but can now even be grown on British soil.

England

Tregothnan Estate in Cornwall began supplying England's first and only tea in 2005.

Kenya

One of the oldest African producers and becoming one of the most important, Kenyan teas are most often found in blends.

Tanzania

The legacy of German colonisation, these teas are bright in colour and flavour, making them ideal in blends.

Malawi

The pioneer of tea growing in Africa and now well known for their speciality teas. Some very good ones are being produced on estates around Thyolo Mountain.

Japan

Famous for their ritualised tea ceremonies, the country is the second largest green tea producer after China.

China

The birthplace of tea and the biggest of the world's green tea-producing nations. The country also produces some black tea, often known as 'red' for the colour it gives in an infusion.

Taiwan

Producers of some very good-quality green, black and oolong teas. Some teas are still marketed under the island's former name, Formosa.

Indonesia

Generally only found in blends; however, there are some good-quality Sumatran teas that are similar to assams.

India

Tea production was introduced to India by the British, who wanted to corner the tea market, in the 1680s. The country has three main styles: citric south Indian, strong north Indian assams, and light, fragrant darjeelings from the foothills of the Himalayas.

Sri Lanka

Black teas are the speciality, but the country also produces some very good green and highly prized 'silver tip' white teas, often marketed under the island's previous name, Ceylon.

Which Tea to Buy?

•••

Loose Whole Leaf

Many tea aficionados espouse the benefits of loose leaf tea. With loose tea you are paying for the quality of the leaf rather than a packaging process. Really good-quality tea can actually be used over several infusions, making each spoonful worth triple that of a standard tea bag.

Tea Bags

Invented by an American tea broker in the early 20th century, tea bags didn't take off in Britain until the 1970s. Often regarded as containing just the 'sweepings from the factory floor', tea bags have come a long way, with quality tea merchants developing high-tech tetrahedral bags and including much better leaves.

Decaffeinated Tea

This is achieved by 'washing' the tea leaves with a solvent during the production process. The process is strictly governed, but no washing will remove every trace of caffeine. Look out for organic, if possible.

Single Estate Teas

Teas that come from only one tea estate or garden, as opposed to being a blend from a number of estates. Teas from single origins will have specific characteristics from their geography, the tea-making process and the season they were picked. Particular vintages can be identified as a result.

Seasonality

Teas picked at different times have varying characteristics and flavours. Tea varieties differ hugely, but first-flush teas, harvested following the spring rains, can often be lighter in flavour and colour. The second flush, usually gathered in June, tends to be more amber and full bodied, while the autumnal flush can be darker and more rounded.

Blended Teas

The majority of teas sold in bags – and a lot of other teas sold in the West – are now blends. Blending can be of a very high quality, creating teas with many more complex flavours, but it can also be used to cover the inferior taste of cheaper varieties.

Ethical Sourcing

The importance of giving back to tea-growing communities means many tea brands support ethical sourcing, which targets the communities' needs with health services and economic development.

• •

Caffeine and Tea

There are several myths surrounding the caffeine content of tea, one of the biggest being that green teas and other lighter-coloured teas contain less caffeine than black tea. This is not the case. Within a few grams of each other, all teas made from *Camellia sinensis* and *Camellia assamica* plants contain 40–75 mg of caffeine, depending on brew strength, whether using black, green, white, oolong or anything in between.

Bagged teas do contain slightly less caffeine than loose teas. However, this is probably more due to tea bags containing poor-quality broken leaves than anything else.

If you are drinking a good-quality whole-leaf tea and using the leaves to create several infusions, you get a huge decrease in caffeine content from the first brew (around 50–70 mg/cup) to 15–25 mg/cup in the second and only 5–10 mg/cup in the third.

Surprisingly, tea contains more caffeine per gram than coffee by dry weight. But, as making tea uses far less dry material than you need to make coffee, the 100–200 mg caffeine in a cup of coffee overtakes that of tea, making it more than twice as caffeinated.

Tea and Health

Tea's health benefits have been debated for hundreds of years. Wealthy 18th-century philanthropists worried that tea drinking among the working classes would lead to 'weakness and melancholy'.

However, tea is full of flavonoids and antioxidants, which are increasingly noted for their role in protecting against conditions such as stroke, heart disease and cancer by combating free-radicals in the environment. The particular antioxidants in tea are plant-derived polyphenols, which are also found in nuts, fruits, vegetables, cereals and red wine.

Green tea has been the focus of many health studies in recent years. As it is not as processed, it differs in chemical composition from black tea, with increased simple flavonoids called catechins, reputed to be linked to reduced body fat and a decrease in artery-clogging LDL cholesterol. White tea, being the least processed of all, contains even more.

The Perfect
Cup of Tea

•••

Despite our fame as tea drinkers, those of the more refined tea-drinking Eastern tradition feel it's still almost impossible to find a decent cup on our shores. Tea is actually easier to make and less easy to ruin than coffee. Here are some simple tips to ensure you always get the best out of your leaves:

Water Temperature The amino acids which produce flavour in tea dissolve at lower temperatures than tannin, so tea made with water at 100°C will be more astringent and less sweet. For black and green tea, use water around 85°C; white teas around 70°C. With oolong, conversely, hotter temperatures bring out interesting top notes.

Water Quality Always use freshly drawn water and don't reboil the kettle as this reduces oxygen in the water. Tea's delicate flavours can easily be masked by the deposits in tap water, so if you are spending money on good-quality tea it's worth investing in a water filter.

Brew Time Always follow the recommended brew times on your tea. Anything else is throwing money down the drain, as you will not be getting the full character of the tea leaf. With a black or semi-fermented tea such as oolong you are looking to develop the dry, astringent tannins, also found in red wine, that give the tea its flavour. With a green or white tea, the correct brew time will bring out the tea's delicacy and floral notes. With a good-quality whole leaf, the best flavour comes from a high leaf-to-water ratio and short infusion times. Put a lot of tea in a small amount of water and let it infuse for only 20–60 seconds, then pour off the tea completely. This way you can reuse the leaves over several infusions, while getting the best nutrients, flavour and value from your tea.

Two Tea Pots Method The first tea pot is used to brew the tea. Once the tea has brewed to perfection, strain the tea into the second warmed pot. This stops any risk of a 'stewed' flavour.

Warm Cup Method Pour fresh-boiled water into the number of tea cups required. Pour the water from the cups to the tea pot with the tea, cooling the water to the right temperature and ensuring the correct amount for the leaves used.

Tea Bags Good-quality tea bags will give the leaves plenty of room to expand and infuse. Leave bags in the boiled water, without disturbing them too much, for the brewing time stated. There is no need to squeeze the bag.

ANISEEDS

BASIL

CHAMOMILE

CARAWAY SEEDS

DILL

DRIED LIQUORICE

FENNEL SEEDS

GINGER

GREEN CARDAMOM

HIBISCUS

LAVENDER

LEMON BALM

LEMON GRASS

LEMON VERBENA

MARJORAM

MINT

NASTURTIUMS

NETTLES

PANSIES

OLIVE LEAVES

OREGANO

RASPBERRY LEAVES

ROSES

ROSEMARY

SAGE

THYME

VIOLETS

Herbal Teas

...

A herbal tea, infusion, or tisane refers to any drink made from a decoction of herbs, flowers, leaves, seeds or roots, but not from tea leaves. They tend not to contain caffeine and, traditionally, they have been drunk for their therapeutic effects. Some, such as ginseng, are stimulating and can replace coffee as a livener; others, such as chamomile, have calming, relaxing properties; flowers such as lavender are very useful sedatives.

Hundreds of varieties of herbal tea line our supermarket shelves with weird and wonderful-sounding flavours, but how many of them actually contain the real thing? Sadly a surprising number are filled with fruit, flower and herb 'flavourings' rather than the actual ingredient; chemically enhanced and not perhaps what you imagined you might be consuming in something sold under the banner of 'herbal'.

There are of course very good natural herbal infusions out there; though the old saying that you get what you pay for applies here, too. Look out for brands using real dried and, if possible, whole ingredients. Organic brands – or those containing certified organic ingredients – will tend, but not always, to give a good-quality tea. It's best to look out for small-batch artisan, hand-produced teas, whose ingredients have been carefully sourced and cared for during their growing and processing.

Making Your Own Herbal Teas

Home-made herbal infusions are incredibly easy to make. With just a little practice and experimentation you can come up with an array of delicious concoctions to use throughout the day, evening and into the night to suit your mood and your specific need: to give you a lift in the afternoon; help you drift off to sleep; or ease a full belly after a good meal.

We find that growing herbs, flowers and leaves in pots and window boxes is the easiest way to guarantee an easy 'pickable' supply, and using them fresh certainly adds to the enjoyment of drinking the resulting teas. You can, however, buy good-quality dried herbs, flowers and leaves for the purpose online and from good health food shops.

Herbs and flowers have long been used for their medicinal properties. Those we have listed overleaf, however, have been chosen for their flavour and ease of use, rather than attempting to list every edible herb or teach their specific therapeutic function:

Steeping Herbs

1

Carefully wash any herbs, flowers, leaves and so on that you have gathered from the garden (use those from your own garden or sources you know to be pesticide-free).

2

Use a sparkling clean tea pot and fill it with the ingredients (be careful to remove any tannic stains clinging to the pot from your morning cuppa, which could taint delicate flavours).

3

Bruise any roots, seeds or hard pieces and scrunch the soft fresh ingredients in your hands a little to release their flavour-giving essential oils.

4

Pour over boiling water (the water must be boiling to sterilise the fresh ingredients and ensure they are safe to drink).

5

Cover with a lid to prevent any of the oils evaporating and leave to steep for two to five minutes, depending on the strength you want.

6

Remove the ingredients, or take out the strainer section if you don't want to drink straight away, or drink it, then use the same ingredients for one or two more brews.

Our Favourite Herbal Infusions

These are some of our favourite combinations, which can be grown in pots or bought dried as whole flowers, petals, leaves or roots. If your local health store doesn't stock them, then a simple search will find them online. The quantities make a small- to medium-sized pot of tea that you can refresh with boiling water a couple of times throughout the morning, afternoon or evening. Use these ratios as a base and adjust the amounts of flavourings to suit your tastes and the strength of your ingredients:

Cleansing and Refreshing

Post-supper or 'Morning-after' Tea

12 large mint leaves
(a combination of apple mint and
spearmint is lovely, as is peppermint
if you want a really punchy flavour)

½ tsp fennel seeds

2 crushed green cardamom pods

Calming and Relaxing

Evening Tea

4 fresh or 8 dried lemon verbena leaves

6 fresh or dried chamomile flowers

Uplifting and
Zesty

Morning or Afternoon 'Slump' Tea

2 cm bruised lemon grass stalk

8 lemon balm leaves

2 cm lightly bruised liquorice root

3 slices of root ginger

Sleep-inducing

Bedtime Tea

6 fresh or dried chamomile flowers

1 small lavender head

2 cm lightly bruised liquorice root

Fruity and
Floral

Everyday Tea

2 dried hibiscus flowers

12 rose petals
(from a fragrant variety; traditional
old roses often have the best aroma)

6 fresh or dried raspberry leaves

Cooking With Tea

•••

Tea is a surprisingly versatile cooking ingredient; just think of the aromas and flavours found in it, from floral to astringent, to herbal, smoky, fruity, sweet, pine and woody scents, earthy and even leathery notes... and that's before you've even started on fruit and herb infusions. Here are some of our favourite ways to use tea in cooking:

Infusing with Tea

A great way to get flavours into milk or cream. Lemon verbena makes a lovely addition to pannacotta; indeed anything creamy or custardy can benefit from the addition of a carefully chosen tea. Try lapsang-infused sultanas in an ice cream swirled with Pedro Ximenez, or matcha to make a very interesting flavour addition to crème brûlée (colouring it a brilliant green at the same time).

Poaching with Tea

Poach whole peaches in peach tea and white wine to intensify their taste and make an elegant pudding to serve with crème fraîche, or try late raspberries and blackberries in hibiscus tea to make a floral-scented fruit compote to eat with yogurt and granola.

Rehydrating with Tea

Soak dried fruits in Earl Grey to impart a bergamot flavour before adding them to a cake batter. Or try a strong assam for prunes, a delicate floral darjeeling for dried pears, or a jasmine tea with semi-dried apples. In each case, allow the teas to infuse the fruit with their distinct flavours before adding them to your cooking.

Baking with Tea

Add loose black tea leaves and chai masala spices to a shortbread or biscuit recipe. A classic British tea loaf uses tea to impart flavour, richness and moistness. Or use a fragrant tea to infuse a buttercream to ice a cake.

Marinating with Tea

Pork ribs will not only take on the flavour of the tea, the meat will also be tenderised. Try a robust assam or smoky lapsang souchong that can stand up to other marinade flavours.

Smoking with Tea

Tea smoking imparts interesting flavours to oily fish and poultry. (Try hot-smoking duck breasts with jasmine tea and jasmine rice.) It is not the same as cold smoking and can be done quickly and easily at home.

Try experimenting with teas – floral darjeelings for fish and robust oolongs for meat – adding spices such as star anise, cinnamon and allspice to stand up to the smoky notes and brown sugar to enhance the flavours:

Tea Smoking Tips

1

Line a deep frying pan or wok with a tight-fitting lid with several layers of foil, ensuring there are edges overhanging to make a seal.

2

Spread an equal mixture of your chosen tea and raw rice into the pan and sprinkle with cold water to stop it smoking too much.

3

Heat the tea and rice until they smoke, then place a wire rack a few centimetres over them, followed by the meat or fish. Cover with the lid, seal with foil and cook.

4

Fish will cook in a matter of minutes, meat takes longer. A meat thermometer will give you an accurate gauge when it is ready.

Bara Brith (A Welsh Tea Loaf)

•••

This recipe evokes memories of when we opened our shop in Primrose Hill. Our friend Debbie, of Welsh ancestry herself, would arrive at 5 pm after the other chefs had left and turn out this 'bread', baked in our unruly gas oven, night after night. Serve buttered with a nice cup of tea.

Makes 1 loaf

Ingredients

unsalted butter, for the tin
175 g wholemeal flour
100 g plain flour
1¼ tsp baking powder
300 ml hot strong tea (such as lapsang, darjeeling, assam)
120 g currants
120 g sultanas
120 g raisins
175 g demerara sugar
1 unwaxed lemon
1 egg, lightly beaten
2 tsp mixed spice

Equipment

900 g loaf tin
baking parchment
sieve
mixing bowl
tea pot or jug
saucepan
zester

Preparation

Butter a 900 g loaf tin and line with baking parchment.

Sift the flours and baking powder into a bowl.

Make the tea.

Method

Pour the tea over the fruit and sugar in a saucepan, set over a medium heat and stir until the sugar dissolves. Leave to cool for a few hours.

Once cooled, add the lemon zest, working over the pan to catch the lemon's essential oils.

When ready to bake, preheat the oven to 150°C/300°F/gas mark 2.

Add the beaten egg to the fruit mixture, then gently stir in the sifted flour mixture and mixed spice. Don't over-work this mixture or the bread will be chewy. Scrape the mixture into the prepared tin.

Bake for 1½ hours in the centre of the oven. Check for readiness with a skewer; it should emerge clean. Cool and serve, or wrap carefully in cling film and store in an airtight container for up to five days.

19

VINEGARS

An Introduction to Vinegars

Is vinegar the unsung hero of the kitchen cupboard? Many of us think of it in one of two ways: sprinkled liberally with a good dose of salt on our chips; or mixed with olive oil as a salad dressing. As delicious as these are, vinegar deserves far more attention and appreciation. It can play a vital and wide-ranging role in our kitchens and its flavours can be complex.

Vinegar is a key ingredient in marinades, dressings and sauces. Confident cooks can create extra depth and layers of flavour by adding it to their food, even if it's not mentioned in the recipe.

For centuries, vinegar has been used to preserve foods through pickling as, due to its acidity, it keeps bacteria at bay. Pickled eggs may not be to everyone's taste, but among the panoply of foods pickled by different cultures, we promise there's a pickled something for you to enjoy!

What is Vinegar?

The word is derived from the French *vin aigre* or 'soured wine'. During the natural process of souring, the wine changes – through the introduction of airborne bacteria and a process of oxidation – into acetic acid.

However, not all vinegars are the same. Vinegar can be made from any of several alcohols, including wine, ale, sherry or cider, or any liquid initially containing sugars or starch that can be fermented, then left to oxidise and sour. These bases give the vinegar its particular flavour.

How it's Made

Today most commercially produced vinegars are made under controlled laboratory conditions that speed up the process, so that rather than taking months or years to produce, they can be created in a day.

However – as is the case with wine – patience, care and old-fashioned ways can produce vinegar of superior quality. Traditional and artisanal methods aim to do things slowly, thus retaining more of the original character of the wine or other base used. Look out for these slower processes – revealed by the key words Solera, Orleans or Schützenbach on the bottles – when choosing your vinegars.

Which Vinegar When?

•••

	Dressings	Sauces	Marinades	Pickling	Bases for Flavoured Vinegars
Balsamic	●	●	●		
Red wine	●	●	●		
Malt				●	
Sherry	●	●	●		
Cider	●	●	●	●	●
Rice	●	●	●	●	
White wine	●	●	●		●
White				●	

Types of Vinegars

•••

Balsamic Vinegar Perhaps surprisingly, this is made not from wine, but from the grape 'must' (skins, flesh, stems and juice) of Trebbiano grapes. It has a sweet and sticky quality and carries a high price.

Real balsamic vinegar comes from two areas of Italy and they will be noted on the label: *aceto balsamico di Modena* and *aceto balsamico tradizionale di Reggio Emilio*. They will have been aged in oak casks for a minimum of 12 years – and some for up to 100 years – hence the high prices. Both have DOP (Protected Designation of Origin) status.

Of course, vinegar makers and food producers have taken advantage of the high prices and started making vinegars of a similar style but much more quickly. Balsamic-style vinegars are plentiful and relatively cheap. Used in Italy as a condiment, the complexity of traditional balsamic means it can be drizzled neat over meats, vegetables, cheeses, salads and even fruits such as strawberries and peaches. You can use balsamic-style vinegar in a similar manner; it won't have the depth of flavour, but will do the job.

Cider Vinegar Found, unsurprisingly, in the apple-growing areas of Europe and America, this light-coloured vinegar is suited to a variety of uses. It has an apple-like flavour with honey notes that makes it perfect with autumnal dishes, well suited to pork and anything served with apple. Many consider it the perfect base for pickling and chutney making. It also provides a perfect host to make all types of fruit vinegars (see page 446). It can be bought, unpasteurised, with the 'mother', which is essential to make your own vinegar (see page 445).

Malt Vinegar Once known as 'alegar', because ale was soured to make it; now known as malt, due to the type of barley used. It is most commonly used to douse chips, or in pickling. Don't bother mixing it with oil to dress salad; it tastes harsh and wrong. It is mostly produced commercially, but is also now obtainable from a UK-based artisan company who've revived the traditional way of making it.

Rice Vinegar Typically used in Asian cooking. White rice vinegar is less acidic than most Western vinegars; red rice vinegar is powerful and aromatic; black rice vinegar is deep-flavoured, sweet and rich. Some are aged in wooden casks.

Generally they are less pungent than vinegars from the West. Vinegars from northern China are thought of as being superior to those of the south. Japan also produces a very fine vinegar – genmai mochigome su – made from unpolished glutinous rice.

Sherry Vinegar This is increasingly popular. Made from the must of those grape varieties traditionally used to make sherry, the vinegar is aged in oak casks and really good versions use the Solera method of production. It's made in Spain and in particular in the 'sherry triangle' around Jerez. A sherry vinegar with DOP status will have been aged for at least six months in oak. Rich, complex and full of fruity flavours, some would say it offers more variety than other vinegars. Just sip a teaspoon and you'll get an idea of the complexity of the flavours involved: sweet, sour, fruity, floral. And you can now find sherry vinegars made from a single grape variety. The Pedro Ximenez (or PX) grape variety is considered by some as a worthy (and less expensive) alternative to balsamic. Use in salad dressings, or drizzle over sun-ripened tomatoes, or add a few splashes to gazpacho.

Wine Vinegar Most of us know wine vinegars as either 'red' or 'white' and probably use white wine vinegar to make salad dressing, mayonnaise or hollandaise and red wine vinegar in stocks and stews. However, look a little further on the supermarket shelf and you'll find a range of wine vinegars in which a single type of grape has been used to create a more distinct flavour: Chardonnay, Riesling, Champagne and Muscatel, or Merlot, Cabernet Sauvignon and Chianti. Each have their own distinct notes and, by tasting, you'll find favourites that suit your style of cooking, in the same way that you have your preferred wines to drink. Experiment and find your wine vinegar of choice. We really do encourage you to spend just a little extra and get a vinegar that actually tastes of something.

White Vinegar Not to be confused with white wine vinegar, this is usually made from distilled malt vinegar. It's often used in commercial pickling, particularly when you don't want the pickled ingredient to be coloured by the vinegar.

Storecupboard Stars

SHERRY VINEGAR	CIDER VINEGAR	MOSCATEL VINEGAR (White Wine)	CABERNET SAUVIGNON VINEGAR (Red Wine)
For dressings and sauces	For pickling and dressings	For mayonnaise and dressings	For stock, stews and sauces

Making Your Own Vinegar

•••

All you need to make your own vinegar is time, patience, some alcohol, a muslin cloth and a large jar.

Method 1

Pour a bottle of good wine (not the cheapest nor your best) into a clean 2-litre glass Kilner jar. Cover it with a muslin cloth and secure it with string so it can breathe. Leave it in a dark, ventilated corner of the house for several months, while the alcohol ferments slowly into acetic acid. It is this acid that gives vinegar its kick and also its preservative qualities.

Method 2

Introduce a 'mother' to wine, found in unpasteurised cider vinegar that can be bought from health food shops; it looks like jelly suspended in the liquid. It is a living organism that is destroyed in all pasteurised vinegars. Don't be alarmed by it, it is what sourdough starters are to bakers and will create all your vinegar for years to come if you look after it.

Mix 250 ml of the mother vinegar with 750 ml good wine, red or white, whichever you prefer, into a clean 2-litre glass Kilner jar. Don't skimp, as you are investing in the future. Cover it with a muslin cloth and secure it with string so it can breathe. Leave it in a dark, ventilated corner of the house for two or three weeks, then taste. Replace the muslin and leave for another week. The wait will be worth it; it will be better than any shop-bought vinegar. Repeat the tasting until you are happy with the flavour. You'll be surprised how much it develops and, the longer you leave it, the more it improves. Once you and the vinegar are ready, strain half through a fine sieve to remove any of the mother, and bottle. Leave the rest to mature further, or add more wine and continue to brew.

Flavoured Vinegars

•••

These are an easy way to 'bespoke' your larder, by choosing a flavour or ingredient that you enjoy and simply adding to either a white wine vinegar, or a cider vinegar, or if you've gone to the trouble of making your own vinegar, even better. Vinegars are living things and usually improve with age; they also become infused very easily with the ingredient you're adding, so that it becomes the dominant flavour.

Typical flavourings fall into three groups:

Fruits

Blackcurrant

Elderberry

Raspberry

Strawberry

Spices and
Other Things

Chilli

Honey

Herbs and Flowers

Basil

Dill

Mint

Nasturtium

Rose Petal

Tarragon

Vinegar Reduction

Use a lower-grade balsamic that lacks the depth of aged balsamics (taste it before you start). Gently boil the vinegar with a little sugar, a bay leaf if you have one and a cinnamon stick, until syrupy, reducing up to 75 per cent depending on the quality and age of the vinegar. Strain and cool. It adds a burst of flavour over tomato salads or rich meats. A couple of drops on grilled peaches and ice cream will do magical things to the dish.

Tarragon Vinegar

Take a 500 ml glass Kilner jar and place 1 bunch of washed and picked tarragon leaves in it and cover with good white wine vinegar and leave on a window-sill for a month, shaking from time to time. Strain into sterilised bottles (see page 408). Adding a sprig of tarragon is pleasing; it also helps with ID!

Pickling

•••

Our pantry seems to grow its own jars of pickles. While rummaging around for that piece of cheese you know you bought last Friday, you inevitably find a jar of pickles you didn't know you had. Onions, cucumbers or crabapples, they're all welcome with that piece of cheese, or a pork pie, or added to a sandwich to give that surprise crunch and flavour explosion. They all add a little extra 'spice' to our food and are a requisite for us all.

Pickling is a way of preserving, whether it's eggs, fish or even meat. We're more in favour of pickled vegetables and fruits and find ourselves in summer and early autumn surrounding ourselves with jars, vinegars, sugar, spices and the fruits or vegetables to be pickled. Pickling allows us to enjoy the seasons now passed.

Trade Secrets

The more interesting and better quality the vinegar, the better your results will be. Don't use 'non-brewed condiment' often found in greengrocers for the sole purpose of pickling; it's actually the stuff that fish and chip shops use on your chips. Check the acid percentage of the vinegar: it must be more than five per cent.

Use best-quality fruit and vegetables. Don't be tempted to use those going soft or past their best, as they will start to break down much more quickly in the pickling solution.

Ensure the equipment you're using is squeaky clean. That means pans, spoons, jars, lids... everything. (See page 408 for how to sterilise them.) Vinegar and sugar are the two essentials in a chutney or relish, acting as the preservative. Most fruits and vegetables can be transformed into chutney or relish and that often gives the cook a chance to experiment.

Generally, you then cook them in a solution of vinegar and sugar with spices. Some chutneys require long, slow cooking, while others can be ready in minutes. The same principles apply for jarring and storing as for pickling.

If you're a novice chutney or pickle maker, follow a recipe at first, but you'll soon be adept at creating your own combinations. Try adding them to sauces and stews to give extra flavour. A spoonful is good in gravy.

1

Make a pickling solution by simmering vinegar with spices for 5 to 10 minutes.

2

Remove the spices. If using sugar, dissolve 1 part to 5 parts infused vinegar. Cool.

3

Prepare your fruit or vegetables (some vegetables may need to be cooked first, such as beetroot) by washing and, if necessary, cutting into bite-sized chunks.

4

Once all items are cool, place the fruits or vegetables in sterilised jars (see page 408) and pour over the vinegar solution. Seal the jar with a tight-fitting sterilised lid and leave in a cool dark place for at least a month.

5

After a month or maybe longer, the pickle will mellow and taste less acidic and the fruits or vegetables will take on the flavours from the spiced vinegar.

Quick Pickled Breakfast Radishes

Sometimes, you want a pickle in minutes, rather than waiting a month. It won't keep as long as pickle produced in a traditional way, but it's a great standby. Slice 150 g of breakfast radishes and 1 shallot very thinly. Mix with ½ tsp of brown mustard seeds. Pour 150 ml of white wine vinegar, 50 ml of water and 40 g of granulated sugar into a saucepan, and add 1 tsp of green peppercorns and 1 tsp of coriander seeds. Bring to the boil, stirring to dissolve the sugar, then strain over the vegetables. Stir in 1 tsp of sea salt and set aside for a few hours. Excellent with terrines and very pretty in a seafood salad. In a sterilised jar (see page 408), these keep, chilled, for a month.

M

Asparagus
Beetroots
Broad Beans
Cabbages
Cauliflowers
Celery
Cherries
Courgettes
Crabapples
Cucumbers
Damsons
Eggs
Fennel
Garlic
Gherkins
Ginger
Grapes
Herrings

Lemons
Mushrooms
Olives
Onions
Peaches
Pears
Peas
Peppers
Plums
Prunes
Quinces
Redcurrants
Rhubarb
Salmon
Salsify
Samphire
Shallots
Walnuts

Pear Piccalilli

•••

This is a bit of a Melrose and Morgan classic and gained a cult following. Even if you are averse to the idea of piccalilli, this version has the power to convert you. Give it a try; it's sweet, sour and fruity...

Makes 5 x 340 g jars

Ingredients

1 cauliflower (500 g prepared
  weight without leaves)
1 red onion
100 g fine green beans
225 g courgettes
3 tbsp sea salt
450 ml white wine vinegar
125 g unrefined granulated sugar
45 g cornflour
2 tsp turmeric
2 tsp mustard powder
1 tsp brown mustard seeds
¼ tsp chilli flakes
1 tbsp honey
2 Conference pears
thumb of root ginger

Equipment

5 x 340 g jars
sharp knife and chopping board
colander
whisk
saucepan
Microplane grater

Preparation

Clean the jars, then sterilise them (see page 408).

Method

The day before, cut all the vegetables (not the pears) neatly into small pieces. Wash, drain, place in a colander and cover with the salt. Cover and leave overnight in a cool spot in the kitchen.

Next day, whisk the vinegar, sugar, cornflour, spices and honey in a saucepan. Place on the heat and slowly bring to the boil, whisking as the sauce thickens.

Continue to cook until you have a thickened sauce. Rinse the salt from the vegetables and drain them well. Peel and chop the pears. Peel and grate the ginger.

Place the vegetables, pears and ginger in the sauce and return to the boil, then remove from the heat and pot into the clean jars while the mixture is still hot.

Put the lids on tightly and keep in a cool spot for a month before consuming.

Pickled Dill Cucumbers

•••

A classic combination of dill and cucumber. Perfect with poached salmon.

Makes 3 x 500 ml jars

Ingredients

3 cucumbers
30 g sea salt, plus 1 tsp
bunch of dill
1 red chilli
600 ml white wine vinegar
100 g caster sugar
1 tsp coriander seeds
1 tsp yellow mustard seeds

Equipment

sharp knife and chopping board
mixing bowl
3 x 500 ml jars with screw-top lids
saucepan
very large saucepan

Preparation

Wash the cucumbers and cut into batons that are the length of the jar or just shorter. Place in a bowl, dredge with the 30 g of salt, cover and leave to brine for one hour.

Wash the dill and divide it into fronds.

Halve the chilli and remove the seeds, then cut it lengthways into strips.

Sterilise three 500 ml jars and lids (see page 408).

Method

Pour the vinegar into a saucepan and add the sugar, coriander and mustard seeds. Bring to the boil, then cool and stir in the 1 tsp of salt.

Rinse the cucumber batons and pack into the jars with fronds of dill and chilli.

Pour over the vinegar solution almost to the top of each jar, leaving 1 cm space. Screw on the lids.

Seal the jars: fold two tea towels and place in your largest saucepan. This will protect the jars from direct contact with heat. Fill with water and bring to the boil.

Submerge the jars, covering each by two-thirds. Cover the pan and cook for 45 minutes. Check the seal on the jars is good before cooling them in the pan.

Once cooled, remove and store away from direct sunlight. Consume within six months and store each jar in the fridge once opened.

Poaching an Egg

Vinegar aids coagulation of the egg white. Bring a saucepan of water to a rolling boil and briskly whisk to create a 'whirlpool'. Crack an egg into a tea cup, splash a few drops of malt or white wine vinegar, then slide it into the vortex. Cook for three minutes, then remove with a slotted spoon. Serve, or chill in ice-cold water. (To reheat, bring a pan of water to the boil and add the egg for one minute, then serve.)

M

Adding Depth to a Sauce or Casserole

Add 1 tsp of wine vinegar to a pan of sweating onions as you start to make the sauce or casserole and cook for a few minutes, allowing the acid to cook off.

M

Four Simple Salad Dressings

•••

Salad leaves should form part of all good meals, especially throughout the summer. So keep these dressings in a sealed bottle: they will live happily somewhere cool in the kitchen and will just need a shake before serving. Experiment with different oils and vinegars until you find one you like. Substitute part or all of the vinegar with lemon juice if you want a citrus finish to your salad.

Blue Cheese

8 tbsp extra virgin olive oil
½ tsp honey
2 tbsp cider vinegar

40 g blue cheese
pinch of freshly ground black pepper

Place all the ingredients in a blender and blitz. Check the seasoning and add salt if needed.

Asian-style

This works well on a crunchy salad or coleslaw.

2 tbsp rice wine vinegar
2 tbsp miso paste
1 tbsp soy sauce
1 tsp toasted sesame oil
1 small garlic clove, crushed or finely grated
1 tsp finely grated root ginger

Whisk together all the ingredients with 1 tbsp of water.

Sherry Vinegar and Shallot

We use this to dress Bread salad
(see page 26) as it's quite acidic and cuts
through the creaminess of the cheese.

3 tbsp extra virgin olive oil
1 tbsp sherry vinegar
1 small shallot, finely chopped
sea salt

Whisk and emulsify the oil and vinegar
and, once combined, add the shallot
and season with salt.

Classic French

The honey is optional,
but gives balance to the acidity
of this dressing.

Makes 160 ml

2 tbsp white wine vinegar
1 tsp Dijon mustard
½ tsp runny honey (optional)
¼ tsp sea salt
8 tbsp olive oil

Mix the vinegar, mustard, honey
(if using) and salt in a bowl, then slowly
whisk in the oil in a gradual stream
until you have an emulsified dressing.
Taste and adjust the seasoning.

Acknowledgements

This book is the result of 10 years of shop keeping and cooking and therefore would not exist without the loyal customers who have supported us during these years. To all of you: Thank you.

And it certainly would not exist without the encouragement and support of Elizabeth Hallett of Saltyard Books who championed us and had such a clear vision of what this book could be. And to the rest of the team at Saltyard Books, particularly Kate Miles who has patiently endeavoured to keep us all on track.

To our editor, Lucy Bannell, for her straightforward, no-nonsense approach to get the job done, her fastidious eye for detail and for instilling us with confidence as we compiled the book.

Our designers at Studio Frith, particularly Frith Kerr and Ben Prescott, who over the past 10 years have shaped the way we look. Your work sets this book apart. And to Nina Chakrabarti for her delightful and considered illustrations.

Charlotte Robertson at United Agents, for her enthusiasm and careful guidance and for spurring us on.

To our PR team at Samphire PR, particularly Amy Williams and Danielle Sidders.

To our suppliers who've shared their knowledge and skills in the day-to-day running of our shops, but also those who particularly helped in the compilation of these chapters: Danny Davies and the team at Climpson's Coffee; the baker John Rolfe; Ausra Burg of My Cup of Tea; Henrietta Lovell of Rare Tea; and cheesemaker Margaretha Herman. We've only been able to share a small amount of the wealth of knowledge you all hold.

Add to the list: Martha Swift for her valued advice and introducing us to our agent; Diana Henry for her encouragement when this book was just the germ of an idea. Not forgetting Jenny Parker, May James, Jonathan Hall, Tracey Bellow and Sarah Gonzalez, all of whose help has been much appreciated and needed as we've been writing.

To Mr Alan Bennett for his generosity in the words he wrote at the front of this book.

To all of the people who've worked with us in our shops and kitchen since 2004. There's a little bit of you all in this book. But special thanks to some of the chefs whose skill and creativity can be seen in some of the recipes here: Rose Sykes and Sylvan Jamois, Steve Williams, Flori Johnson, Jane Rawson, Daniel Karlsson, Brian Mulcahy and Mauro Mateus. In addition, to our retail managers who've represented us to our customers so well, particularly Martin Cohen, Joshua Talmud and Andrew Davies.

We'd be nowhere without the initial goodwill and faith of a small group of friends and family bestowed on us: Michelle and Steve Kirby, May and Don James, Guido Palau, Dave Woolf, Maggie and Peter Zownir. We are eternally grateful.

Finally to all our friends and families who have supported us and put up with us, both in the writing of this book and the running of our company.

Louisa, Nick and Ian.

First published in Great Britain in 2014
by Saltyard Books
An imprint of Hodder & Stoughton
An Hachette UK company

1

Copyright © Melrose and Morgan 2014
Illustrations © Nina Chakrabarti 2014

A CIP catalogue record for this title is available from the British Library.

ISBN 978 1 444 78932 4

Design and Art Direction by Studio Frith

Proofreaders Margaret Gilbey and Kate Truman
Indexer Caroline Wilding

Printed and bound by L.E.G.O. Spa

Hodder & Stoughton policy is to use papers that are natural,
renewable and recyclable products and made from
wood grown in sustainable forests. The logging and
manufacturing processes are expected to conform to
the environmental regulations of the country of origin.

www.saltyardbooks.co.uk

1 Gallon
=
160 Fluid Ounces

Tub of Butter = 84 lb

1 Bushel
=
8 Gallons

1 QUART

40 FLUID OUNCES

2 PINTS

3 Barleycorns = 1 Inch

4 POPPYSEEDS = 1 BARLEYCORN

180°C
=
350°F